Social Protection in Africa

Frank Ellis

Professor, School of Development Studies, University of East Anglia, UK

Stephen Devereux

Fellow, Institute of Development Studies, University of Sussex, UK

Philip White

Research Fellow, School of Development Studies, University of East Anglia, UK

Edward Elgar

Cheltenham, UK • Northampton, MA, USA

Published by
Edward Elgar Publishing Limited
The Lypiatts
15 Lansdown Road
Cheltenham
Glos GL50 2JA
UK

Edward Elgar Publishing, Inc.
William Pratt House
9 Dewey Court
Northampton
Massachusetts 01060
USA

A catalogue record for this book
is available from the British Library

Library of Congress Control Number: 2008939770

PEFC
PEFC/16-33-111
CATG-PEFC-052

ISBN 978 1 84844 258 0 (cased)
ISBN 978 1 84844 364 8 (paperback)

Printed and bound in Great Britain by MPG Books Ltd, Bodmin, Cornwall

Contents

Abbreviations   vii
Preface   x

PART I   THEMES

1   Overview   3
2   Vulnerability   23
3   Targeting   40
4   Delivery   54
5   Coordination and coverage   70
6   Cost-effectiveness   85
7   Market effects   98
8   Asset protection and building   111
9   Lesson learning: strengths, weaknesses and the state of the
    art   124

PART II   CASE STUDIES FROM SOUTHERN AFRICA

10   Introduction to the case studies   143
Case Study 1   Old Age Pension, Lesotho   154
Case Study 2   Food Subsidy Programme, Mozambique   161
Case Study 3   Public Works Programmes, Malawi   169
Case Study 4   Dowa Emergency Cash Transfer, Malawi   179
Case Study 5   Social Cash Transfers, Zambia   187
Case Study 6   Urban Food Programme, Zimbabwe   195
Case Study 7   Food Assistance Programme, Mozambique   204
Case Study 8   School Feeding, Lesotho   211
Case Study 9   Neighbourhood Care Points for orphans and
                vulnerable children, Swaziland   219
Case Study 10   Education Material Fairs, Mozambique   226
Case Study 11   Input Subsidy Programme, Malawi   234
Case Study 12   Food Security Pack, Zambia   244
Case Study 13   Input Trade Fairs, Mozambique   253

Case Study 14   Chiefs' Fields for orphans and vulnerable
                 children, Swaziland   261
Case Study 15   Small Livestock Transfers, Zimbabwe   269

References   276
Author Index   286
Subject Index   288

Abbreviations

AAI	ActionAid International
ACC	Area Coordination Committee (Zambia)
ADMARC	Agricultural Development and Marketing Corporation (Malawi)
AFSC	Area Food Security Committee (Zambia)
ART	Anti-retroviral therapy
BI	*Bilhete de identidade* (national identity card, Mozambique)
BMI	Body mass index
CCT	Conditional cash transfer
CERF	Central Emergency Relief Fund (United Nations)
CRS	Catholic Relief Services
CSB	Corn-soya blend
CSI	Coping strategy index
CWAC	Community Welfare Assistance Committee (Zambia)
DA	District Assembly (Malawi)
DECT	Dowa Emergency Cash Transfer (Concern Universal Scheme, Malawi, 2005–06)
DFID	Department for International Development
DSWO	District Social Welfare Officer (Zambia)
DWAC	District Welfare Assistance Committee (Zambia)
EPA	Extension Planning Area (Malawi)
FAO	Food and Agriculture Organization
FPE	Free Primary Education
GDP	Gross Domestic Product
GTZ	Gesellschaft für Technische Zusammenarbeit (German technical cooperation agency)
HIPC	Highly Indebted Poor Countries
HSNP	Hunger Safety Net Programme (DFID-funded programme, northern Kenya, starting Nov. 2008)
IGPWP	Income Generating Public Works Programme (Malawi)
INAS	National Institute of Social Action (Mozambique)
JICA	Japan International Cooperation Agency
LAMP	Local Authority Managed Project (Malawi)

LEAP	Livelihood Empowerment Against Poverty (Ghana)
MACO	Ministry of Agriculture and Cooperatives (Zambia)
MASAF	Malawi Social Action Fund
MCDSS	Ministry of Community Development and Social Services (Zambia)
MDG	Millennium Development Goal
MINAG	Ministry of Agriculture (Mozambique)
MINSAU	Ministry of Health (Mozambique)
MMAS	Ministry of Women and Social Action (Mozambique)
MOAC	Ministry of Agriculture and Cooperatives (Swaziland)
MoARD	Ministry of Agriculture and Rural Development (Ethiopia)
MOET	Ministry of Education and Training (Lesotho)
MoFNP	Ministry of Finance and National Planning (Zambia)
MVAC	Malawi Vulnerability Assessment Committee
NCP	Neighbourhood Care Point (Swaziland)
NERCHA	National Emergency Response Council on HIV and AIDS (Swaziland)
NGO	Non-governmental organization
NPA	National Plan of Action (for OVC)
OIBM	Opportunity International Bank in Malawi
ORAP	Organization of Rural Associations for Progress (Zimbabwe)
OVC	Orphans and vulnerable children
PAM	Programme Against Malnutrition (Zambia)
PARPA	Action Plan for the Reduction of Absolute Poverty (Mozambique)
PMTCT	Prevention of mother-to-child transmission
PoS	Point of sale
PPM	Pay Point Manager (Zambia)
PRP	Protracted Relief Programme (Zimbabwe)
PSNP	Productive Safety Net Programme (Ethiopia)
PSWO	Province Social Welfare Officer (Zambia)
PWAS	Public Welfare Assistance Scheme (Zambia)
PWP	Public works programme
RHVP	Regional Hunger and Vulnerability Programme (DFID-funded programme, southern Africa 2005–10)
ROSCA	Rotating savings and credit association
SANHA	Food, Nutritional Security and HIV/AIDS group (Mozambique)
SC-UK	Save the Children UK

SETSAN	Technical Secretariat for Food and Nutritional Security (Mozambique)
SFFRFM	Smallholder Farmers Fertilizer Revolving Fund Malawi
SPRINT	Special Programme for Relief and Investment in Needy Times (Malawi)
SSRP	School Self-Reliance Project (Lesotho)
TLC	Technical Learning and Coordination Unit (PRP, Zimbabwe)
VAM	Vulnerability Assessment Mapping
VDC	Village Development Committee (Malawi)
WFP	World Food Programme

Exchange Rates

The exchange rates given below provide conversions to the US$ in 2007 for the currencies in the countries from which the Part II case studies are drawn.

Country	Currency	Rate to the US$ 2007
Lesotho	maloti (M)*	M7.0
Malawi	kwacha (MK)	MK140
Mozambique	metical (Mtn)	Mtn26.0
Swaziland	emalangeni (E)*	E7.0
Zambia	kwacha (ZK)	ZK4000
Zimbabwe	dollar (Z$)	Z$30000**

Notes:
* These currencies are pegged to the South African rand (R).
** Figure refers to the official rate in September 2007; however, the unofficial rate in that period was around Z$250 000.

Preface

This book arises from the involvement of its authors in the Regional Hunger and Vulnerability Programme (RHVP) in southern Africa, funded principally by the UK Department for International Development (DFID) with co-funding from the Australian Agency for International Development (AusAID). RHVP began in mid-2005 and its first three-year phase of funding ended in mid-2008. A second phase lasting for two years through to 2010 has since got underway. RHVP was created in order to move forward the policy debate about how best to tackle persistent poverty and vulnerability, following a period of recurrent food security crises in the southern African region necessitating frequent recourse to emergency responses with their attendant high and unpredictable costs. By 2005, many personnel in DFID were becoming persuaded that regular social transfers to the persistently poorest and most vulnerable ('predictable funding for predictable needs') would avoid a considerable proportion of emergency responses, the latter then only being required for catastrophic events with wide adverse impacts.

RHVP was set up with three overlapping components, which were support to vulnerability assessment capabilities, evidence gathering (the research component), and policy advice and advocacy (feeding new ideas into policy processes in country governments). The authors of this book acted as mentors of the research component and established a regional network of country researchers who conducted an initial analysis of knowledge gaps and then proceeded to explore these gaps through the medium of case study social protection schemes and programmes. The research component was known as the Regional Evidence Building Agenda, and it established a template for undertaking case study research comprising six modules, which were vulnerability, targeting, coordination and coverage, cost-effectiveness, asset effects and market impacts. These same modules also formed the basis for comparative lesson learning across case studies. This book retains this core framework as originally devised for RHVP, with the modules becoming the theme chapters in the first part of the book, and a selection of the schemes and programmes that were studied providing the case studies in the second half of the book.

The work conducted under the auspices of RHVP since 2005 can be accessed at the programme website known as www.wahenga.net. *Wahenga* is a Swahili word meaning 'those who can be relied upon to give sound advice'. The website is a useful resource for all matters related to hunger, vulnerability and social protection in southern Africa and more widely in sub-Saharan Africa, and includes commissioned studies, outputs from the research programme, training materials, news items, video clips, and links to other sites covering the same or closely adjacent topics. In the early phases of the programme there was some debate about whether hunger and vulnerability (implying a specific focus on secure access to food) was quite the same as social protection (with its broader remits about rights, social justice, labour standards and so on). It soon became evident that little is achieved by treating this as an important distinction, and this is illustrated especially well by predictable cash transfers to the extreme poor that are becoming mainstream in social protection in Africa, and which have the fundamental purpose of reducing the chronic hunger and vulnerability of their recipient families. The book provides information on larger scale predictable social transfer programmes outside southern Africa in the form of boxed examples, including the Productive Safety Net Programme (PSNP) in Ethiopia, the Hunger Safety Net Programme (HSNP) in Kenya and the Livelihood Empowerment Against Poverty (LEAP) programme in Ghana.

The authors of the book owe a substantial debt to DFID and RHVP for providing the institutional framework, the logistical support, and the funding that enabled the research underlying the book to take place. Needless to say, the book represents the views of its authors, not those of RHVP or DFID. Two individuals deserve special mention and these are Nicholas Freeland, the director of RHVP, and John Rook, the programme manager, both of whom were instrumental in creating the space that allowed the research component of RHVP to flourish, and in supporting it throughout the evidence gathering process. From 2006 to 2008, RHVP was organized in part on the basis of 'country coordinators' who acted as the facilitators and networkers on social protection in each participating country (Lesotho, Malawi, Mozambique, Swaziland, Zambia, Zimbabwe). The country coordinators were critical to the success of the research and we are very grateful to them. They were Chaka Ntsane (Lesotho), Duncan Samikwa (Malawi), Anabela Mabota (Mozambique), Patricia Musi (Swaziland), Emmanuel Ngulube and Chosi Nkhata (Zambia), and Ngonidzashe Mararike (Zimbabwe). The case studies and thematic chapters of the book represent the final synthesis of material that was collected and written up by country researchers. The institutions involved were: for Lesotho, the Institute of Southern African Studies, National University; for Malawi, Wadonda Consult and Centre for Social Research, University of Malawi; for Mozambique, several independent researchers; for Swaziland, the Coordinating Assembly of Non-Governmental Organisations (CANGO); for Zambia, RuralNet Associates; and, for Zimbabwe, Centre for Applied Social Sciences (CASS), University of Zimbabwe.

Many thanks are due to all those institutions and the individuals within them who undertook the research, listed in alphabetical order by country as follows: in *Lesotho*, Nthabiseng Chaka, David Croome, Dr Itumeleng Kimane, Moipone Letsie, Matseliso Mapetla, Thope Matobo, Makabi Matsoai, M. Molisana, Dr M. Nteso, Prof. Andrew Nyanguru, Tsoeu Petlane, Limakatso Ranko, Prof. E.M. Sebatane, Caleb Sello and Dr Setoi Setoi; in *Malawi*, Dr Ephraim Chirwa, John Kadzandira, Dr Milton Kutengule, Dr Peter Mvula and Duncan Samikwa; in *Mozambique*, Nicia Giva, Dr Paulo Mole, Nelia Taimo, Rui Vasco and Rachel Waterhouse; in *Swaziland*, Armstrong Dlamini, Gideon Dlamini, Dr Solomon Dlamini, Thembinkosi Dlamini, Thembumenzi Dube, Zakhe Hlanze, Magalela Ngwenya and Dr Sabina Silaula; in *Zambia*, Fison Mujenja, Mwila Mulumbi, Neo Simutanyi and Stephen Tembo; and, in *Zimbabwe*, Ebbie Dengu, Dr Vupenyu Dzingirai, Dr Sithabiso Gandure, Dr Jeanette Manjengwa, Dr Prosper Matondi, Dr Billy Mukamuri and Katrina Wallace-Karenga. The finishing work on the book manuscript was ably assisted by Alexander Walmsley.

It seems appropriate to end this preface on an optimistic note. When RHVP started its work, there was great confusion concerning the best way forward for achieving more secure access to food and basic needs for the poorest of the poor in sub-Saharan Africa. Strongly polarized stances were at that time being adopted with respect to such questions as needs against rights, food against cash, conditionality against non-conditionality, targeting against universal provision and so on. In the intervening period, these discussions have moved on, and it is apparent that there is no single and definitive solution to providing effective social protection, but rather a range of options that can potentially be drawn upon in a lot of different ways in order to achieve social assistance and livelihood promotion outcomes. While the shift from emergency food to predictable cash constitutes a fundamental change in thinking, it is not the end of the story, and the future provides great scope for innovation in the effective provision of social protection in Africa. By examining patterns of experience and distinguishing features that work from those that plainly do not, it is hoped that this book can make some small contribution to this quest.

PART I

Themes

1. Overview

THE PURPOSE OF THE BOOK

Social protection is moving up the development agenda in Africa. The reason is a growing recognition that too many people in Africa are mired in chronic poverty and vulnerability, such that even small shocks to agricultural outcomes or cash incomes cause disproportionate distress and hunger. In the past, governments, aid donors and non-governmental organizations (NGOs) have responded to adverse events in Africa primarily through emergency transfers to those most seriously affected. Most of this humanitarian relief has been food aid, and the unpredictability yet frequency of its occurrence and scale has been costly as well as failing to address the underlying causes of vulnerability. Aid donors are moving towards the notion of 'predictable funding for predictable needs'. In other words, if the most vulnerable people in African countries were provided with regular cash transfers to underpin their access to food and basic needs, then emergency measures could be avoided in most instances, being required only in the event of catastrophic emergencies on a broad scale.

This policy agenda is a lot more complicated than it may appear at first sight. Decisions to provide vulnerable people at national scale with regular social transfers must ultimately be made by governments and have political force behind them or they stand little chance of success. Nevertheless, sufficient cases of such political will do exist across Africa to provide the basis for taking the agenda seriously. For example, seven sub-Saharan African countries have proper old age pension schemes, guaranteeing in law the right of all citizens on reaching a certain age to obtain a regular monthly or quarterly pension payment. Social pensions are one amongst a wide potential range of cash and other transfers to vulnerable people that deserve to be considered. While recent literature has tended to set cash against food transfers and find the latter wanting in most respects, it is premature to write off a future role for food in social transfers, especially as the world enters an era when global food supplies are predicted to fail to meet rising demand, resulting in rising real food prices in the long term. A cash transfer is as good for its recipient as the food it is able to buy.

The purpose of this book is to make accessible to a broad audience the ideas, principles and practicalities of establishing effective social protection in Africa. The readership of the book is envisaged mainly as practitioners and implementers of social protection policies in Africa, including civil servants, donor personnel and NGO staff. This is not a theoretical or deeply academic book. It seeks to pose its arguments and findings in a clear and straightforward way, while at the same time remaining faithful to the more abstract ideas that sometimes underlie them. The book has a structure divided between seven topics or themes in social protection in Part I and 15 social protection case studies in Part II. There is a continuous interplay between these two parts of the book, so that the synthesis of ideas that occurs in each theme chapter draws on and signposts examples represented by the case studies. Examples of major sub-Saharan African social transfer programmes not covered in the case studies are provided as separate boxes in the text.

This chapter proceeds to provide some building blocks pertinent to the themes and case studies of the rest of the book. A first such building block is the adoption of a workable definition of social protection. This then leads, second, into a consideration of the differences, interactions and overlaps between social protection and emergency responses. The third building block is to define and distinguish different forms of transfer to beneficiaries that social protection can take. The fourth is to identify actors, institutions and stakeholders that are central to the adoption and implementation of social protection. The fifth is to introduce the reader to the logic behind the themes of social protection that make up the remaining chapters in Part I of the book, and also provide the framework guiding the way the Part II case studies are researched and presented. The sixth is to summarize the big strategic issues about tackling vulnerability to hunger and other deprivations in Africa that underlie and inform discussion and debates about the future of social protection in the continent. The final section of this chapter provides a brief preview of the Part II case studies, as well as of boxed examples of major sub-Saharan African social protection schemes that are not part of the case study set.

THE DEFINITION OF SOCIAL PROTECTION

Social protection in low-income countries has been around for a long time, even if not described as such (Midgley, 1997), and has placed emphasis on different levers of policy in different eras. In the 1960s and 1970s subsidising retail food prices was popular as a means of ensuring that all citizens could afford enough to eat, and certain countries were regarded as iconic in the enthusiasm with which they pursued low staple food consumer prices (rice in Sri Lanka; wheat in Egypt; maize in Tanzania). In some well-known cases, these low consumer prices were made possible by very large transfers of food aid (Bangladesh). Interestingly, consumer price subsidies represented social protection at scale, a goal now being pursued energetically by different means, and they also aligned political interest and social transfers in a way that appears more difficult to replicate in the current era.

Food subsidies as a form of social protection fell out of favour for many reasons: bureaucratic management of markets lost credence, subsidies were fiscally unaffordable, they favoured urban consumers above rural producers, and world food prices began a long run decline, making it cheaper to buy food from world markets than subsidize the consumption of domestic supplies. Nevertheless rising real prices in world food markets in 2007–08 could put this social protection policy back on the table, depending in part on whether the new substantially higher real prices of maize, wheat and rice are sustained in the future. Already by 2008 some countries have turned to issuing vouchers to poorer citizens, enabling them to purchase food rations from government outlets at prices well below market levels.

In the 1980s, social protection switched to a minimalist stance, best captured by the notion of 'safety nets' that would play a limited role in protecting vulnerable citizens from the removal of previous state supports (like food and input subsidies), the higher risks associated with liberalized markets, and seasonal food deficits in the hungry season before the next harvest. Not only the coverage but also the delivery cost of safety nets should be minimized, hence the popularity of 'self-targeting' mechanisms of beneficiary selection, typified by food-for-work schemes that set the food ration at a level below the quantity that anyone able to produce food themselves, or already earning enough wages to secure food, would be interested in doing the hard physical work to acquire.

The safety net idea is predicated strongly on the notion that the economy as a whole is moving forward, living standards are rising, but nevertheless there are pockets of people especially in rural areas who confront seasonal or unexpected food deficits that need to be addressed. India has one of the earliest and best-known safety nets, now called the National Rural Employment Guarantee Scheme, and this remains a central plank of India's public response to inadequate income and consumption at household level in rural areas. In sub-Saharan Africa, too, safety nets have been the main response to temporary or seasonal deprivation since the mid-1980s, as exemplified by public works programmes in which self-selected participants provide labour in return for food rations, cash wages or agricultural inputs (McCord, 2008).

In many ways, the limitations of safety nets provide the point of departure from which contemporary social protection preoccupations emerge. In particular, safety nets proved unequal to the task of protecting the minimum acceptable food consumption of populations in countries exhibiting rising vulnerability across a broad front, prone to devastating droughts or floods or civil conflict, and where economies were not growing fast enough to make hunger and destitution a residual problem affecting just a few people left behind while the rest of society moved to higher ground. In sub-Saharan Africa, the inadequacy of safety nets became plain in ever rising requirements for supplementary and emergency measures to ensure the food security not of small groups but of entire populations and zones persistently or intermittently finding themselves on the brink of unacceptable hunger and deprivation. Most of these supplementary and emergency measures have been delivered in the form of food, and they are seriously high cost to put in place each time they are required.

The period from the mid-1980s to the mid-2000s saw an immense widening and deepening of our understanding of vulnerability, its causes and consequences. The touchstone was the publication in 1981 of the celebrated book by Amartya Sen on poverty and famines that introduced the idea of 'entitlements to food', and recast the interpretation of famines as failures of entitlement or access rather than failures in food supply (Sen, 1981). Devereux (2006) uses Sen's entitlement framework as a way of classifying different social protection mechanisms: production-based entitlement can be boosted by free input packs or fertilizer subsidies, labour-based entitlement by food-for-work or cash-for-work schemes, trade-based entitlement by food price stabilization (shades of the past), and transfer-based entitlement by social transfers (for example, food aid or cash transfers).

The notion of entitlements leads in a few steps to why some people are more prone than others to entitlement failures. The risk of adverse events occurring is evidently a critical factor, but risk alone is not enough since even moderately well off people are able to deal with adverse events considerably better than very poor people. It is risk combined with a lack of ability to deal with a shock that jointly constitutes a definition of vulnerability (Chambers, 1989; Dercon, 2002). The lack of ability to deal with a shock if it occurs is to do with the depleted asset status and lack of options of the household. Asset depletion occurs when poor families sell assets in order to maintain food consumption in the face of a shock, a process referred to as 'coping' (Corbett, 1988). The failure to rebuild assets after a shock (or to rebuild sufficiently before the next shock occurs) increases vulnerability, and explains the rising trend in vulnerability observed in very poor, risk-prone, countries and environments.

These vulnerability sequences have been explored fairly exhaustively in a number of settings (see, for example, Dercon, 2005). Some powerful extensions to the basic model recognize the jointly debilitating effects of household and community-wide shocks occurring simultaneously or sequentially (Dercon, 2005); the existence of thresholds or poverty traps that make it exceptionally difficult for those who have descended into chronic poverty to climb out (Barrett & Swallow, 2005; Carter & Barrett, 2006, 2007; Carter *et al.*, 2008); and the limitations of informal insurance (or 'community coping') for providing support when shocks occur (Morduch, 1999; Morduch & Sharma, 2002; Ellis, 2006a). Much conceptual and empirical work has also been done concerning the impact of AIDS mortality in spreading and intensifying vulnerability in populations with a high prevalence of people living with HIV and AIDS (Barnett *et al.*, 2001; de Waal & Whiteside, 2003; Chapoto & Jayne, 2005; Slater, 2008).

Viewed through the lens of risk and vulnerability, and associated particularly with events and trends in Africa over the past ten years or so, social protection can be interpreted as offering the potential means for addressing the multiple factors causing persistent poverty and rising vulnerability. A helpful classification is one that distinguishes the three social protection functions of protection, prevention and promotion (Guhan, 1994). The first refers to protecting the minimum acceptable consumption levels of people who are already in difficulty. The second refers to preventing people who are susceptible to adverse events and shocks from becoming more vulnerable (by stopping them from having to sell their assets). The third refers to promoting people's ability to become less vulnerable in the future (by helping them to build assets and achieve stronger livelihoods), and is therefore directed at escape from poverty traps. A fourth, or transformative, function of social protection is to promote social justice through building the rights and empowerment of the poor and vulnerable (Devereux & Sabates-Wheeler, 2004; Sabates-Wheeler & Devereux, 2007, 2008).

There has been much debate concerning narrow versus wide definitions of social protection, as also between pure welfare (or social assistance) and livelihood promoting definitions (Conway & Norton, 2002; Norton *et al.*, 2002). Safety nets correspond closest to a narrow, purely welfare, remit for social protection. Yet safety nets are full of holes (Morduch, 1999; Devereux, 2002), and one of the biggest of these is the able-bodied labour requirement of food-for-work and cash-for-work schemes which exclude hungry and destitute people who are unable to work (the elderly, disabled, women caring for small children, etc.) (McCord, 2008). The scale and persistence of the deprivation problem in many low-income countries point in the direction of a wider remit, but this also then makes it difficult to know where to draw the line between social transfers and development policies. For example, fertilizer subsidies to vulnerable small poor farmers rather awkwardly straddle the interface between social protection and development policy.

Another branch of the definitional discussion has concerned itself with whether social protection should be argued primarily from a needs or a rights perspective (Morduch, 1999; Devereux & Sabates-Wheeler, 2007; Munro, 2008). A great proportion of the vulnerability literature is concerned with material deprivation and the risk of becoming unable to secure adequate food. From this perspective, social protection is an instrument to secure food security and possibly more durable enhancement in future livelihood capabilities. An alternative view is that freedom from hunger and destitution is an inalienable human right that should be legislated as such by national governments (as, indeed, it is in many instances) and delivered as a legal obligation of the state. While a lot of heat is generated by different stances taken in this discussion, the two views (like many intermediate positions) are essentially complementary to each other, and the responsibilities of governments towards ensuring that all citizens have freedom from hunger and access to basic needs can be grounded in both sets of arguments.

An existing definition of social protection that takes into account many of the foregoing considerations, and is considered adequate to the task for this book, is stated as follows:

> Social protection describes all public and private initiatives that provide income or consumption transfers to the poor, protect the vulnerable against livelihood risks, and enhance the social status and rights of the marginalised; with the overall objective of reducing the economic and social vulnerability of poor, vulnerable and marginalised groups.
>
> (Devereux & Sabates-Wheeler, 2004)

This definition offers a number of pertinent features. It allows for a wide range of social transfers to be included under the rubric of social protection. For the purposes of this book such transfers can include categories such as the provision of inputs to poor farmers or transfers of livestock to vulnerable rural dwellers, even though such transfers rather awkwardly straddle the conceptual divide between welfare payments and development policies. In addition it embodies the principle of rights to support for individuals and families whose circumstances comply with guidelines or thresholds established in law. As so defined social protection includes public policy measures such as minimum labour standards or gender equality in the workplace that go beyond social transfers. However, this book restricts its scope to the social transfer dimensions of social protection, since these lie at the centre of innovatory approaches to reducing chronic poverty and food insecurity in Africa.

SOCIAL PROTECTION AND DISASTER RESPONSE

Some definitions of social protection would include emergency or disaster responses as one category among the array of social transfers that can occur over a wide variety of different circumstances and timescales. However, the protection and prevention functions of social protection seem to indicate some utility in distinguishing policy measures that seek in advance to prevent or minimize the disruption to people's food security caused by unexpected shocks, from those that are brought into play when food security failure occurs precipitously. Thus preventative social transfers do differ significantly in style and intent from the responses that swing into action when disaster occurs and people suddenly lose their means of survival (as occurs with floods, earthquakes, severe droughts, armed conflict, etc.).

This book maintains some degree of separation between social protection and disaster responses. This is, indeed, already implied by the emphasis on protection, prevention and 'predictable funding for predictable needs', in distinction to the unpredictable and short term character of emergency responses. Nevertheless, it is recognized that social protection and disaster relief overlap in many important ways, and some types of social transfer (for example, responses to seasonal food deficits that can occur unpredictably each year in different places within countries) sit uneasily between being preventative in character and being immediately reactive to localized food security stress.

Disaster relief and social protection often follow each other sequentially in the aftermath of an event that seriously impairs the ability of a population to reconstruct the former basis of their livelihoods. This then raises complex policy issues about the duration of support, the appropriate form of that support, and whether the population affected will eventually be able to graduate from requiring assistance in the future, given that perhaps they did not require it in the past. Thus while it is not possible to draw a sharp set of distinctions between social protection and disaster response, nevertheless there are dimensions of duration and purpose that differ sufficiently for them to occupy somewhat different policy spaces. This difference recurs in a variety of ways throughout this book and reappears later in this chapter under the heading of 'big strategic issues'.

FORMS OF SOCIAL TRANSFER

Social protection can be delivered to its intended beneficiaries in a wide variety of ways utilizing many different forms of transfer. For the purposes of this book, four categories of transfer are recognized as encompassing most types of delivery that can be devised, and these are:

- cash
- food
- inputs
- assets

Of course there are countless ways that each of these forms of transfer can be handled in practice, especially where cash transfers are concerned. Cash can be handed out as bank notes, or put in a bank account, or credited to an electronic card (a smartcard), or texted to a mobile phone. In addition, any number of cash surrogates can be devised, such as books of vouchers that have cash values stamped on them, with those vouchers only being redeemable in certain outlets or for the purchase of a prescribed range of goods. Food too can take different forms. It can be delivered as grain or flour or prepared food, it may be pre-mixed to attain certain nutritional objectives (such as corn–soya blend, CSB), or put together in packages of different items representing a balanced diet (for example, vegetable oil, beans and maize flour). Cash and food transfers overlap when beneficiaries are provided with a voucher of a certain cash value redeemable against a restricted range of items in designated retail outlets. They also overlap when both food and cash are used in some combination in order to ensure desired food security outcomes (see, for example, the Ethiopia PSNP described in Box 2.3).

Inputs typically refer to home garden or farm inputs, and social protection in this area rarely envisages inputs to do with manufacturing or industrial processes. Transfers can be made of seeds, root materials (cassava, seed potatoes) and fertilizers. These can be packaged with specific objectives in mind such as mixed vegetable production or crop diversification in farmers' fields. Inputs may also be delivered against a coupon, where the cost of the coupon to the beneficiary is some fraction of the full market price of the same inputs.

The question arises whether input transfers or subsidized inputs can be properly regarded as social protection rather than as development policy. If social protection is fundamentally thought of as comprising welfare transfers, then this would tend to exclude explicitly livelihood building transfers such as seed and fertilizer packages given to small poor farmers. However, such distinctions can rarely be made definitively, and they depend in part on the entry point to the discussion. When input transfers are designed to overcome the food deficits and material deprivation of particular categories of highly vulnerable urban dwellers (backyard gardens) or farmers, then they seem inarguably part of social protection. On the other hand, a subsidy that nevertheless leaves the price of fertilizer at a level only accessible to better off or rich farmers may be more properly considered a development policy. Since an infinite number of intermediate possibilities exist between these two options, the assignment of input transfers as between social protection and development policy cannot be unambiguously resolved, and this book tends to view most such transfers as part of the social protection discussion.

Social transfers can also take the form of assets, for example farm implements or livestock, and since these are productive assets the same ambiguity applies here as for free or subsidized inputs. Livestock transfers recognize the multiple roles in successful livelihoods of livestock in rural African livelihoods. They typically take the form of small stock (chickens, guinea fowl, perhaps goats) and provide the potential to multiply numbers upwards through successful breeding. Beyond these immediate asset transfers, some social transfers have broader and longer term asset building in view. For example public works programmes (food-for-work, cash-for-work) create physical infrastructure, most often as roads, but sometimes in other forms such as irrigation or drainage works (canal digging). Some types of transfer focus on human capital (school fee vouchers, school feeding, health clinic access vouchers, etc.), and seek to foster the intergenerational reduction of hunger and vulnerability.

The categorization between these four basic forms of social transfer is useful up to a point, but particularly among small social transfer schemes managed by NGOs multiple forms of social protection delivery in a single bundle are quite common. The forms are at their purest in single objective national programmes such as social pensions (pure cash transfer) or a national fertilizer subsidy (pure inputs). However, it is not at all uncommon for an NGO project aimed at a particular constituency of vulnerable people to provide cash, food, inputs and assets in various combinations within a single social protection scheme. By doing this the intention may be to achieve multiple different goals over different time horizons (for example, immediate hunger relief combined with livelihood building for the future).

ACTORS AND INSTITUTIONS IN SOCIAL PROTECTION

In low-income countries in Africa, many different actors are involved in devising and delivering social protection, giving social transfers both within and across countries a distinctly 'patchwork' character. Individual NGOs, UN agencies, quasi-state agencies and public bodies deliver a diverse range of social transfers to different social groups, according to criteria that are internal to each organization or follow the shifting priorities of funding agencies. The accidental character of this social protection means that both duplication (particular beneficiaries being targeted by two or more different agencies) and exclusion (deserving individuals being missed entirely from all types of social transfer) can occur.

The question of whether improved coordination between actors would result in improved social protection practice is left to a later chapter (Chapter 5). Here, the aim is simply to identify the main cast of characters as they appear in a typical sub-Saharan African country, with some notes on organizational links that are relevant to other parts of the book:

Governments

These typically have a ministry or a department with a title like Department of Social Welfare; however, it is rare in sub-Saharan Africa for these to do much more than oversee civil service pensions, and administer legislation that applies to the 'formal' private sector (job security, sickness benefits, etc.). Mostly, this type of government department has an oversight role for activities that are conducted mainly by international and national NGOs, but the degree of such oversight can vary from moderately well coordinated to virtually no coordination at all. In recent times, some countries have adopted social protection strategies or frameworks intended to improve coordination across government departments and NGOs carrying out differing types of social protection, as well as to conduct public cash transfers, funded in part through general budget support.

International and Bilateral Aid Donors

Donor agencies play a dominant role in funding most emergency and social protection activities that go on in sub-Saharan African countries. These include specialised UN agencies like the World Food Programme (WFP) and the UN High Commission for Refugees; the World Bank (which in the past has financed a lot of social action funds that conduct public works pro-grammes); and individual bilateral donors like the UK's DFID. Under the new modalities for delivering aid, donors often nowadays participate in joint coordinating committees with government concerning matters such as food aid, food security, hunger and social transfers. In a few cases social protection is recognized as requiring such a committee in its own right, and more formal coordination between the aid agencies and governments concerning the future shape of such social transfers is beginning to be put in place.

NGOs and Civil Society Organizations

International and some national NGOs are the most active and energetic participants in social protection throughout sub-Saharan Africa, conducting between them the entire array of social protection types encountered in this book. All the big international NGOs are typically represented: ActionAid, CARE, Concern Worldwide, Oxfam, Save the Children and so on. Some of these, such as Save the Children, have multiple presences depending on country of origin (SC-UK, SC-US, etc.). NGOs are typically funded by donors to conduct specific operations in particular districts (or parts of a country), arising from projects put forward and gaining funding from particular donors. These projects are typically limited in geographical coverage and in duration. It is rare for funding to continue beyond two to three years, and in some cases it may be a lot shorter than this (for example, funding for a single lean season). NGOs often cluster into 'groups' for particular social protection purposes, or may coordinate at national scale, when serious longer term programmes are being funded (for example, the Ethiopia Productive Safety Net Programme). International NGOs often work through networks of local partner NGOs or other civil society or community-based organizations in the delivery of social transfers.

Private Sector

The private sector, mainly local enterprises, has a specific role in various aspects of social protection delivery, for example:

- logistics of delivering food or inputs to rural areas in a country (hauliers, traders)
- logistics of delivering cash to remote areas (banks, credit unions, etc.)
- use of electronic technologies for effecting cash transfers (cellphone companies, banks)
- redeeming vouchers for farm inputs (agricultural input suppliers and merchants)
- redeeming vouchers for food and retail goods (retail chains, or individual retail shops in district towns)

In addition some large international companies may conduct forms of social protection on their own account, typically under the rubric of 'corporate social responsibility', and usually in connection with commercial activities that they are already conducting in the geographical areas where the social transfers take place.

IDENTIFICATION OF THEMES

In this book, all types of social protection are recognized as having certain attributes concerning their objectives, functioning and outcomes for the well-being and livelihoods of their beneficiaries that can be compared across different schemes and programmes. These attributes are referred to in the book as social protection themes, and they form the basis of the next seven chapters of the book (Chapters 2–8), as well as, in slightly modified form, the evidence structure of the 15 case studies in Part II of the book. In their briefest description these themes may be stated as follows:

1. vulnerability
2. targeting
3. delivery
4. coordination and coverage
5. cost-effectiveness
6. market effects
7. asset impacts

The vulnerability theme seeks to discover the nature of the vulnerability that a social protection scheme sets out to address (for example, the vulnerability to hunger of older people addressed by a social pension). It also differentiates between ameliorating the effects of chronic vulnerability, principally by providing transfers to overcome people's 'hunger gap', from attempting to tackle the root causes of vulnerability, for example by stimulating rising yields in small farm agriculture.

The targeting theme addresses the precepts and methods by which the beneficiaries of a social protection scheme are selected. The targeting process results in a list of designated beneficiaries, or in a self-selected group of beneficiaries (self-targeting in public works schemes), or in a beneficiary category (for example, everyone over 70 years of age). Targeting is prone to inclusion errors (beneficiary names on the list who do not meet the criteria for inclusion) and exclusion errors (inadvertent or deliberate exclusion of people who do fit the selection criteria).

The delivery theme refers to the different delivery methods deployed by social transfer schemes. This includes the form of the transfer that is being delivered to beneficiaries, and as already discussed four categories are more or less exhaustive of the main forms that delivery can take: cash, food, inputs and assets. It has already been noted that important variations can occur within each of these main categories: for example, cash can be delivered as bank notes or in the form of a voucher with a given cash value; while inputs can be delivered as a physical package (seeds and fertilizers) or be purchased with coupons representing entitlement to a particular quantity of a particular input. In addition, the technology of the delivery can vary, with electronic technologies offering the scope for entirely new ways of effecting social transfers, especially for cash transfers.

Coordination refers to the inter-agency coordination of social protection efforts, that is, between government departments, between NGOs, between aid donors, and between all these bodies and institutions and each other. Coverage refers to the spatial and temporal distribution of social protection beneficiaries that arises due to decisions made by different agencies about where, when, how and to whom to provide social transfers. Coverage differs from targeting since it refers to the combined outreach resulting from the actions of many different players. Coordination and coverage come together as a theme because coordination failure (between different agencies engaging in social transfers) can also result in coverage failure (duplication of coverage for the same vulnerable groups, or failure of particular vulnerable people to be addressed by any measures).

The cost-effectiveness theme brings together two aspects of social protection that are closely linked together, but differ in the depth and duration of the impacts being considered. One aspect of cost-effectiveness (the input side) is the efficiency of social protection delivery, that is, the total cost of delivering US$1 worth of transfers to beneficiaries. The other aspect of cost-effectiveness (the output side) concerns the relationship between stated intentions and actual outcomes achieved, including the sustainability of those outcomes, for example the achievement of sustained higher yields as the result of delivering free farm inputs to small poor farmers.

The market effects of social transfers can take two opposing directions. There is the influence of the transfers on food, farm input, and labour markets; and there is the influence of market prices, especially the price levels of staple foods like maize and rice, on the value of the transfer. In brief, cash transfers represent an injection of expenditure into local markets, thus stimulating trade and supporting local prices. Food transfers may have the opposite effect on local food prices. However, these effects on markets are in practice complicated and location and time specific (they vary in different places and different seasons). Meanwhile, the effect of market price trends on the real purchasing power of a cash transfer can be critically important, for example if the transfer is spent by recipients mainly on maize, and the price of maize doubles, then the transfer will only buy half the previous quantity of maize.

Social transfers can have three main positive impacts on household assets, either directly or indirectly. First, both food and cash transfers can protect against the distress sale of assets. Second, many social protection schemes explicitly create assets at the individual level (for example, education and skills), the household level (for example, livestock, farm tools) or the community level (for example, roads, village grain banks). Third, recipients of social transfers often choose to allocate some transfer income to savings or purchases of productive assets.

BIG STRATEGIC ISSUES

The mid-2000s saw a massive surge of interest in cash transfers as the principal vehicle for delivering social protection. This occurred in part because of the recurrence of food crises in eastern and southern Africa dating from 2000 onwards, and the limited range of policy levers available to deal with these crises, beyond food transfers of which over half are organized by the World Food Programme (WFP). Emergency food operations are unpredictable and costly, and lead to exit strategy problems once the initial crisis has passed. Moreover, they do not address and may even worsen the vulnerability contexts that cause them to occur, for example by undermining local food markets. It began to be argued that, since the vulnerability problem being addressed seemed to be widespread and persistent, and due to multiple causes small and large, it might be better addressed by some form of continuous transfer that would enable beneficiaries to withstand minor and routine shocks, thus necessitating food aid only in the event of serious catastrophes of wide geographic scope. And so the principle of 'predictable funding for predictable needs' emerged, with regular cash transfers to the poorest and most vulnerable members of society replacing (except in exceptional circumstances) ad hoc and intermittent deliveries of food aid.

Some important distinctions underlie the notion of 'predictable funding for predictable needs'. An initial distinction is between transient and chronic hunger, with the former referring to seasonal or 'shock' reasons for hunger, while the latter refers to a persistent inability to obtain minimum acceptable levels of food. The persistently hungry are the main category of vulnerable people for whom cash transfers are considered more appropriate than emergency food supplies. Nevertheless, if seasonal hunger is observed to recur every year to a predictable number of households, it too becomes a predictable need better addressed by a routine annual response than by emergency procedures. For example, the Productive Safety Net Programme (PSNP) in Ethiopia (Box 2.3) responds to predictable seasonal hunger and provides transfers to beneficiaries for a maximum of six months, while the Hunger Safety Net Programme (HSNP) in Kenya (Box 4.1) responds to chronic hunger and provides transfers to recipients throughout the year.

In a rather polarized debate about the relative merits of cash and food transfers, positive qualities of cash have been contrasted with negative qualities of food (see contributions to the collection edited by Farrington & Slater, 2006). Cash is argued to be lower cost to deliver, provide choice and empowerment (over its expenditure) to its beneficiaries, and support rather than undermine local markets. Nevertheless, these conceptual qualities are not necessarily easy to realize in practice and they do not cover all circumstances. Security of delivery is a major issue with cash. Moreover, in remote locations with insufficient food supply and poorly working markets, there is a risk that cash will provoke rising food prices. In the meantime, this debate has had the interesting consequence of modifying the operational behaviour of WFP towards local rather than remote food purchases and recognition of a role for cash transfers in its own programming (Gentilini, 2007a, 2007b).

The current enthusiasm for cash transfers in Africa represents, in part, the transmission of ideas from the Latin American experience with conditional cash transfers (CCTs) (Handa & Davis, 2006; Slater & Schubert, 2006). During the 1990s, pilot CCT schemes in Brazil and Mexico were scaled up to national programmes (the *Bolsa Família* and *Oportunidades* respectively). CCTs broke with traditional forms of social assistance in Latin America by providing transfers as small monthly cash payments rather than as goods; paying money directly to mothers of young children, rather than to household heads; and requiring beneficiaries to comply with conditionalities, typically to do with attendance at schools or health clinics, although in some instances very much more complicated conditions apply (Britto, 2008). Evaluations of the big Latin American CCTs have generally been positive with minor caveats across a range of indicators (Rawlings & Rubio, 2005) such as low corruption, accuracy of targeting, poverty impacts, school attendance (human capital benefits), and empowerment of women beneficiaries (Molyneux, 2007). CCTs have been adopted in many Latin American countries, becoming the preferred model for implementing social transfers in the region.

However, when translated to African contexts, the conditionality has rather quickly been dropped from the cash transfer, with many commentators strongly opposed (Freeland, 2007). One argument is that conditionalities are inappropriate in circumstances where the social services on offer are of such limited capacity and poor quality as to make imposing conditions to attend them quite infeasible and irrelevant. A broader argument locates itself more in individual freedom to make responsible choices. In social transfer pilot projects in Zambia (see Case Study 5 in Part II) and Malawi, the notion of conditionality is reversed, with families given an extra incentive payment if their children attend school (e.g. Schubert &

Huijbregts, 2006), as contrasted with the CCT condition of school attendance as a requirement for getting the basic transfer. Like other contemporary debates in social protection, the conditionality discussion at times seems rather excessively polarized by the efforts of different authors to put clear water between each other. In fact, many types of transfer impose a condition of one sort or another. For example, social pensions require a condition (reaching a certain age) in order to participate, as also does a food- or cash-for-work project that requires participation in a work gang.

A further ongoing strategic debate in social transfers concerns dimensions of dependency and graduation (Matin & Hulme, 2003). The pessimistic view is that social transfers render people increasingly incapable of building or rebuilding their own livelihoods (dependency), and therefore they become ever less likely to 'graduate' from requiring transfers. Some governments are concerned a lot about graduation, since they would prefer to consider the financial commitment to supporting people who are unable to meet their minimum food and basic needs requirements as temporary, and they would therefore also like to see an exit strategy built into the design of any large scale transfer programme.

As with all topics in social protection, there are different angles and entry points to dependency and graduation. For food transfers, there is some evidence to suggest that the dependency hypothesis is overstated (Abdulai *et al.*, 2005). Some types of cash transfer, for example social pensions, clearly cannot have any expectation of graduation; however, their budgetary provision is predictable given known age threshold and mortality parameters. Cash transfers to the chronically hungry seem likely to represent mixed prospects for graduation since some categories of the chronically hungry may have capabilities to lift themselves from ultra-poverty while others do not. One argument made in favour of cash transfers (as opposed to food transfers) is the ability of recipients to choose to save and invest rather than consume part of the transfer. However, a transfer of sufficient size for this to happen may be prone to causing the income of beneficiaries to jump above that of non-beneficiaries who are nearly as poor (see further discussion of this problem in Chapter 9).

While cash transfers seem to have decisively come out on top in the food versus cash comparison, a new consideration in the form of a worldwide tightening of food supplies and rising real food prices may lead to a re-evaluation of these arguments as the impact of rising food price trends makes itself felt in individual national economies, especially in the more food deficit-prone parts of Africa. Cash transfers at a given nominal level provide protection against food insecurity only when food prices are relatively stable, unless clever mechanisms are put in place to adjust transfer amounts to changing food prices. While this may seem an obvious and easy thing to do, there are few countries anywhere in the world where the level of a regular cash transfer like a social pension or a child benefit is repeatedly altered on a monthly basis to reflect changes in its relative purchasing power. Food delivery avoids this problem, shifting the risk of adverse food price changes back from the beneficiary to the supplier of food.

Potentially disastrous rises in real food prices for food deficit vulnerable people are also linked to environment and climate change issues. The contemporary rise in real food prices worldwide is driven in part by the switching of land and crops into sources of biofuel, made more attractive as real oil prices rise, and climate change predictions suggest that many parts of Africa may incur even more frequent droughts than has been the case in the past (although there is a great deal of imprecision in such predictions). Social protection seems likely to play a critical future role in helping African populations deal both with high food prices and with adaptation to climate change (Davies *et al.*, 2008).

This book, with its emphasis on the practicalities of implementing social transfer schemes, is therefore set in a context where large scale adverse events and trends overshadow efforts to achieve significant and sustained poverty reduction in Africa, at a pace that will begin to make inroads into the absolute numbers of people existing persistently at the edge of failing to achieve minimum acceptable levels of food and basic needs. Social protection offers a potential way forward to reach vulnerable groups and populations directly, rather than through the indirect and uncertain route of pro-poor economic growth. Social protection well executed should also boost such growth in addition to protecting the minimum consumption levels of its beneficiaries. This book makes a contribution to this important strategic dimension of poverty reduction in Africa, by looking carefully at what works and what does not work in social protection, and identifying strong points, weak points and opportunities for innovative solutions in the future.

PREVIEW OF THE CASE STUDIES AND BOXED EXAMPLES

The second half of this book contains a set of 15 social protection case studies drawn from schemes and programmes researched in southern Africa in 2006–07. For ease of comparison each case study is set out according to a common template comprising overview, vulnerability, targeting, coverage, coordination, cost-effectiveness, market effects, asset building, strengths, weaknesses and policy lessons. The comparison of these attributes across different social protection schemes provides the basis of the theme chapters that follow on from this chapter. In addition three boxed examples of major social protection schemes in other sub-Saharan African countries are located at appropriate points in the text. A brief preview of these case studies and boxed examples is provided here as a short description:

Southern African Case Studies

Case Study 1: Old Age Pension, Lesotho
The Old Age Pension (OAP) in Lesotho is what is called a categorical social transfer, the category being people living above an age threshold, in this case 70 years. The OAP is a social pension, meaning that it is provided as social assistance without prior contributions. It is also legislated as a right in law.

Case Study 2: Food Subsidy Programme, Mozambique
The Food Subsidy Programme (FSP), known as the Programa de Subsidios de Alimentos (PSA) in Portuguese, is a state-financed cash transfer to the destitute in Mozambique. Until the mid-2000s its coverage was nearly exclusively urban. It provides a very small transfer indeed, enough to buy two to three days' food supply.

Case Study 3: Public Works Programmes, Malawi
Public Works Programmes in Malawi are classic seasonal safety nets. They provide food-for-work or cash-for-work for a limited number of days to self-selected beneficiaries who turn up to join work gangs on public infra-structure projects, in the lean season before the next harvest.

Case Study 4: Dowa Emergency Cash Transfer, Malawi
This scheme was a seasonal cash transfer provided to beneficiaries in a par-ticular food deficit part of Dowa District, Malawi, in the lean season of 2006–07. It was an innovative project that indexed transfers to the price of maize, delivered cash through mobile ATMs, and issued women with smartcards.

Case Study 5: Social Cash Transfers, Zambia
Zambia has had no fewer than five different pilot social cash transfer schemes, each testing different modalities of delivering cash on a routine basis to destitute beneficiaries. All five schemes regard lack of able-bodied labour in the household as a fundamental criterion for beneficiary selection.

Case Study 6: Urban Food Programme, Zimbabwe
The Urban Food Programme in Zimbabwe is interesting as an example of how to provide food and basic needs to beneficiaries under conditions

of hyperinflation. This is achieved by providing beneficiaries with a coupon, redeemable for an agreed basket of goods in participating super-markets.

Case Study 7: Food Assistance Programme, Mozambique
This is a WFP and Ministry of Health programme designed to provide AIDS patients beginning anti-retroviral therapy (ART) with the optimum nutrition for their physiological adaptation to the medication.

Case Study 8: School Feeding, Lesotho
School feeding is a classic social protection programme that provides food rations to primary school children in order to improve their attendance and nutrition status. An interesting comparison in Lesotho is between WFP and government-led schemes that work in differing ways.

Case Study 9: Neighbourhood Care Points for orphans and vulnerable children, Swaziland
Neighbourhood Care Points are a uniquely Swaziland response to the problem of social exclusion of orphans and vulnerable children (OVC). They build on a traditional reciprocity towards people in need in Swazi communities, and allow the provision of food and activities for OVC at a central point.

Case Study 10: Education Material Fairs, Mozambique
The intention of this pilot scheme is to encourage children in rural desti-tute households to attend school. Beneficiary children are provided with a voucher, enabling them to buy school supplies (including clothes) at a one-day fair to which traders have been invited. A secondary aim is to stimulate more market activity in rural areas.

Case Study 11: Input Subsidy Programme, Malawi
This programme comprises heavily subsidized seed and fertilizer supplies for small poor farmers in Malawi. Coupons giving recipients access to two types of fertilizer at about one-third of their world market prices are at the centre of the programme.

Case Study 12: Food Security Pack, Zambia
This is a long-running scheme in Zambia that provides the poorest small farmers with free inputs, in the form of an input package. While suppos-edly being nationwide in coverage, its budgetary provision has been highly erratic, so that actual coverage has varied greatly from year to year.

Case Study 13: Input Trade Fairs, Mozambique

Like the Education Material Fairs, these input fairs work by creating a market day at a specific rural location at which poor farming beneficiaries can exchange a coupon of a specified value for a wide variety of farm inputs and implements (seed, fertilizers, hoes, machetes, etc.).

Case Study 14: Chiefs' Fields for orphans and vulnerable children, Swaziland

In this scheme, chiefs in Swaziland have been asked by the country's king to make available a 3-hectare plot that can be communally farmed by orphans and vulnerable children, under the guidance of willing helpers from the communities. Half-hectare plots are also made available to individual orphan-headed households, up to 26 in each chiefdom.

Case Study 15: Small Livestock Transfers, Zimbabwe

This is an asset transfer scheme that provides small stock (chickens, guinea fowl, goats) to beneficiaries either as direct transfers or via a livestock trade fair similar to those described above. An innovative feature is 'pass-on', whereby a proportion of the increased flock or herd size is donated to other beneficiaries, thus expanding the coverage of the scheme.

Boxed Examples

Box 2.3: Productive Safety Net Programme, Ethiopia

This is a scaled up seasonal safety net programme, providing cash or food transfers to 7.3 million beneficiaries for a maximum of six months in the lean season each year. In terms of number of beneficiaries it is the largest social protection programme in sub-Saharan Africa.

Box 4.1: Hunger Safety Net Programme, Kenya

This programme addresses chronic hunger in northern Kenya and provides a regular cash transfer to 60 000 families (300 000 people) in a first phase up to 2011, funded entirely by the UK DFID. It is intended that coverage in a second phase should eventually reach 300 000 households, with funding from the Government of Kenya as well as a consortium of donors.

Box 5.2: Livelihoods Empowerment Against Poverty, Ghana

The LEAP programme is a CCT directed at the extreme poor left behind by the relatively successful growth record of Ghana. It aims to reach 165 000 beneficiaries by 2012 and is resourced entirely through the government budget using savings earmarked from Highly Indebted Poor Countries (HIPC) debt relief.

2.   Vulnerability

VULNERABILITY AND SOCIAL TRANSFERS

Vulnerability tends to be a term that is used rather loosely; consequently it is often confused with, or used as a synonym for, ultra-poverty (being unable to meet even minimum food needs); or its descriptive meaning varies with the context in which it appears. Here, vulnerability is taken to mean both that people experience high risk of events that have adverse impacts on their livelihoods, and that their ability to deal with risky events when they occur is impaired (Devereux, 2002; Ellis, 2006b). Risky events, or shocks as they are often called, can occur individually (accident, illness, death) or community-wide (drought, floods, plant or animal diseases) (Dercon, 2002). Ability to deal with them when they occur, and thus avert livelihood collapse, depends much on the asset status of households. A household with strong and diverse assets (land, family labour, savings, livestock, tools, etc.) is better able to cope with a shock than a household with weak or depleted assets.

Note that both sides of the vulnerability definition are relevant: the degree of risk of adverse events occurring, and the inability to cope. High risk on its own is not a good indicator of vulnerability (for example, for families that have plentiful resources and many options), and depleted assets would less often lead to livelihood failure in a low risk environment. It follows that vulnerability rises owing either to rising risk or to falling ability to cope, or to some combination of both those factors. People become more vulnerable over time owing to insufficient rebuilding of assets after each successive shock. This can occur for many reasons, including depletion of key assets needed to generate a living (e.g. lack of able-bodied labour), lack of opportunity for generating cash incomes (perhaps due to stagnation or decline of the national economy), poor agricultural performance, and shorter time intervals between shocks. Poverty predisposes people to vulnerability, and the deeper and more persistent the poverty the more this is the case.

As discussed in Chapter 1, the aim of social protection is to reduce hunger and other forms of extreme deprivation. It does this primarily by providing welfare support and underpinning people's livelihoods so that they are protected against a collapse in their food consumption, and are

prevented from having to sell their assets in order to secure minimum
acceptable levels of nutrition and other basic needs. Social protection thus
acts on both the risk and the ability-to-cope branches of the vulnerability
definition. It reduces risk by giving people some form of backup should a
shock occur to them, and it stops the erosion of assets that otherwise leads
to people becoming more vulnerable in the future. Further than this, some
forms of social protection set out to augment people's assets directly (for
example, by giving them livestock) or to assist them to build stronger and
more resilient livelihoods by boosting the productive activities in which
poor and vulnerable people engage (for example, by subsidizing farm
inputs).

This chapter considers what can be learnt about vulnerability to hunger
and ways of effectively addressing it from experience across Africa and particularly from the 15 social transfer case studies contained in Part II of the
book. The chapter is organized around how vulnerability is interpreted for
the purposes of devising social protection responses, across different social
transfer schemes. This is referred to as the 'concepts of vulnerability'
addressed by different schemes. These different vulnerable circumstances
are then examined in terms of the way different social transfer schemes set
about tackling them, and the relative success or failure experienced in
achieving vulnerability reduction goals. The final section of the chapter
seeks to draw out lessons from the examples and case studies about ways of
thinking through vulnerability to hunger, and effectively helping people to
overcome or ameliorate the vulnerability factors to which they are most
prone.

VULNERABILITY CIRCUMSTANCES ADDRESSED BY SOCIAL TRANSFERS

Across Africa, diverse social protection schemes set out to provide support
to different vulnerable groups or populations, over differing time periods,
and some of them seek to ameliorate vulnerability without tackling its
causes, while others seek to tackle perceived causes of vulnerability without
offering an immediate improvement in access to food and basic needs. It is
found that most social transfers in Africa are susceptible to being classified
into seven main categories in relation to the approaches to vulnerability
they represent, and these seven categories are listed in Box 2.1, followed by
a discussion of each of them, drawing particularly on the case studies of
Part II of the book.

BOX 2.1: SOCIAL TRANSFERS IN AFRICA
GROUPED BY VULNERABILITY
APPROACH

A. Food and basic needs deprivation of older people
B. Food and basic needs deprivation of the extreme poor or
destitute
C. Food consumption gap of those facing seasonal food deficits
D. Low yields and output due to wrong or low inputs
E. Intergenerational transmission of poverty
F. Adverse impacts of AIDS on household livelihoods
G. Asset depletion arising from personal or community shocks

Food and Basic Needs Deprivation of Older People

The vulnerability to hunger of older people in poor countries and settings
is verified in numerous studies. Older people may no longer be able to carry
out cultivation and other onerous physical activities, they are prone to
bouts of ill health requiring rising medical costs, and they can become
socially excluded even in tightly knit societies. Mortality associated with
AIDS places particular burdens on older members of affected families,
since they both lose the care that they might have received in old age from
their own children and end up looking after orphaned grandchildren.
These AIDS impacts were put forward, for example, to justify the introduction of an Old Age Grant in Swaziland (see Box 2.2).

There are seven sub-Saharan African countries that have social pensions
and these are Botswana, Lesotho, Mauritius, Namibia, Senegal, South
Africa and Swaziland. This list contains several of the better off sub-
Saharan African countries; however, Lesotho and Senegal are two quite
poor countries that have taken on public responsibility towards the vulnerability of older people in this way. The origins and working of the Lesotho
Old Age Pension is described in Case Study 1 in Part II of the book.

Social pensions are national entitlements to a regular cash transfer, subject
to the single criterion of an age threshold. The age threshold differs across
countries that have social pension schemes (for example it is 60 in Swaziland
and 70 in Lesotho). A process of registration is required for eligibility to be
conferred, and this involves a mixture of written identification (if available)
and verification by traditional leaders (chiefs). In Swaziland, the initial idea
was that better off people would be excluded from registering; however, this

---

BOX 2.2:   SPEECH BY THE KING OF SWAZILAND
           MAKING WAY FOR THE OLD AGE
           GRANT, 2005

*'One outcome of the HIV and AIDS pandemic is the effect on our
elderly. HIV and AIDS continues to kill a lot of our young people
who leave behind orphans and uncared for elderly parents. Some
of these elderly people sometimes go without basic support and
yet they are expected to also care for the orphans . . . It is in the
light of such difficulties, in which our elderly people live, that government has decided to increase the annual allocation to the
social security fund to E30 million for the benefit of our elderly poor
citizens.'*

(HMK, Mswati III, 2005, Speech from the Throne)

---

is not a line that it has proved possible to hold in practice. In both the countries mentioned, public servants on government pension schemes are
excluded from the state pension.

Social pension schemes essentially work rather well. Indeed, in Lesotho
and Swaziland they have confounded pessimistic predictions about their
budgetary sustainability and the safety of pensioners collecting cash. The
success of such schemes relies on ensuring that the pension amount is
adjusted for price rises in food and other essential goods and services,
for otherwise the vulnerability protection conferred will be eroded over
time.

Social pensions involve a trade-off between age threshold, coverage and
budgetary cost. An age threshold of 70 (the Lesotho OAP) means fewer
families are supported and for a shorter duration than an age threshold of
60 (the Swaziland OAG). Data for Lesotho shows that the OAP corresponded to roughly 3 per cent of government recurrent expenditure in
2006/07, and it has been estimated that lowering the age threshold to 65
would raise this to 5.2 per cent. Reluctance to do this is likely to be more to
do with establishing rights (on the part of older people) and obligations (on
government) than to do with cost factors taken in isolation.

Food and Basic Needs Deprivation of the Destitute or Extreme Poor

Destitution is a difficult concept to pin down, since it is relative to other, less
severe, degrees of poverty and vulnerability. By addressing the needs of the

Table 2.1   Concepts of vulnerability addressed in the 15 case studies

Case Study	Acronym	Concepts of Vulnerability Addressed
1	OAP	Insufficient food access of older people, plus OVC caring role
2	PSA	Food consumption gap of the urban destitute
3	PWPs	Seasonal and local food consumption gap
4	DECT	Seasonal and local food consumption gap
5	SCTs	Food consumption gap of the destitute
6	UFP	Food consumption gap of the urban destitute
7	FAP	Special nutritional needs of AIDS patients on ART
8	SF	Food access of primary school children; barriers to school attendance
9	NCPs	Vulnerability to social exclusion of OVC
10	EMFs	School attendance of deprived children; poorly working markets
11	ISP	Food consumption gap due to poor yields
12	FSP	Recovery from farm shocks (drought), low and unstable yields
13	ITFs	Recovery from farm shocks (floods, drought); poorly working markets
14	CFs	Food consumption gap of OVC
15	SLTs	Asset depletion (livestock) due to previous shocks

Note: See Table 10.1 for the full list of countries and case study project names.

destitute, a presumption of ultra- or extreme poverty (typically defined as not being able to secure enough food even if all household income were spent on food) and unusually high vulnerability to hunger is made. Destitution is typically approached through proxy indicators such as only being able to afford one meal per day, lack of income earners in the household, small households comprising single widows or disabled people or orphans, or large households with many dependants and no income earners.

The Kalomo Scheme in Zambia (Schubert & Goldberg, 2004 and Case Study 5) pioneered the notion that the destitute make up about 10 per cent of that country's population. This figure was empirically based. It constituted the proportion of households found in the Zambia 2004 Living Conditions Monitoring Survey to have a per capita food consumption under 1400 kilocalories per day, and that in addition lacked able-bodied labour. This category of households is referred to in some of the social protection literature as the 'non-viable' poor, an unfortunate characterization since it seems to imply that disabled people, for example, are unable to engage in productive livelihoods even if given the opportunity to do so. The 10 per cent rule has acquired some authenticity, though not without debate (Ellis, 2008), and has been used as the cut-off point defining the most vulnerable in other Zambia cash transfer pilots, as well as in more recent Malawi cash transfer schemes (Schubert & Huijbregts, 2006).

Destitution features as a criterion determining eligibility for social transfers across a wide variety of different social protection schemes. Amongst the southern Africa case studies, three schemes have tackling destitution as the primary focus. One of these has both rural and urban components (Case Study 5), while the other two are mainly urban (Case Studies 2 and 6). The first two of these provide regular cash transfers to the destitute, following the axiom of 'predictable funding for predictable needs'; however, in the Zambia case these were pilot projects designed to explore the modalities of scaled up social protection for the extreme poor, and therefore they had limited duration. The last scheme mentioned was a project funded by the DFID Protracted Relief Programme (PRP) in Zimbabwe, and it utilized food vouchers as a delivery mechanism to a limited number of the urban destitute.

The experience of schemes in this category is mixed. The original Zambia cash transfer pilot (the Kalomo scheme) was considered to have worked well, thus inspiring replication (with variations in approach) in the form of four further pilots. A feature of all such schemes has been the intensity of involvement of donors and NGOs in scheme design and implementation, to an extent that could not be realistically replicated at a broader scale. More recent experience has indicated lurking difficulties around beneficiary selection, delivery motivation, and governance. The Mozambique PSA possesses some positive organizational features, but the amount of the monthly cash transfer is so small (perhaps enough to purchase meals for two to three days) as to make negligible difference to the hunger circumstances of its beneficiaries. The Zimbabwe urban food vouchers scheme works well for its beneficiaries, but is spread thin, covering 2000 households across five cities.

Food Consumption Gap of Those Facing Seasonal Food Deficits

The occurrence of seasonal food deficits in rural areas of sub-Saharan Africa is a well-established phenomenon (Chambers *et al.*, 1981; Sahn, 1989). In many parts of the continent seasonal migration patterns are closely associated with food scarcity in the lean season. Seasonal migration both removes mouths to feed from rural households under food stress, and opens up the possibility of remittance income that can help families get through to the next harvest. A standard social protection response to seasonal food gaps over the past 10–15 years has been the institution of food-for-work or cash-for-work schemes, exemplified by public works programmes in Malawi (Case Study 3) and Ethiopia (Box 2.3).

Where seasonal hunger is unpredictable and springs up in different places from one year to the next, social transfer responses to seasonal hunger tend to be short duration. In Public Works Programmes (PWPs), either food or cash is provided on a self-targeting basis in return for work on public infra-structure or community projects. These can be put in place just for those locations where vulnerability assessments indicate that a severe but transient hunger problem is developing. A ceiling number of days' work by any particular individual is often applied. For example, in one of the Malawi PWPs, the transfer amount was US$1.6 for an eight-hour task unit, up to a maximum of ten such task units (allowing for a maximum cash income earning of MK2000 or US$16 per person); in the Ethiopia PSNP (Box 2.3), households are allocated up to 30 days' work per month, based on a maximum of five days per individual household member.

When seasonal hunger is predictable and is known to create a given case-load of families requiring assistance year after year, the potential exists for treating this as a chronic problem requiring a long term approach. The PSNP in Ethiopia (Box 2.3) does just this, providing around 7.3 million people with food or cash transfers for up to six months each year in the lean season. In terms of absolute numbers of people covered, this makes the PSNP the largest social protection programme in sub-Saharan Africa. About 90 per cent of PSNP beneficiaries must engage in PWPs in order to receive their transfers, but beneficiary selection is by community targeting of those most in need, rather than by self-targeting. This programme is interesting on many other counts, including the coordination of such a large programme and its efforts to enable recipients to graduate from requiring support after three years.

The Dowa Emergency Cash Transfer (DECT) project (Case Study 4) had a different and innovative design, providing monthly unconditional cash transfers through a smartcard system and mobile ATMs, with women being given ownership of the smartcards. In the DECT project, cash transfers were made monthly for five months and varied to keep the real purchasing power of the transfer the same (in terms of the retail price of maize) across the duration of the intervention (Devereux *et al.*, 2007). The DECT project is regarded as having been successful at achieving its limited seasonal and locational objectives in Dowa District in Malawi in the 2006–07 lean season.

Public works programmes have been the most popular instrument for providing fallback positions for able-bodied participants in the hungry season in numerous settings, and do provide some, albeit temporary and

BOX 2.3:   PRODUCTIVE SAFETY NET PROGRAMME, ETHIOPIA

The Productive Safety Net Programme (PSNP) in Ethiopia provides a particularly clear illustration of key themes in social protection in Africa that arise throughout this book:

- distinguishing chronic from transitory hunger;
- for the chronically food deficit, replacing emergency responses by routine transfers ('predictable funding for predictable needs');
- coordinating the transfers of many different agencies (government, NGOs, WFP, etc.) under a single administrative structure;
- distinguishing beneficiary households between those with and those without able-bodied labour;
- addressing the duration of transfers, and prospects for beneficiaries to graduate from needing them in the future.

Food insecurity in Ethiopia is mainly chronic in nature. Around 7–8 million people (10 per cent of the population) require assistance every year irrespective of agricultural outcomes, and these numbers increase steeply in drought years. In the past no distinction was made between chronic and transitory hunger, and almost all transfers to those in need were met through annual emergency appeals. The PSNP sets out to separate chronic from transitory hunger, addressing chronic hunger by integrating predictable transfers with other rural development initiatives in a multi-year programme. In this way, annual emergency appeals should diminish very considerably in size, eventually only being for food shortfalls caused by unpredictable crisis events.

The PSNP was devised in 2003–04 and became operational in February 2005. In 2006 and 2007 it reached 7.3 million people, and in 2008 8.2 million, to which it transferred per beneficiary a maximum of US$3.50 per month or US$21 over six months, in either food or cash or some combination of both. The PSNP is nested in a broader strategy called the Food Security Programme overseen by the Ministry of Agriculture and Rural Development (MoARD) and comprising grants to districts for resettlement, agricultural services, and other food security interventions in addition to the PSNP. The programme itself is managed by an agency within MoARD called the Food Security Coordination Bureau (FSCB).

The PSNP has the following interesting features from the viewpoint of comparisons with other social protection examples provided in this book:

- It has covered up to 8.2 million recipients as compared to 1.9 million for the means-tested social pension in South Africa or 100000 for the Food Subsidy Programme in Mozambique (Case Study 2).
- Transfers to beneficiaries are for a maximum of six months in the lean season.
- Transfers may be in food or cash, or can be switched between cash and food mid-season.
- It has both a public works (conditional) transfer component and a direct support (unconditional) transfer component.
- The direct support transfer is available only to individuals lacking able-bodied labour and with no other means of support, e.g. from children or relatives.
- In practice, only about 10 per cent of beneficiaries receive direct support payments, the rest being assigned to public works.
- The public works component is not self-targeted – beneficiaries selected by community targeting must turn up to work in order to qualify for their transfers.

The PSNP places considerable emphasis on graduation. Its aim is not just to meet the immediate consumption needs of transfer recipients, but to facilitate them to exit from the programme if they are able to do so. It is hoped that this can be achieved through the preventive dimension of transfers (preventing distress sales of assets), the infrastructure created by public works (community asset building), the role of complementary rural development activities coordinated at district level, savings and investment by beneficiaries themselves, and provision of sequential measures such as credit to graduating beneficiaries. The programme has the following definition of graduation: 'a household has graduated when, in the absence of receiving PSNP transfers, it can meet its basic food needs for all 12 months and is able to withstand modest shocks'.

Graduation is operationalized through annual reviews of the circumstances of recipients conducted at the community level, for which a set of federal graduation benchmarks have been devised; although these have yet to be adjusted for the diverse regions of Ethiopia.

The mix of food and cash in the PSNP provides unusual flexibility for responding to local market circumstances. In 2006–07 there was a roughly 50:50 overall split between cash and food. At the local level, districts are advised to supply food when local supplies are tight and cash when local supplies are plentiful. Within the limitations of delivery to remote rural areas, they can switch between cash and food as the lean season progresses and food stocks at family and community level run low. In 2006, for example, about one million beneficiaries were switched from cash to food during the disbursement cycle. By 2008, however, a strong shift in beneficiary preferences towards food occurred, resulting in the phasing out of cash transfers in most places. This was because the daily cash wage rate provided under PSNP had only risen by 33 per cent since inception, as compared to a 350 per cent rise in food prices over the same period.

The size of the PSNP means that a massive administrative and logistical exercise was required to put into place all the community, district and regional level committees and bodies and accounts and procedures in order to put the programme into effect. This was mainly well executed, and targeting is considered to have worked fairly well to date. Nevertheless, the programme faces continuing challenges:

- Timeliness of both food and cash transfers to districts has been an issue, with late transfers meaning delays in reaching beneficiaries in serious need.
- Rising world food prices and diminishing stocks in 2007 and 2008 caused disruption of the Ethiopia food pipeline, with corresponding adverse effects on the integrity of the programme.
- Graduation remains an elusive goal, since other events such as substantial emergency operations in 2008 have meant that the achievement of a smooth progression towards the exit of recipients from the programme after two to three years has not been feasible.

Sources: Ethiopia (2004); FEWSNET (2006); Devereux (2007); IDL Group (2007)

ad hoc, protection from hunger. However, they also possess significant weaknesses (detailed in Case Study 3), which include the able-bodied labour requirement (the poorest households lacking able-bodied labour are not reached), the high start-up costs of public works (requiring civil engineers, etc.), and the often low quality of the public works maintained or constructed. For these reasons, enthusiasm for them has been waning across Africa (except in Ethiopia), and the growing preference is to provide regular cash transfers to chronically hungry people continuously through the year.

Low Yields and Output Due to Low Input Use

The vulnerability addressed here is the inability of poor small farmers to produce enough to satisfy their families' food consumption needs over a calendar year. Social protection in this category therefore sets out to overcome a major perceived root cause of vulnerability (low yields and output), not just the symptoms of vulnerability (as applies to the preceding categories).

Several of the case studies contained in Part II of this book are centred on the delivery of free or subsidized inputs to small poor farmers; however, there are substantial differences in the scope and duration of individual schemes and programmes. Both Zambia and Malawi (Case Study 11) have re-established national fertilizer subsidies, thus going against the grain of received wisdom about the benefits of free markets in this regard. In addition to a national fertilizer subsidy, Zambia has an input package scheme specifically aimed at farmers who are too poor to purchase fertilizer, even at subsidized prices (Case Study 12). More modest input schemes with limited or dubious impacts are represented by Input Trade Fairs in Mozambique (Case Study 13) and Chiefs' Fields for orphans and vulnerable children (Case Study 14).

In the Malawi Input Subsidy Programme, fertilizers attract a roughly two-thirds subsidy, and farmers purchase vouchers for fixed quantities of fertilizer at one-third the border price of imports (Dorward *et al.*, 2008). A huge logistical exercise is required for the countrywide distribution of vouchers as well as seed and fertilizer distribution. In Case Studies 12 and 13, the aim is to provide free inputs (up to a voucher value or as a delivered package) for especially vulnerable small farmers facing difficulties recovering from previous shocks.

In order to reduce vulnerability, input subsidies in rainfed agriculture require complementary circumstances to be helpful rather than hostile; in other words, the amount and pattern of rainfall must be favourable for crop growth and maturation across the growing season. In three successive seasons beginning in 2005/06 Malawi was especially fortunate in this regard. When events are not so favourable, input subsidies can be an expensive way of funding crop failure. Some of the Input Trade Fairs (ITFs) in Mozambique as well as similar experiments in other African countries have failed owing to adverse natural events of this kind. Moreover, the once only and non-repeating formula of the ITFs means that the cumulative effect on vulnerability reduction for their beneficiaries is negligible.

Input subsidies have a chequered history as a means of raising rural incomes and lowering rural vulnerability. In an earlier era, they were regarded as making a significant contribution to sustained yield growth in Asia (the Green Revolution), but experience in Africa was mixed and often disappointing. On a national scale, they can take a heavy toll on government budgets, and politically they become more difficult to lower or remove the longer that farmers become accustomed to paying artificially low fertilizer prices. One emerging view is that transitional (or 'market-smart') subsidies can play a role in reviving smallholder agriculture when the use of purchased inputs has fallen to exceptionally low levels (World Bank, 2007, p.152; Dorward *et al.*, 2008).

Intergenerational Transmission of Poverty

Social protection that prevents malnutrition in children and improves their chances of acquiring education and skills has intergenerational effects that will not be perceived until the children grow up and are hopefully able to create better life chances than their parents. All social protection that successfully targets very poor families and provides a sufficient level of transfer to benefit the children in the household has this potential effect. Nevertheless, some forms of social protection specifically aim at this intergenerational goal. Amongst the social transfer case studies in Part II, School Feeding in Lesotho (Case Study 8), Education Material Fairs in Mozambique (Case Study 10), and social transfers to OVC in Swaziland (Case Studies 9 and 14) correspond to this type of social protection.

Schemes listed in this category exhibit widely varying methods for achieving their aims of keeping children in school and ensuring their adequate nutrition. The Education Material Fairs (EMFs) in Mozambique (Case Study 10) were pilot projects that utilized vouchers in connection with one-day trade fairs to provide a limited number of vulnerable children with a single chance to improve their life chances through participation in education. OVC initiatives in Swaziland include providing OVC with more stable social reference points, as well as food (Neighbourhood Care Points), school fee waivers, school feeding, and a chance to gain agricultural skills through collective and individual farming. Lesotho school feeding (Case

Study 8) involves universal delivery of food rations to primary school children throughout the country, as well as take-home rations for herd boys of school age in mountainous areas.

Success in this category is difficult to assess since tracking studies of children who benefit from such transfers are virtually unknown. The arguments in favour of school feeding at primary schools seem compelling (Del Rosso, 1999; Bergeron & Del Rosso, 2001), and Lesotho has a long history of near enough complete coverage in this area. The Education Material Fair pilots in Mozambique are thought to have improved school retention for those children who received vouchers, but the non-repeating character of such fairs means that they are subject to the same limitations for vulnerability reduction noted for input trade fairs.

Adverse Impacts of AIDS on Household Livelihoods

HIV and AIDS have many negative consequences for livelihoods and vulnerability. Foremost amongst these are the costs of providing medication and care for those falling ill from AIDS-related illnesses, and the loss of able-bodied labour in the household due to illness and death. A lot of social protection in Africa addresses this latter outcome, with lack of labour frequently being used as the marker to determine which families are most in need of assistance.

Out of 33.2 million people worldwide estimated to be living with HIV/AIDS, 22.5 million or 68 per cent are in sub-Saharan Africa. The HIV prevalence rate for sub-Saharan Africa overall is 5 per cent of the total population. However, prevalence rates vary across the continent, with the highest rates in the world found in southern Africa (Table 2.2). Here, Lesotho, Swaziland and Zimbabwe have (with Botswana) the highest four HIV infection rates in the world (rates above 20 per cent of the 15–49 adult population). Mozambique and Zambia are in the next tier of rates between 10 and 20 per cent of the 15–49 population. The demographic effects of rising HIV rates through the 1990s and early 2000s have yet to be fully experienced in individual country populations. It is estimated that AIDS was responsible for over half a million deaths across the six countries listed in Table 2.2 in 2005. AIDS deaths result in growing numbers of orphans, and these are estimated by UNAIDS to have numbered around 3 million aged 0–17 in 2005, or 5 per cent of the total population across those six countries.

Many social protection schemes across Africa are designed to address the nutritional and basic needs of families containing individuals with AIDS-related illnesses, or the social and consumption needs of children orphaned by AIDS. Amongst the southern African case studies, this category includes the Food Assistance Programme in Mozambique that

Table 2.2   HIV data for selected southern African countries, 2005

RHVP Country	Adults (15–49) '000	Adults Infected '000	Infection Rate %	AIDS Deaths '000	AIDS Orphans '000	Orphans % Pop
Lesotho	1 078	250	23.2	23	97	5.4
Malawi	6 028	850	14.1	78	550	4.3
Mozambique	9 938	1 600	16.1	140	510	2.6
Swaziland	629	210	33.4	16	63	6.1
Zambia	5 882	1 000	17.0	98	710	6.1
Zimbabwe	7 463	1 500	20.1	180	1 100	8.5
Totals and Averages	31 018	5 410	17.5	535	3 030	5.0

Source: UNAIDS (2006a)

provides food rations for families in which one or more members were receiving ART (Case Study 7), as well as the projects in Swaziland that address the well-being of OVC (Case Studies 9 and 14). While these case studies address AIDS and its deleterious impacts as their main focus, in truth a considerable proportion of all social protection schemes take into account AIDS impacts in the criteria that they establish for eligibility to scheme benefits. Thus households lacking able-bodied labour owing to AIDS-related deaths, households containing OVC, and the elderly looking after orphaned grandchildren all describe circumstances that tend to enter the multiple criteria utilized by different agencies to target the most vulnerable people in society.

Based on the case studies, schemes that address AIDS impacts directly seem prone to short time horizons, insufficient funding and poor scheme design. The six-month cut-off point in the Food Assistance Programme in Mozambique, for example, was rather arbitrary, especially when taken in conjunction with uneven ration supply during the delivery period. OVC farming schemes in Swaziland are poorly coordinated and designed, with multiple different entry points overlapping each other in different schemes, an undue reliance on purported community reciprocity for scheme success, token redistributions of land, and lack of clarity regarding beneficiary needs and their availability to engage in farming.

Asset Depletion Arising from Personal or Community Shocks

A well understood feature of the dynamics of vulnerability is that households that have experienced one or more shocks, and have depleted their assets to cope with those shocks (for example to buy medicine or food), are often unable to rebuild their assets before the next crisis occurs, resulting in a spiral downwards into destitution. Some social transfer projects seek to reverse this sequence directly by providing assets or strengthening the capability of families to acquire assets. The allocation of land to child-headed households (Case Study 14) and the transfer of livestock to small poor farmers (Case Study 15) fall within this category of social protection.

The methods used to address asset depletion vary considerably between case studies. In the simplest case, livestock are provided to vulnerable families as direct transfers to beneficiaries, or via vouchers that can be spent on livestock at special fairs convened for the purpose (Case Study 15), and note the similarity of mechanism to the ITFs and EMFs (Case Studies 10 and 13). In the Chiefs' Fields (CF) scheme in Swaziland (Case Study 14) land is allocated to listed beneficiaries by area chiefs, and this is framed partly in terms of the restitution of land rights lost owing to the premature death of parents and the associated failure of land inheritance.

This is a category in which success is difficult to assess, although for different reasons to those cited under other categories. The livestock transfers scheme in Zimbabwe contained the innovative idea of 'pass-on', whereby successful breeding would result in additional livestock being passed on to other listed beneficiaries in recipient communities. This builds on a traditional practice, known as *mafisa* in northern Namibia but also occurring in many other countries, whereby someone agrees to rear livestock for a friend or relative in return for a share of the offspring. On the other hand, livestock transfers throughout Africa display mixed outcomes owing to the complexity of the contingent factors that need to be in place for scheme success (skills in livestock husbandry, access to grazing or feed, veterinary support services).

LESSON LEARNING ABOUT APPROACHES TO REDUCING VULNERABILITY

This chapter has examined vulnerability as a cross-cutting theme in social protection, drawing on 15 case studies in southern Africa as well as examples from other African countries. Three different vulnerability attributes of schemes were explored: the concept or understanding of vulnerability that schemes set out to do something about, usually linked to the circumstances of a specified social group; the approaches or methods used by the schemes to tackle these forms of vulnerability; and their relative success or failure at reducing the vulnerability of their chosen beneficiaries. The lesson learning set out here is about these dimensions of vulnerability and its mitigation.

Vulnerability is rarely a short term phenomenon. In many parts of Africa, it is thought to have deepened and become more persistent over time owing to factors that have depleted people's assets and eroded their options to generate incomes from a variety of sources. Droughts, floods, soil depletion, AIDS, shrinking migration options and many other factors are implicated. Chronic vulnerability means that small adverse events can push people into food deficit, hunger and other deprivations. This highlights the inadequacy of taking short term positions with respect to vulnerability reduction in social transfer projects, and this is one amongst a number of lessons about duration, scope and timeliness with respect to addressing vulnerability that emerge from the southern Africa case studies and other examples:

1. There is an evident advantage to having a clear vision of the vulnerable circumstances that are being addressed, and older people (in relation to social pensions) or primary school children (in relation to school feeding) are exemplary in this regard.

2. Under social protection, as contrasted to emergency response, there are few circumstances where short duration responses to vulnerability are appropriate, the only exception being seasonal hunger and deprivation, which may crop up in different places in different years and therefore need a capability to anticipate their occurrence and respond in a timely and effective manner (the DECT project in Malawi was a model of good practice in this respect).

3. The whole point about chronic vulnerability is the role of risk and unpredictability in undermining people's capability to secure enough food to eat and other basic necessities; therefore the worst possible features to allow to surface in social transfer schemes are inconsistencies or unpredictabilities, whether of funding, commitment, duration or coverage (and unfortunately quite a lot of social protection in Africa falls short in regard to one or other of these attributes).

4. Nor in most cases can vulnerability be reduced through medium-term, two- to three-year social transfer projects: in the case of welfare transfers to the chronically hungry, cessation after an interval of a few years merely means that beneficiaries are thrown back into the hunger that they were temporarily protected from; while in livelihood building initiatives (for example, providing farm inputs or livestock) a longer duration commitment is typically required to ensure that the full benefits of the transfer are realized (many NGOs have come to understand this, but they are often hampered by the unwillingness of their donors to take longer term positions).

5. It is doubtful that one-off instantaneous transfers of the type typified by Input Trade Fairs make much difference at all to the underlying inci-

dence of vulnerability; the idea that a single opportunity to acquire inputs or implements in a fair that only occurs once in any one location could make a serious difference to people's vulnerability to hunger seems deeply flawed.

6. While limited geographical coverage may be unavoidable for NGO schemes with small budgets, design in such cases should at least ensure that all vulnerable people who fulfil targeting criteria can be included, for otherwise social transfers are socially divisive, and seriously inequitable for those who are excluded from the project or programme.

7. The most successful social transfer programmes are those that are national in character, underwritten by legislation and permanent in duration: these satisfy the principle of 'predictable funding for predictable needs' and they bring features of consistency, coherence, duration and coverage to reducing the vulnerability of beneficiaries.

Amongst examples provided in this book, three comparatively recently instituted programmes targeted at the extreme poor comply in varying degrees with these desirable attributes. These are the Ethiopia PSNP (Box 2.3), the Kenya HSNP (Box 4.1), and the Ghana LEAP (Box 5.2). In addition, social pension schemes in a limited number of countries also fulfil these requirements, and often with the additional benefit of being legislated as an inescapable right to which all citizens who reach the designated age threshold are eligible.

In summary, vulnerability to hunger and other forms of severe deprivation is in most instances a persistent phenomenon, the result of gradual erosion of people's livelihoods over many years, and therefore not susceptible to instant turnaround through the medium of short-burst social transfers. With respect to the vulnerability dimension of social transfers, consistency, predictability and long duration are preferred principles upon which to design schemes and programmes.

3.   Targeting

INTRODUCTION

Targeting has been defined as 'the process of identifying the intended beneficiaries of a program, and then ensuring that, as far as possible, the benefits actually reach those people and not others' (Sharp, 2001, p.1). This may sound straightforward enough, but in practice targeting is far from simple, and can be broken down into a series of at least seven discrete choices. First is defining eligibility in theory – who is entitled to benefit from this programme? (often this is vaguely defined, for example 'the poor', or 'vulnerable groups', or 'the disabled'). Second is operationalizing eligibility in practice – what criteria will be used to decide who is entitled? (agreeing on robust indicators of poverty, for instance, is a challenge in itself, while proxy indicators of need such as having a disability or being female are often inaccurate). Third is identifying and selecting beneficiaries – how will all the people in the programme area who meet the eligibility criteria be found?

Fourth, registration procedures – how will beneficiaries be registered? (and, since many programmes are targeted on households rather than individuals, which person should be registered?). Fifth, verification tests – how will it be confirmed that the correct individuals are collecting benefits? (this might require senior community members to be present, to verify the identity of claimants). Sixth, grievance procedures – will a mechanism be provided for people who feel unfairly excluded from the scheme to appeal for their inclusion? Finally, there are graduation and re-targeting – what if some beneficiaries no longer need assistance, or if new people meet the eligibility criteria, during the lifetime of the programme? (for example, in a social pension that targets people over 60 years of age, people who are 59 are not registered, but will become eligible to register the following year).

In this chapter the intention is to explore the ways that different social transfer schemes seek to overcome or resolve these seven challenges. Clearly it is rare, if not impossible, to resolve all of them simultaneously in a single scheme; therefore most social transfers focus on just the two or three of these challenges that they consider most important for scheme success. As in other chapters of the book, examples are drawn from the 15 southern Africa case studies provided in Part II, as well as from experiences in other parts of Africa. The chapter proceeds by considering alternative targeting mechanisms, then exploring key issues and principles that arise from these alternatives, and finally deriving lessons that emerge from the experience of targeting in a wide variety of different social transfer schemes.

TARGETING MECHANISMS

An extraordinarily diverse range of targeting approaches can be found across social protection schemes in Africa, including geographic targeting, categorical targeting, means tests, proxy means tests, community selection and self-selection. Typically, more than one mechanism is used; for instance, the first level of targeting is often geographic (even 'universal' programmes are limited by national boundaries). This discussion explores the strengths and limitations of each approach to targeting, drawing on actual experiences with applying these mechanisms, especially as provided by the case studies, the targeting approaches of which are summarized in Table 3.1.

Geographic Targeting

This is the simplest targeting mechanism of all. Benefits are concentrated in certain parts of a country, either administrative districts or areas defined as vulnerable (drought zones, arid regions, floodplains, etc.). Geographic targeting is very common in emergency programmes, where the cause of vulnerability is a natural disaster or conflict that affects an identifiable area (for example, the DECT project in Malawi was confined to part of a single district affected by drought). A purely geographic approach would imply having complete coverage at the area level. This might be quick and easy to administer but the cost of providing transfers to people who do not strictly require them has to be weighed against the cost of more rigorous targeting. The key variable is the percentage of population affected. Most pilot projects use geographic targeting as a 'first level' criterion; however, this is often for circumstantial reasons (communities where the implementing NGO happens to be active), rather than resulting from needs assessment. This introduces arbitrariness and randomness into targeting, unless NGOs purposively select the poorest and most vulnerable communities as their programme areas. However, even if this is done, such projects tend to have limited geographical coverage, so that from a national level perspective exclusion errors are extremely high. Politics can also enter geographic targeting, such that assistance may be dependent on support for government, or places hostile to the government get social transfers as a form of 'votebuying'.

Table 3.1   Targeting in the 15 southern Africa case studies

	Country	Social Protection Scheme	Targeting Mechanisms
1	Lesotho	Old Age Pension	1. Categorical (all citizens over 70)
2	Mozambique	Food Subsidy Programme	1. Categorical (older people; people with disabilities; the sick) 2. Means test (monthly income <Mtn 70)
3	Malawi	Public Works Programmes	1. Self-targeting (low wage +work) 2. Categorical (women) 3. Geographic (vulnerability mapping)
4	Malawi	Dowa Emergency Cash Transfers	1. Geographic (drought-affected district) 2. Community selection (+ triangulation)
5	Zambia	Social Cash Transfers	1. Geographic (pilot project districts) 2. Proxy means test (indicators of destitution)
6	Zimbabwe	Urban Food Programme	1. Means test (households with income <US$1/day)
7	Mozambique	Food Assistance Programme	1. Multiple eligibility criteria (vulnerable AIDS patients) 2. 'Medical means test' (eligible for ART)
8	Lesotho	School Feeding	1. Categorical (primary school children, herd-boys, orphans)
9	Swaziland	Neighbourhood Care Points	1. Categorical (orphans) 2. Multiple proxies (vulnerable children)
10	Mozambique	Education Material Fairs	1. Categorical (vulnerable children in school)
11	Malawi	Input Subsidy Programme	1. Multiple eligibility criteria (farmers; land owners; cash-for-work participants)
12	Zambia	Food Security Pack	1. Proxy means test (<1 ha land; unemployed; female- or child-headed; caring for orphans; terminally ill; disabled; the elderly)
13	Mozambique	Input Trade Fairs	1. Multiple eligibility criteria (drought-affected, female-headed, poor, farming)
14	Swaziland	Chiefs' Fields for OVC	1. Categorical (orphans) 2. Multiple proxies (vulnerable children)
15	Zimbabwe	Small Livestock Transfers	1. Geographic (drought-affected rural districts) 2. Proxy means test (no livestock) 3. Categorical (widows)

Categorical Targeting

This requires identifying distinct groups of people who are generally poorer or more vulnerable than others. Examples include people with disabilities, orphans and older persons. Sometimes the target category is defined by the nature of the programme. For instance, the obvious beneficiaries of agricultural input subsidies in Malawi or Input Trade Fairs in Kenya are farmers. Categorical targeting is popular because it is cheap and simple, but it is subject to inclusion error (non-needy members of that category), and also to two types of exclusion error: (a) neglect of other vulnerable people who do not fit the category (countries that deliver social pensions and child support grants, like South Africa, provide little social assistance to poor people aged between 16 and 60), and (b) thresholds can be set to exclude all but a small proportion of a category (for example, setting the age threshold for an old age pension at 70 excludes vulnerable older people between 60 and 70 years of age).

Categorical targeting is not always as simple as it first appears. Interventions targeted at orphans must first define 'orphan' (for example, a child under 18 who has lost both parents), and then verify that applicants indeed meet these criteria. Seemingly simple categories often add qualifying conditions (for example, widows 'without support' or 'living alone'), which then necessitate more careful assessment and monitoring. Categories selected as target groups often relate to the objectives of the intervention. In highland Lesotho, for example, herd-boys and orphans are given monthly take-home rations conditional on school attendance, which is intended to provide incentives for their families to keep the boys in school (they have lower enrolment and higher drop-out rates than other children, because herd-boys are needed by their families to look after livestock, while orphans are more likely than other children to be kept at home to help with household chores).

Means Tests

These can be implemented by requiring applicants to complete a questionnaire regarding their incomes and assets, and if their 'means' fall below a minimum threshold they are entitled to receive social assistance. In Mozambique's Food Subsidy Programme (actually a cash transfer), monthly income per capita must not exceed Mtn 70. In Zimbabwe's urban food subsidy, eligible households are those 'obtaining less than US$1 per day from all sources'. Means tests are generally agreed to be the most accurate targeting mechanism, but also the most expensive and complicated, being susceptible to under-reporting of income and assets by applicants, or collusion between applicants and officials to register ineligible beneficiaries. These risks of fraud and corruption can only be mitigated with close monitoring and double-checking, which raises administrative costs. Also, because the livelihoods of poor people are insecure and their incomes are unpredictable, the validity of means tests is debatable. Individuals can move in and out of poverty from year to year, or even from month to month, requiring repeated income assessments, which of course raises these administrative costs even further. A final problem associated with means testing, as also with several other targeting approaches, is that it creates incentives to modify behaviour to become eligible (for example, to 'import' relatives into the household for grants that are proportionate to household size, or to stop looking for work to qualify for unemployment-related grants, which is a 'dependency' effect).

Proxy Means Tests

These are applied to avoid the cost and complexity of income assessment, by identifying local indicators of poverty that are considered robust (accurate) and easier to observe than income. This is similar to categorical targeting, except that multiple categories are often involved, and these are not always as visible as age, gender or disability. In Swaziland's 2006 National Plan of Action for orphans and vulnerable children (OVC), children are eligible for assistance if they meet one or more of several proxy indicators of poverty and vulnerability. These include parents or guardians who are incapable of caring for them; staying alone or with poor elderly grandparents; living in a poor sibling-headed household; having no fixed place of abode; being physically challenged; lacking access to health care, education, food, clothing and psychological care; lacking shelter from the elements; being exposed to sexual or physical abuse; engaging in child labour. Table 3.2 contains several other examples of proxy indicators used as targeting criteria.

Community Selection

This involves communities themselves in selecting beneficiaries (this occurs in several of the case studies of this book, and is also a feature of larger programmes such as HSNP Kenya – Box 4.1, and LEAP Ghana – Box 5.2) in order to draw on local knowledge and ensure social acceptance of targeting decisions. For example, OVCs who benefit from Neighbourhood Care Points in Swaziland are selected by their communities, in consultation with traditional leadership structures and community-based workers such as rural health motivators. The targeting works well because community members understand the situation of local children, and caregivers make

*Table 3.2   Examples of proxy means tests in the southern Africa case
            studies*

Case Study	Country	Project or Programme	Proxy Criteria
2	Mozambique	Food Subsidy Programme	Destitute: proxy indicators include: ● older people (men over 60, women over 55) ● unable to work ● people with disabilities ● chronically sick ● living alone or heads of destitute households
5	Zambia	Social Cash Transfers	Poorest 10%: proxies include: ● eating one meal per day ● begging from neighbours ● having malnourished children ● very poor shelter and clothing ● owning no valuable assets ● caring for large numbers of children ● elderly-, sick-, disabled- or female-headed
6	Zimbabwe	Urban Food Programme	Urban poor: criteria include: ● bedridden home-based care clients ● families with several orphans ● single-parent households ● households with no able-bodied adult
12	Zambia	Food Security Pack	Poor farmers: ● access to land ● cultivating less than one hectare ● having adequate labour for farming ● not in gainful employment
15	Zimbabwe	Small Livestock Transfers	'People struggling to survive': ● rural households with no livestock ● women widowed by AIDS ● destitute families with small children ● caregivers to the chronically sick ● elderly with no support and no remittances

house-to-house visits to ensure that all deserving children are identified and participate in the programme.

On the negative side, unless community institutions are representative, inclusive and democratic there is a risk of 'elite capture', that is, committees favour their relatives and friends and exclude socially marginalized groups. Targeting and verification procedures need to be independent of each other, or the risk of 'elite capture' is high. In rural Zimbabwe, traditional leaders participated in the compilation of beneficiary lists for the Small Livestock Transfers project, which targeted destitute rural households, but several beneficiaries had to be de-registered after they were discovered to be from wealthy families, including village headmen. Genuine community participation is time-consuming, resource intensive, and challenging to scale up; for example, if community wealth ranking is used to identify poor groups, this is a relative measure that is not comparable across communities.

Self-Selection

This is popular with donors because in theory it reduces targeting costs and social tensions and improves accuracy. Instead of assessing individual need or trying to find robust proxies for poverty, incentives are structured so as to attract needy individuals and discourage non-needy applicants. Self-targeting works by lowering benefits transferred or raising costs of accessing benefits. Public Works Programmes (Case Study 3) exploit both sides of this equation. They have high access costs (commitment of manual labour and time) and relatively low benefits (wages set below local market rates, or payment in food rather than cash). But self-targeting often does not work in contexts of widespread and severe poverty, because benefits cannot be set low enough, or access costs high enough, to discourage people from applying. On most public works in rural Africa, for instance, wages cannot for ethical reasons be set low enough to equalize the supply and demand for labour. Job rationing and discretionary allocation of workplaces inevitably follow, causing inclusion and exclusion errors. Public works also embody other exclusion errors since recipients must be capable of hard physical work, implying that the old, the ill, people with disabilities, or women looking after orphans and vulnerable children are not reached by these 'self-targeted' social transfers.

KEY ISSUES AND PRINCIPLES

Targeting raises a number of issues, quite apart from the decision about how to do it. Three key issues that are examined here are: first, the case for targeting *versus* universal coverage; second, inclusion and exclusion targeting errors; and, third, politicization of targeting (for example, 'patronage bias' in geographical targeting).

Targeting or Universal Coverage?

A prior question, before thinking about how to do targeting, is whether to target at all (Hoddinott, 2007). In most cases this is not a realistic choice: resources are constrained and it is cost-effective and equitable to channel these resources to people who need assistance most. But objections to targeting can be raised: that it is inequitable and discriminatory, that it contradicts 'rights-based' approaches, or that the poorest cannot be easily identified and separated out ('we are all poor here'). In the Small Livestock Transfers project in Zimbabwe (Case Study 15), resentment from people who were excluded but felt strongly that they deserved to benefit caused fights to break out in project villages. In such contexts an argument for universal coverage is often made, but of course this incurs substantial 'leakages' to people who do not really need assistance.

In cases where the extent of need is high and the costs of targeting are significant, the case for universal distribution is stronger. In the DECT project in Malawi, more than 70 per cent of households were drought-affected in parts of Dowa District, and the argument was made that implementing community-based targeting was so expensive that it would have been simpler and even cheaper to register all households in the district. This was not in fact true, since the cost of targeting amounted to US$53000 while expanding the programme to 100 per cent coverage would have cost an additional US$186000 (Devereux *et al.,* 2007, p.23). However, there is also an argument about the political costs of targeting. 'Benefits meant exclusively for the poor often end up being poor benefits', said Amartya Sen (Sen, 1995, p.14), meaning that programmes that benefit everyone gather political support from influential and wealthy people, which is often an important determinant of programme success. In the case of DECT, a decision to exclude headmen from the benefits caused resentment and loss of support from several of these gatekeepers to local communities. Several people interviewed during the DECT evaluation argued that a rule of thumb should be applied: if the people eligible for assistance in any community exceeds 70 per cent of the population, universal coverage should be preferred to avoid the economic and social divisiveness of targeting.

At the other extreme, projects like the cash transfer pilots in Zambia (Case Study 5) applied a '10 per cent rule', defining only the poorest decile of the population as eligible for social transfers. In such cases the debate about universal coverage does not arise, but different challenges arise, notably how to apply such an arbitrary quota fairly in contexts of wide-spread and severe poverty that vary across locations and communities.

Of course, very few 'universal' programmes are not targeted in some sense, even if they are universal within a district, like the proposal for the DECT project (=geographical targeting) or within an age group, like a universal social pension (=categorical targeting). Instead of 'targeted' versus 'universal' programmes, perhaps we should talk about 'light' versus 'heavy' targeting, or 'simple' versus 'complex' targeting. Light or simple targeting means choosing a single indicator (for example, all citizens over 70, as in Lesotho's Old Age Pension). Heavy or complex targeting implies multiple criteria (see Table 3.2 for several examples), or targeting procedures that are time-consuming and expensive (for example, the Public Assistance Grant in Swaziland, where each applicant is visited by a social welfare officer who assesses their income, assets, food consumption and health status).

Targeting Errors

The debate about whether to target (that is, to exclude some members of the population) or to opt for universal coverage (to include everyone) naturally raises the issue of targeting errors. Programme staff are usually pre-occupied with minimizing inclusion error or 'leakage', which is caused by targeting people who do not really need assistance. This is very important, not least because it wastes scarce budgetary resources and can deprive needier people of assistance. Recipients of the Food Security Pack in Zambia are selected in a way that results in a high degree of leakage. Beneficiary lists are first drawn up by village headmen, and then reviewed by Community Welfare Assistance Committees (CWACs) or Area Food Security Committees (AFSCs). 'This method is prone to inclusion and exclusion errors owing to elite capture by kin and cronies of headmen' (Case Study 12). Similarly, input subsidies in Malawi were delivered in the form of coupons that were allocated in a non-transparent manner: 'leaders, police, chiefs, friends and relatives received the bulk of the coupon allocations' (Case Study 11). In Lesotho's Old Age Pension, it was reported that 'ghost beneficiaries' were created by corrupt officials, and that pensions continued to be paid out for several months after pensioners had died. Verification procedures have since been tightened up to reduce these sources of fraud and corruption. Low civil service salaries in many countries have contributed to a reported increase in petty corruption by officials, some of whom see social transfer programmes as a source of supplementary income, by cheating beneficiaries out of part of their entitlements.

Equally (or even more) important is ensuring that everyone who needs assistance is reached by the programme – that is, minimizing exclusion

---

**BOX 3.1 EXCLUSION ERRORS IN THE
MOZAMBIQUE FOOD SUBSIDY
PROGRAMME**

The Food Subsidy Programme in Mozambique is a government programme with national coverage. The programme makes regular cash transfers to destitute Mozambicans who are unable to work. Target groups include older people (90 000 beneficiaries in 2006), people with disabilities (5600) and chronically ill people (933). Because of budget constraints and limited administrative capacity in rural areas, the programme has been restricted to all major urban centres, though the intention is to expand coverage to rural districts.

There are approximately one million men and women over 60 years old in Mozambique, and the national poverty rate is 54 per cent. Since poverty is typically higher than average among older people, this implies that there are at least 540 000 elderly poor, but only 90 000 are receiving the FSP, a coverage rate of 17 per cent, and an under-coverage or exclusion error of 83 per cent.

Source: see Case Study 2

---

error – because the consequences of excluding desperately poor people from social assistance programmes can be very serious, even fatal. Under-coverage is high on locality-based pilot projects (which provide islands of access for a tiny minority of needy people), and where budget constraints limit beneficiary numbers (Zimbabwe's urban food subsidy, for instance, reaches only 10 per cent of people who meet the eligibility criteria: 'Thus exclusion is substantial owing to limited budgets').

A major source of exclusion error arises when budget constraints require quotas or rationing to be imposed, as in Malawi's Public Works Programme (discussed above). In Zambia's Social Cash Transfers projects, an explicit quota was introduced in the targeting process: households were ranked by level of need, and a cut-off was applied at 10 per cent. The technical justification was that the poorest 10 per cent of the population in rural Zambia are destitute and demonstrably worse off than everyone else, according to survey data, but this is a spurious argument for setting a quota at the level of individual communities. For project budgeting and planning purposes, a quota keeps things simple, but this can result in the exclusion of many households that clearly meet the eligibility criteria for assistance.

An alternative to quotas or rationing is 'dilution' of benefits. This is a common practice on public works projects, where participants are 'rotated' after only a few weeks or months, in order to maximize coverage, but at the cost of reduced impact at household level. The dilemma facing project staff is, therefore, wide coverage but limited impact, or limited coverage but deeper impact. Alternatively, beneficiary communities can themselves choose to dilute benefits: when communities are given a limited number of bags of food or fertilizer and seed packs and instructed to allocate these to the poorest households, they sometimes split these resources equally among all community members.

Just as there are real consequences to mis-targeting, so there are real costs to achieving accurate targeting, which can be modelled as a trade-off, since the more accurate the targeting the higher the costs of doing the targeting. These costs arise not only in the identification and selection of eligible individuals, but also in registration and verification procedures, which will improve programme efficiency if done properly, but take time and money. Verification has two aspects: proving eligibility and proving identity. Examples of verification procedures include:

- *age:* ID card (Lesotho Old Age Pension);
- *residence:* verified by local administration (Zambia pilot cash transfers);
- *clinical status:* 'the disabled, the chronically sick and malnourished pregnant women' (Mozambique Food Subsidy Programme);
- *medical criteria:* 'patients must be certified by a medical practitioner as requiring and being able to benefit from ART, including testing for CD4 count and having a body mass index (BMI) of 16 or under' (Mozambique Food Assistance Programme);
- *spot checks:* follow-up visits on 10 per cent of beneficiaries (Zimbabwe Urban Food Programme).

Conversely, less rigorous methods might be cheaper (for example, choosing visible proxy indicators like disability instead of conducting detailed means testing), but there will almost certainly be much higher inclusion and exclusion errors. For example, a popular proxy indicator of vulnerability is the female-headed household, but many female-headed households are not poor (for example, if the woman is a wealthy trader, or has an employed son or daughter sending her remittances), while many women in male-headed households are extremely poor and vulnerable. In any society there are many more male-headed than female-headed households, but women in male-headed households will be omitted from any programme that targets female-headed households in an attempt to reach poor women.

Politicization of Targeting

Any assessment of the strengths and weaknesses of different targeting mechanisms should include a discussion of the degree to which there is (or can be) political influence over the targeting process. Access to social grants is too often seen as a philanthropic gesture by the state or foreign donors and NGOs, rather than as a right that all poor citizens are entitled to claim from their government. This welfarist approach allows programmes to be targeted on a discretionary basis, where eligibility is based partly on objective criteria, partly on chance and partly on patronage, which is where the politics comes in. Politicization of social grant programmes occurs when, for instance, transfers are targeted not on the basis of need but on geographic areas (for example, the President's home district) or population groups (for example, the dominant ethnic group that supports the incumbent administration), or groups that the administration is trying to attract (by 'winning hearts and minds' through handouts).

The broader issue here is the contradiction that can exist between 'social rules of allocation' (patronage, ethnicity, etc.) and 'administrative rules of allocation' (poverty, vulnerability, etc.), which can result in perceptions of mis-targeting by programme administrators (if 'social rules' dominate) or by communities and local elites (if 'administrative rules' with which they disagree dominate). In Zambia, for instance, a substantial number of Food Security Packs were allocated on a patronage basis, which ignored the prescribed eligibility criteria. In other cases mechanisms are found for minimizing the patronage bias that diverts resources away from intended beneficiaries, such as the community triangulation method used in Malawi to identify eligible households for the DECT intervention.

Politicians view social protection ambivalently. On the one hand, handouts and subsidies are always popular with voters, especially in the run-up to elections when these instruments are routinely exploited to 'buy votes'. The Government of Malawi first claimed political credit for delivering farm input packages to Malawian farmers in the late 1990s and then turned on the donors who supplied these packages when cutbacks in the programme were blamed for causing the 2002 famine. The government also attempted to influence the decision about which districts should receive input packages, when the programme was scaled back from national to one-third coverage. Similarly, the Government of Zambia raised objections to the five districts that were selected by international NGOs for pilot cash transfer projects, and proposed alternative districts that were politically more strategic.

Many African governments are deeply sceptical about predictable large scale social transfer programmes, arguing that they are unaffordable and breed a 'dependency culture' among beneficiaries. For this reason they often favour programmes that support 'productive' groups like farmers, who are expected to invest their transfers (for example, fertilizer subsidies) and generate economic growth that will ultimately reduce their dependence on social transfers. Recently, however, there has been an expansion of social grants to older ('non-productive') citizens, with non-contributory pensions schemes spreading from South Africa and Namibia to Botswana, Lesotho and Swaziland. One advantage of favouring simple demographic indicators like age (or gender, or disability) is that they are not susceptible to falsification or political manipulation. There have been no reports of political interference with Lesotho's Old Age Pension; instead the pension became subject to 'positive politicization' when parties contesting the general election in 2007 attempted to woo 'grey votes' by promising to raise the pension level if they were elected.

Finally, Cliffe (2006) makes the point that politicization can distort allocations of social grants at several stages in the process, from defining eligibility criteria to registration and delivery. A crucial element here is 'the institutions chosen for making lists and handling delivery. Does provision go through corrupt channels, reinforce patronage networks or miss out the poor?' In several of our 15 case study projects, traditional leaders (chiefs, headmen and elders) are centrally involved at all stages, but as we have seen this can produce ambiguous results.

LESSON LEARNING ON TARGETING

This review of experiences with targeting social transfers confirms the findings of an exhaustive global review of targeting mechanisms that there is no 'magic bullet' for good targeting; the outcomes depend not on which approach is adopted but on how well it is implemented (Coady *et al.*, 2002). Several specific lessons on targeting can be extracted from the case studies and examples drawn on in this chapter:

1. There is no single best approach to targeting social transfers. Every targeting mechanism has its strengths and weaknesses, and in many cases trade-offs are involved that require subjective judgements to be made – between targeting costs and targeting accuracy, for instance, or between 'complex but accurate' individual assessments and 'simpler but less accurate' proxy indicators.
2. Although programme officials typically focus their efforts on minimizing inclusion errors (leakages), in contexts of severe need it is arguably even more important to minimize exclusion error (under-coverage). To build social consensus and political support for pro-poor social

transfer programmes, some degree of 'leakage' to influential elites might be an acceptable and even necessary cost, provided this does not deprive very needy individuals and households of receiving social assistance.

3. Complex concepts like 'vulnerability' and multiple eligibility criteria aim at sharpening targeting accuracy, but create opportunities for different interpretations and manipulation by different actors involved in programme delivery, elite capture within beneficiary communities, and discretionary allocations, all of which raise both inclusion and exclusion errors.

4. Simple, single criteria that are not easy to falsify or manipulate (for example, age thresholds or health status) usually work well in terms of transparency, community understanding and acceptance, minimizing inclusion errors and keeping targeting costs low (identification as well as verification). However, broad categories, such as all citizens over 65, overlook many other population groups who also need social assistance, so complementary programmes are also needed that target other vulnerable groups.

5. Politicization can distort the allocation of social assistance, for instance if eligibility is determined by 'patronage bias' rather than indicators of need. Possibilities for political interference increase if national or local political elites are involved in defining eligibility, drawing up beneficiary lists or delivering benefits. As noted above, local leaders are the gatekeepers of their communities so their support is needed, but mechanisms need to be implemented to curb their influence and ensure that programme objectives are not compromised.

6. Grievance procedures should be implemented as standard procedure on all social grant programmes, to allow anyone who feels unfairly excluded an opportunity to complain formally. To date very few programmes have included grievance procedures in their design and implementation, but introducing this mechanism, provided it is independent of the institution that made the initial targeting decisions, would address many of the concerns about targeting errors and politicization that have been raised in this discussion. The Kenya HSNP (Box 4.1) built in independent grievance procedures from the outset of the programme.

4. Delivery

INTRODUCTION

The purpose of this chapter is to explore different delivery methods deployed by social transfer schemes in Africa. Delivery of social transfers has several interesting dimensions for lesson learning about good practice. First, there is the form of the transfer that is delivered to beneficiaries, and here, as already discussed in Chapter 1, the four main categories of cash, food, inputs and assets are between them more or less exhaustive of the main forms that delivery can take, even though many variants of delivery approach can be found within each category (vouchers, coupons and so on).

Second, the technology of the delivery can vary, with electronic technologies offering the scope for entirely new ways of effecting social transfers, especially for cash transfers. Third, the organization and logistics of social transfers can vary considerably in terms of the institutions and channels that are used. Fourth, and closely related to the preceding dimension, the scale of the delivery task varies very considerably between national programmes and sub-national or local projects and schemes. Fifth, there are potentially significant issues around the incentives and motivation of the personnel involved in delivering social transfers, especially when those personnel do not see themselves as all that much better off than the recipients of the transfers.

The effective delivery of social transfers overlaps with other themes explored in this book, particularly targeting, coordination and coverage and cost-effectiveness. This chapter focuses specifically on the delivery angle, but connections to other themes are made where appropriate. The next section summarizes patterns of delivery as represented by the southern Africa case studies provided in Part II of the book, partly in order to illustrate the extent of variation in delivery that can be found in practice, and partly in order to explore the strengths and weaknesses of alternative delivery methods. In addition to the case studies, illustrative examples are also provided by the Kenya HSNP (Box 4.1) and the Swaziland Old Age Grant (Box 4.2). The third section considers the difficult and sensitive issue of incentives and motivation in the delivery of social transfers. The final section seeks to draw out some lessons from the examples and case studies about strengths and weaknesses in delivery systems for social transfers, again linking these to the five delivery dimensions listed above.

DELIVERY TYPES IN THE SOUTHERN AFRICA CASE STUDIES

Cash Transfers

Table 4.1 below provides a brief summary of the delivery methods encountered in our 15 southern African case studies. A total of eight schemes involve cash transfers to beneficiaries and, within this collection, four deliver bank notes to beneficiaries, one utilizes smartcards that can be used for cash withdrawal, and three involve vouchers of a given cash value that can be spent on groceries (Urban Food Programme, Zimbabwe), or on farm inputs (Input Trade Fairs, Mozambique), or on educational materials or school clothes (Education Material Fairs, Mozambique).

Variations in implementation are rather more diverse than is suggested in such a summary description of the cash category. Amongst those schemes that end up with cash-in-hand for beneficiaries, some involve withdrawal at designated bank branches (some beneficiaries in the Zambia social cash transfer pilots), some involve pay points placed in post offices, schools or other public buildings on a designated day, perhaps once a month or quarterly (pensions in Lesotho as well as some Zambia SCTs), and some involve cash paid at the end of a specific work shift of four or eight hours (cash-for-work schemes).

Vouchers are a variant of the cash transfer delivery mechanism that can work well in circumstances where cash is for some reason problematic, or the intention of the social transfer is to direct beneficiary expenditure to a limited range of items. The Urban Food Programme run by ActionAid International (AAI) in Zimbabwe utilizes vouchers that represent entitlement over a designated 'basket' of groceries as a means of overcoming the rapidly declining value of cash in a situation of hyperinflation. The Input Trade Fairs (ITFs) in Mozambique provide vouchers with a cash value that can only be exchanged for farm inputs or implements supplied by designated traders at the fairs. The same model was used for the Education Material Fairs (EMFs) project implemented by Save the Children UK, also in Mozambique. In both instances, the goal of the scheme is different from providing a basic consumption capability to destitute beneficiaries; rather it is to encourage improved farm input use for higher outputs (ITFs), or education supplies (including uniforms) in order to encourage children from vulnerable households to attend school (EMFs).

Table 4.1   Delivery methods in the southern Africa case studies

No	Country	Social Protection Scheme	Social Transfer Delivery Methods
1	Lesotho	Old Age Pension	Cash using post offices and other pay points
2	Mozambique	Food Subsidy Programme	Cash using payment team
3	Malawi	Public Works Programmes	Cash or food ration paid for work unit
4	Malawi	Dowa Emergency Cash Transfer	Cash using smartcards and mobile ATMs
5	Zambia	Social Cash Transfers	Cash using pay points and smartcards
6	Zimbabwe	Urban Food Programme	Voucher (cash value) at supermarkets
7	Mozambique	Food Assistance Programme	Food rations for collection at health centres
8	Lesotho	School Feeding	Food rations for primary school children
9	Swaziland	Neighbourhood Care Points OVC	Community caregivers, food rations OVC
10	Mozambique	Education Material Fairs	Voucher (cash value) for use at single fair
11	Malawi	Input Subsidy Programme	Coupons exchanged for inputs at depots
12	Zambia	Food Security Pack	Farm input packs, delivered to villages
13	Mozambique	Input Trade Fairs	Voucher (cash value) for use at single fair
14	Swaziland	Chiefs' Fields for OVC	Enhanced access to land and inputs OVC
15	Zimbabwe	Small Livestock Transfers	Small stock transfer or via fairs; 'pass-on'

Security is clearly a critical issue in cash transfers. The advantage of using the private banking system for withdrawals is that the cash can be assumed to be reasonably safe up to the point of withdrawal. The same holds true for the use of smartcards that can only be cashed against a fingerprint at an ATM (the DECT scheme in Malawi). Pay points involving physical movements of cash are more difficult, and therefore more variable in experience. In Lesotho, the use of post offices to deliver pensions to older people has worked well. However, in Swaziland the same concept proved such a disaster that responsibility was taken away from the post office network within months of trial implementation, being replaced by pay points in other public buildings run directly by the Department for Social Welfare (detailed in Box 4.2). Pay points require clerical verification and a police presence on payout days, which can add up to significant additional delivery costs. In most instances, the whole process of ensuring that cash has been transferred to a withdrawal point, the withdrawal itself, and the disbursement to beneficiaries is a multi-layered, bureaucratic and costly exercise. The Food Subsidy Programme (Programa de Subsidio de Alimentos) run by the National Institute of Social Action in Mozambique represents the most costly end of the spectrum in this regard, with rough estimates of the cost of delivery suggesting that 50 per cent of the budgetary value of the transfer scheme is spent on the delivery function (see Chapter 6).

Low cost of delivery compared to food is purportedly one of the great attractions of cash transfers (Farrington & Slater, 2006), but the case studies examined here suggest that this advantage remains elusive in most cases, the security of cash transfers constituting the greatest barrier to their realization. It is clear that innovative technologies for cash transfer (smartcards, cell phones) have considerable future potential in this regard, as exemplified by the use of smartcards in the DECT project (Case Study 4), and electronic transfers in the Kenya HSNP (Box 4.1) and the Ghana LEAP programme (Box 5.2). The same goes for using the private banking system to effect cash transfers in conjunction with either traditional withdrawals (in person, at the counter) or using new technology for this purpose.

The Kenya Hunger Safety Net Programme (HSNP) provides an interesting example of utilizing the private banking system to effect electronic cash transfers using the latest secure technical options available. In HSNP (see Box 4.1) transfers are made by the private Equity Bank to point-of-sale (PoS) devices distributed to local agents, who are private shopkeepers or traders and who receive a small commission for each transfer. Recipients are issued with a smartcard that is inserted into the PoS device and verified against a fingerprint (using an attached fingerprint reader). As soon as the cash is handed to the recipient, the PoS transmit the transaction to Equity

Bank. Recipients have the option of withdrawing only part of their regular transfer, thus building savings and earning a rate of interest.

Food Transfers

Food deliveries feature in four of the 15 case studies. These are the Food Assistance Programme to AIDS patients beginning ART in Mozambique, School Feeding to primary school children in Lesotho, meals provided to orphans and vulnerable children (OVC) at Neighbourhood Care Points (NCPs) in Swaziland, and food-for-work under Public Works Programmes in Malawi. With the exception of the last of these, plausible arguments can be advanced to support food rather than cash delivery given the purposes of each scheme. In the case of food rations for ART patients, the purpose is to provide a fortified diet in support of the physiological adaptation of patients in the early months of starting ART. In the case of school feeding, a considerable literature attests to meal provision as an effective way of keeping children in school, as well as ensuring a balanced diet and improving attention span in classes (for example, WFP, 2006). Meal provision at NCPs seems to be essential in order to achieve their broader OVC social inclusion goals, since in the absence of food the children just stop turning up.

Delivery of food raises important issues to do with procurement and effects on local markets (Chapter 7). It is now well established that social transfers should support rather than undermine local markets, and therefore food procurement should in most cases take place in the domestic economy rather than relying on food aid imports. Delivery costs are also reduced if procurement happens locally as compared to shipment and importation costs for external supplies, especially for beneficiary locations remote from ports.

While the World Food Programme has become a great deal more sensitive to these considerations in recent years (Gentilini, 2007a), its past history was so steeped in transoceanic food aid deliveries that its default position tended to be towards reliance on external supplies. In the case of the Mozambique Food Assistance Programme, this reliance had adverse effects on the continuity of delivery owing to disruptions in external supply lines. In the Lesotho School Feeding case, delivery responsibilities were split between government and WFP channels, with the government scheme entirely reliant on locally procured ingredients in the vicinity of schools. However, here a different problem came to light, and that is the risk of inferior or insufficient quantities of ingredients being purchased if the money allocated for purchase per pupil turns out to be insufficient to comply with the mandatory composition of rations.

BOX 4.1:   HUNGER SAFETY NET PROGRAMME,
           KENYA

Poverty in Kenya was estimated at 45.9 per cent in 2005/06, with rural poverty at 49.1 per cent and urban poverty at 33.7 per cent (Kenya National Bureau of Statistics, 2007). The proportion of what are termed hardcore poor (those going hungry even if they were to spend all their income on food) was 22 per cent in rural areas, with 934 000 households falling into this category. Poverty in Kenya displays strong spatial patterns, with the semi-arid and arid northern districts of the country having poverty rates ranging from 70 up to 93 per cent (Turkana District), and hardcore poverty averaging around 40 per cent in those areas.

The Hunger Safety Net Programme (HSNP) seeks to address the chronic hunger that prevails in northern Kenya. About 1.5 million people there are regarded as a predictable caseload that requires assistance every year to meet minimum acceptable food and non-food basic needs. In the five years up to 2007, Kenya spent US$420 million on emergency relief in the form of food aid, covering at times up to 3.5 million people. It was estimated in 2007 that a predictable cash transfer would cost less per person than food aid (US$55 against US$79), while at the same time protecting consumption and enabling people to maintain and rebuild assets.

HSNP is funded by the UK DFID as part of a broader programme of support to the Government of Kenya (GoK) costing £122.6 million (US$245 million) over ten years, and comprising the development and implementation of:

- a national social protection policy and strategic implementation framework
- a cash transfer programme for orphans and vulnerable children (OVCs)
- HSNP delivering long-term, guaranteed cash transfers to chronically food-insecure households

The aims of HSNP are to strengthen food security, protect assets and reduce the impact of shocks. Transfers are unconditional. The programme runs alongside other social transfers to which some of the recipients will have access, including ongoing WFP food transfers and an experimental livestock insurance scheme operating in some areas. The cash transfer is regarded as supplementary to people's own livelihood efforts, and to these other transfers. The programme is seen as a cash transfer pilot, albeit a multi-year one that can investigate different modalities and adjust to experience as it goes along.

The HSNP formally began on 1 May 2008; however, it did not become operational until October 2008 when registration, enrolment and issue of parametric cards to beneficiaries were initiated. After some logistical delays, the transfers of cash to beneficiaries were intended to begin in January 2009 with a first 5000 beneficiaries. Thereafter, the programme was to be rolled out, adding 5000 households each month, to reach 60 000 beneficiary households by 1 November 2009. This is 20 per cent of the estimated 300 000 households (1.5 million people) considered to be persistently in need of support in Kenya's arid and semi-arid lands. HSNP is designed in two phases. Phase 1 lasts from 2007 (design) to 2011, stabilizing at the level of 60 000 households (estimated 300 000 individual beneficiaries) covered by DFID-funded transfers. Phase 2 is scheduled to run from 2011 to 2017, in which DFID will continue to fund 60 000 beneficiary households, while other donors in a consortium with GoK will be sought to scale up coverage to the 300 000 household level.

The HSNP is organized into five main components, with different public, donor, private and NGO actors involved in each (see Fig. 4.1). Administration includes targeting, registering and enrolment, undertaken by an NGO consortium comprising Oxfam, Save the Children UK and CARE International. Management Information Systems and coordination are undertaken by donor-funded personnel formally seconded to GoK. Payments (on which more below) are organized through the Financial Sector Deepening (FSD) Trust and implemented by the private Equity Bank. Monitoring and Evaluation (M & E) is contracted out to a private consultancy team. Grievance procedures designed to ensure the rights of prospective and selected beneficiaries are undertaken by the NGO HelpAge International working in partnership with a number of NGOs. It is thought that this separation of functions helps to minimize fiduciary risk; in particular, separation of targeting and payment reduces the risk of elite capture and 'ghost' names in beneficiary lists.

Targeting in the HSNP is the responsibility of the Oxfam GB-led NGO consortium. The intention was to reach three different target groups in different parts of the scheme area (the four districts of Turkana, Marsabit, Mandera and Wajir in Phase 1): (a) the elderly who will in effect receive a pension; (b) community targeting of vulnerable households; and (c) households selected on the basis of high dependency ratios. In planning documents, it was intended to make transfer amounts vary according to household size, with details to be finalized before initiating payments in November 2008. The purpose of this part of the design is to refine ideas about the best targeting criteria for this type of cash transfer.

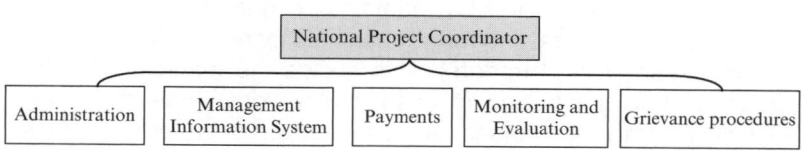

Figure 4.1

The payments system in HSNP is also designed to minimize fiduciary risk, and certainly in Phase 1 occurs entirely outside government financial channels:

- Funding is first transferred from DFID/GoK (the latter rather notionally) to FSD Trust, and from there to Equity Bank.
- Funds are transferred electronically from Equity Bank to registered agents in the districts, using point-of-sale (PoS) devices.
- The agents are shopkeepers and traders ('pay points') in towns and rural trading posts.
- Beneficiaries are issued with parametric cards (smartcards incorporating fingerprint technology).
- The agents pay their listed beneficiaries against a fingerprint, once every two months.
- Pay points in districts are distinguished according to whether they are: A (larger urban areas), B (small urban areas), C1 (moderate sized trading post), C2 (small trading post).
- For budgeting purposes, the average payment per beneficiary household was projected as KShs 2130 (US$20) per two-month payment period, although an inflation adjustment to this may have occurred subsequently.
- Based on budgeting data, a commission was to be paid to agents at the rate of US$0.64 for each transaction.
- Immediately the payment is made by an agent to an individual beneficiary, the transaction is transmitted by the PoS device to Equity Bank.
- In order not to overwhelm agents on a single day each two months, beneficiaries turn up in rotation; for example, a pay

point with 600 beneficiaries can pay out on average ten beneficiaries a day over 60 days.
- Beneficiaries have the option not to draw down their full two-
month entitlement, thus leaving a proportion of it at Equity
Bank as savings that attract an interest rate.

A defining feature of this payments model is its reliance on existing liquidity in the local economy (cash held for normal transactions
by shopkeepers and traders). This avoids the necessity for the
costly and risky carriage of cash into remote semi-arid areas.
However, in the final phases before the launch of the project it was
becoming clear that not all places designated for transfers necessarily had the requisite quantities of cash in circulation, so it
remains to be seen how well this works in practice.

The HSNP has many interesting features for comparative purposes with other case study social protection schemes described
in this book, and especially the PSNP (Box 2.3) and LEAP (Box
5.2) programmes that similarly involve transfers to scale:

- Funding is initially wholly by donors (this is similar in part to
PSNP, but is in contrast to LEAP).
- Organization is almost wholly outside government during a
first phase, with the intention to transfer to government in a
second phase (this contrasts with both PSNP and LEAP, in
which governments have central roles from the outset).
- Delivery of cash transfers occurs wholly outside government
(this contrasts with PSNP, but LEAP similarly uses private
sector services for electronic transfers to post offices).
- Cash transfers are unconditional (in PSNP, 90 per cent of
transfers require physical labour in public works, while in
LEAP broader conditionalities must be met).
- The transfers utilize electronic technologies for reliability and
security (this is similar to the DECT (Case Study 4) and
LEAP, but not PSNP, which relies on old-style financial transfers between central and local tiers of government).
- A variable transfer per household (different from the early
Zambia SCTs (Case Study 5) but similar to other recent high
profile schemes).
- Graduation is mentioned but relatively downplayed (in con-
trast to its high profile in PSNP and LEAP design).

Sources: Kenya National Bureau of Statistics (2007); DFID Kenya (2007a, 2007b,
2007c)

Input Transfers

Four of the case studies are concerned with tackling vulnerability by raising yields and outputs in agriculture via the use of improved inputs (seed and fertilizer), crop diversity and cultivation practices. Two of these are national programmes: the Input Subsidy Programme in Malawi and the Food Security Packs in Zambia. The other two are smaller scale schemes and include the OVC initiatives in Swaziland that involve free input deliveries, and the ITFs in Mozambique, already discussed above in relation to voucher transfers. At national scale, delivering inputs is a very substantial logistical undertaking (see Case Study 11 on the Malawi Input Subsidy Programme).

Each of these schemes takes a very different approach to delivery. The Malawi Input Subsidy Programme involves purchase of coupons by beneficiaries at a cost that is about one third of the import price for the quantity of fertilizer specified on the coupon. The coupons are then exchanged for seed or fertilizer at depots. The Zambia Food Security Packs originally involved physical delivery of a diverse pack of inputs comprising maize and pulse seeds, cassava roots, and two fertilizer types, for which farmers paid a token price. Moreover, this scheme contained many other delivery features including the required adoption of particular cultivation practices by farmers, and reclaiming of a proportion of subsequent outputs in the form of 'recoveries' and seedbanks. Many components of the original scheme have disappeared in subsequent years so that now a more modest pack comprising maize seed and one type of fertilizer is delivered, and the seedbank idea has long since been abandoned.

Timeliness is a critical issue in the delivery of input transfers. If the inputs arrive too late for the onset of the rainy season, then the beneficial effects on yields and output are reduced or lost altogether depending on the degree of lateness involved. All the case study input schemes examined here have at one time or another, or for particular parts of the country, failed to deliver on time, with adverse consequences for project effectiveness. Interestingly, some of the worst performers in this regard are the smallest schemes, with the OVC schemes in Swaziland widely reporting late input delivery, resulting in only a fraction of targeted land being cultivated and very poor output results (other factors are also implicated in these outcomes).

Asset Building

The final category of forms of delivery comprises projects that build livelihood assets. Several social protection schemes mentioned under other headings in this chapter involve asset building. For example, school feeding is intended to increase the human capital of the next generation, transfers related to improving the health of beneficiaries also have beneficial effects on human capital, and public works programmes build infrastructural capital such as roads or terracing or irrigation canals. Cash transfers can also contribute to asset building if the transfer amount is sufficient to permit the saving or investment of some small proportion of the regular transfer. To some degree all types of social transfer can indirectly result in asset protection or building by relieving the pressure on household budgets to be spent wholly on securing enough to eat. The substitution effects of transfers at household levels are an important factor to bear in mind when considering different forms of delivery, and this remains a relatively under-researched area owing to inadequate collection of the requisite data in the impact monitoring of social protection schemes.

A case study included in this book the primary function of which is asset building is the Small Livestock Transfers scheme in Zimbabwe that provides small stock like goats or chickens as transfers, or for purchase with a coupon at a livestock fair (Case Study 15). When making direct transfers, this scheme purchases livestock in local livestock markets, thus seeking to minimize adaptation problems of the stock to the environment in which they will be reared, as well as reducing the transport costs of delivery. When utilizing a livestock fair to make the transfer, the scheme makes use of coupons (a cash transfer equivalent) in the same way as the ITF and EMF examples in Mozambique. Coupons have a nominal cash value, but can only be exchanged for the range of stock that is affordable with that amount of cash at the fair (typically chickens and guinea fowls). This scheme also contains the innovative delivery idea of 'pass-on', whereby initial beneficiaries transfer some of their multiplied livestock numbers after breeding to secondary beneficiaries, thus widening the circle of total beneficiaries at negligible additional delivery cost.

MOTIVATION AND INCENTIVES IN DELIVERING SOCIAL TRANSFERS

As the preceding discussion has shown, much social protection in Africa is delivered by international NGOs, in partnership with local NGOs and personnel from government departments. Notable exceptions include social pensions as adopted in Lesotho, Namibia, Senegal, South Africa and Swaziland as well as nationwide agricultural input transfers exemplified by fertilizer subsidies in Malawi and Zambia. In the case of NGOs and partners, a high level of commitment to success at delivery is typically apparent. This does not only derive from the altruism of individuals attracted to work for NGOs (although that doubtless plays a part); it is also because delivery failure carries the risk of being excluded from future funding for the NGO from donors or governments.

In some government-led schemes, and among government staff involved in implementing schemes led by international agencies, the motivation for effective implementation is less apparent. Most civil servants or local government officers are on the state payroll irrespective of the changing duties that they may be asked to perform. Moreover at lower levels of central government or in local government their remuneration is low and the incentive structures of their jobs are weak. When opportunities occur, 'siphoning off' is not an unusual characteristic of how public service works in practice, and this is often an aspect that no one wants to talk about even though it affects the cost-effectiveness of transfers and can impair or subvert the intentions of social transfer schemes.

Scattered evidence exists regarding motivation and incentive issues around social protection delivery, where the time and energy of public officials, traditional leaders and community committees are concerned. A few that arise from the southern Africa case studies are as follows:

- In the Chipata social cash transfer scheme in Zambia, members of CWACs reached agreement with beneficiaries to pack households with extra children in order to claim and share incentive payments paid to households for having children in school.
- Also in the delivery of social cash transfers in Zambia, District Social Welfare Officers (DSWOs) and district level committee members have several times raised with donors and NGOs the question of their 'unpaid' work in cash transfers, and desire to be remunerated for work performed.
- In the Malawi Input Subsidy Programme, widespread diversions and leakages were found to occur around the delivery of coupons for subsidized fertilizer (see Box C11.1 in Case Study 11, Part II).
- In Malawi in the DECT project, some village headmen and group village headmen took a cut from the recipients of cash transfers, justifying this because they were unremunerated for the time they spent organizing payout days.
- In Lesotho School Feeding, the cash-allocation-per-child approach to funding food purchases by caterers is prone to the purchase of inferior supplies and the delivery of watered down rations to schools.
- In many projects across all countries, traditional leaders regard their presence on beneficiary lists as justified by the work that they put into helping with the delivery of social transfers.

The scale of such problems is typically minimized in small, intensively managed and monitored NGO schemes, thus giving a false impression of their manageability in the absence of the close scrutiny that tends to characterize such schemes. Some social transfer schemes across the continent already build incentives for good performance by stakeholder partners into scheme design. However, neither donors nor government have grappled with the cost implications of dealing with these incentive and remuneration issues, nor where to draw the line between legitimate remuneration for work performed and unstated recompense for inadequate government salaries.

LESSON LEARNING FROM EXPERIENCE

This chapter has examined social transfer delivery methods as a cross-cutting theme in social protection in Africa. Attention was drawn to a number of aspects of delivery that can be compared for lesson learning purposes across case studies. These were the form of delivery (categorized between cash, food, inputs and assets); variations of approach within each of these categories; the technology of delivery; the organization and logistics of delivery; the scale of delivery; and incentives and motivation of the personnel involved in delivering social transfers.

Some patterns emerge. Irrespective of the form of delivery, good delivery involves attributes of reliability, timeliness, low cost, low opportunities for leakage, and ease of access to beneficiaries. In the context of the high risks surrounding the livelihoods of the poor and destitute in Africa, some of these delivery attributes (predictability, timeliness, accessibility) are of great importance to beneficiaries. A contrast can be made, for example, between the mainly predictable monthly cash transfers of the Lesotho pension scheme and the irregular dates as well as burdensome character of quarterly transfers of cheques to a considerable proportion of pensioners in nearby Swaziland (see Box 4.2). Timeliness is a problem in many schemes, but is especially deleterious for subsidized input deliveries to farmers that become increasingly pointless to deliver the later in the season delivery occurs. Overall, the following lessons about delivery can be inferred from diverse African experiences:

1. Effective delivery seems independent of form of delivery – good and bad practice can be observed equally across cash, food, inputs and assets.
2. The same holds true for surrogates of these main categories, such as vouchers and coupons – there are instances where these work well owing to the particular settings in which they are applied, and others where

BOX 4.2: DELIVERY OF THE OLD AGE GRANT (OAG), SWAZILAND

The OAG is funded by the Ministry of Finance and implemented by the Department of Social Welfare (DSW). At its inception in 2005, the task of distributing the OAG was given to the Post Office (Swazi Telecom); however its assignment to this responsibility lasted just three months. The Post Office failed both to cover all the locations for grant disbursement and to distribute the grant on time. There was a public outcry, and DSW was obliged to assume responsibility for distribution itself. This placed a considerable strain on DSW, since no additional resources were allocated by the Treasury to this task. Moreover a proposal by the parent ministry for the creation of a dedicated unit to deliver the OAG was rejected by government. The ministry instead relies on using temporary staff for cash distribution activities, with corresponding risks regarding control and accountability over the funds that are handled.

The OAG is dispensed partly in cash and partly using cheques at designated pay points across the country. Pay points include community civic centres (*Tinkhundla*) and the four regional offices of DSW. This makes the grant widely accessible to its beneficiaries. However, the differential treatment of beneficiaries in different places, some receiving cheques and others cash, creates additional costs for those who receive cheques, as they have to then travel to a bank to cash the cheque. The reason for the cheque–cash discrepancy is simply the ad hoc institutional set-up associated with distributing the grant when the original Post Office trials collapsed. The cost and hindrances associated with cheques are significant. The beneficiaries are charged E5.00 (US$0.70) per transaction; they have to queue up for long periods at the banks without facilities for older people (seats or rest rooms). They also incur travel costs to urban centres, and some beneficiaries report losing cheques along the way. Many older poor are not accustomed to handling cheques, and some have failed to cash them because banks have refused to process cheques that were dirty, folded and crumpled.

The OAG is disbursed quarterly, and this can also cause confusion for older people. The quarterly periods do not have defined future calendar dates for reporting to designated pay points, and therefore recipients are kept guessing as to the exact date they

> should turn up at their pay point. The inability of the DSW to establish a fixed routine for disbursements means that announcements are made shortly before a distribution is made, and of course most older people do not have access to electronic or print media that would enable them routinely to hear such announcements. The quarterly disbursement has the additional disadvantage of delaying cash availability at particular points in the year when some of the cash might be used for productive purposes, for example at the start of the planting season in rural areas.
>
> *Source:* Ellis (2007a)

either the cash or the physical item that the voucher represented might have proved better than the voucher itself as a delivery mechanism.

3. While many social transfer schemes display imaginative innovations in what is delivered and how it is delivered, the use of contemporary electronic technologies is still relatively rare – yet as demonstrated by the Kenya HSNP (Box 4.1) and the Ghana LEAP (Box 5.2) these technologies (smartcards, mobile ATMs, cell phones) hold tremendous promise for reliable, timely, secure and accessible social transfers.

4. As revealed by the Malawi DECT study (Case Study 4), beneficiaries in remote rural areas are amazingly adaptable to new technologies, and very quickly understand how they function and what can be done with them.

5. The organization and logistics of delivery vary widely in competence across different schemes, but there is no particular predictability to this across different main actors in social protection – governments, donors and NGOs can equally manifest themselves as star performers or bad organizers across the range of social protection instruments.

6. The same is also true with respect to the scale of the delivery operation – some of the biggest national programmes are amongst the most competently organized, as also are many of the smaller social transfer schemes where NGOs tend to excel. Equally, poor delivery can be observed at small scale as well as big scale.

7. A critical factor in relation to organizational competence in public sector schemes is the nature of the political commitment to the scheme – where this commitment is driven by electoral considerations and the government seriously feels the need to secure scheme success, then delivery is likely to be managed well; however, where the commitment is more to do with localized power and patronage motivations, then delivery can be very poor indeed.

8. Motivation and incentives are important in all social transfer schemes and are ignored at peril to scheme success – it cannot just be assumed that all stakeholders who become involved are doing so for reasons of altruism or a proper sense of duty, and it is better to anticipate and consider ways of dealing with motivation issues in advance than to wait for them to develop during scheme operation.

9. It is likely that many older schemes operated by semi-autonomous government agencies have been prone to leakages such that quite a considerable proportion of whatever is being delivered ends up in the ownership of other than the intended beneficiaries – this is an aspect of social transfer where new technologies offer considerable potential for improving the security of transfers, as well as lowering the cost of making them.

In summary, an exceedingly diverse range of experience in the delivery of social transfers to beneficiaries can be found across social protection schemes in Africa. This experience reveals that governments can be just as competent at delivering social transfers as anyone else, given the impetus of sufficient political will. It also reveals that strengths and weaknesses observed in different schemes are independent of the type of transfer that is being delivered, so it is not possible to say that one form of transfer is innately superior to another in terms of the effectiveness of its delivery. Nevertheless, it is clear that cash has more potential than other transfers for using new technologies to achieve low cost and secure deliveries, though this potential is only beginning to be realized to any significant degree across Africa. Productive partnerships with private sector players (banks, cellphone companies) are indicated as a way forward for this kind of innovation. From the viewpoint of beneficiaries, reliability, timeliness and ease of access are the key desirable features of delivery, while, from the viewpoint of delivery agencies, cost efficiency and security are important attributes. Social transfer schemes that achieve all these desirable attributes, and keep all their stakeholders happy, are likely to be doing a very good job of delivering social transfers to their beneficiaries.

5. Coordination and coverage

OVERVIEW

Efforts are being made in many African countries to establish improved coordinating mechanisms for social protection. Coordination is about the way that different bodies involved in social protection, within institutions and across institutions, interact with each other to share information, determine roles and competencies, avoid duplication of effort and establish funding priorities. Coordination can have a significant bearing on the adequacy of coverage of different vulnerable groups achieved by social protection. In its absence, coverage is likely to be accidental and patchy, driven more by the diverse interests of NGOs or the unreliable enthusiasms of donors than by a considered oversight of the social and geographical distribution of those most in need in a country.

Coordination is a complicated aspect of social protection because it is needed at many different organizational levels and also requires an understanding of history and politics to explain the forms it takes in different countries at different times. In terms of organizational levels, coordination can occur at levels from an overall overseeing capability in central government down to the practical coordination between partner organizations required to deliver a particular type of social transfer to a defined group of beneficiaries. In between these there are many intermediate levels of coordination that may involve collaboration and information sharing between some institutions but not others. One kind of intermediate level coordination that is prevalent in the region is a national committee or programme centred around a particular vulnerable group; for example, national committees on action related to HIV and AIDS, or national programmes for orphans and vulnerable children (OVC), have been established in several countries.

The historical and political dimensions of coordination have a significant bearing on what is achievable and how well coordination works in practice. In central government, sectoral ministries (finance, health, education, agriculture, etc.) tend to have differing political leverage and also therefore differing claims over government resources. Social transfers are often located in peripheral agencies (departments of social welfare), with weak leverage on central decision making. Inevitably, coordination sometimes springs into life around an upsurge of resources, in which donors play big roles, often with feeble grasps of the political processes that they set in train. In some instances, motives of re-election or consolidation in power by parties in government have proved powerful forces behind the introduction of particular national social transfer programmes (examples are the Old Age Pension in Lesotho and the Input Subsidy Programme in Malawi).

Stronger coordination contains the potential for both positive and negative impacts on the effectiveness of social protection at achieving its objectives. Amongst positive benefits of good coordination are the capabilities:

a. to foster a common understanding across institutions regarding who are the most vulnerable to hunger and how they can best be reached by social transfers;
b. to avoid gaps in coverage caused by inadequate information sharing between agencies about their own coverage, set within national spatial and social patterns of deprivation;
c. to learn lessons from the implementation of different social protection approaches, and to promote best practice across institutions;
d. to avoid duplication of effort caused by different agencies (both inside and outside government) devising their own channels for tackling the same problems of social deprivation.

On the other hand, coordination could potentially aggregate too much power and command over resources in one place. If handled in a particular way, it could stifle diversity of provision and innovation in delivery. It could demand too elaborate involvement of multiple stakeholders to provide a workable framework for efficient delivery of social protection. This can already be seen on the small scale in some social protection schemes that work with so many district, province and central committees and structures that keeping all the stakeholders happy takes more time and human resources than the delivery of the transfer to the beneficiaries itself.

This chapter examines the scope and difficulties of improved coordination in social protection, drawing especially on the 15 southern Africa case studies in Part II. First, it begins by summarizing selected experience around improving coordination at central state level. Second, it identifies patterns of coordination at intermediate and project levels that emerge from the case studies. Third, it examines patterns of coverage represented by the case studies, and links these to the coordination discussion. Finally, it seeks to draw out some lessons about coverage and coordination from the experiences of the case study projects and programmes as well as broader experience across Africa.

COORDINATION AT CENTRAL STATE LEVEL

The deficiencies of uncoordinated responses to emergency events have been recognized for a long time, and most countries now have in place a disaster management unit or equivalent agency that seeks to anticipate such problems before they arise and ensure an orderly approach to crises when they occur. It is widely thought that a parallel capability for social protection is desirable. Although immediacy and continuity differ between disaster management and social protection, in the absence of coordination they are both prone to information inadequacies, duplication of effort and gaps in coverage that can make them substantially less effective at meeting the needs that they set out to address than otherwise could be the case.

It is in line with this thinking that countries have been moving towards a coordination capability for social protection that is broadly equivalent to the role of a disaster management unit for managing crises. However, in the case of social protection, the boundaries around such coordination are not quite as easily defined as they are for disaster management. This is because different central line ministries implement their own forms of social transfer in the context of their own operational mandates, and these can be relatively distinct in terms of transfer approach, form and beneficiary type. A good illustration is the comparison between farm input subsidies falling under the mandate of the Ministry of Agriculture and school feeding to primary school children falling under the mandate of the Ministry of Education. These are both social transfers, but they address such entirely different needs in such very different ways that it is reasonable to ask whether coordination between them is likely to occur, or is even really necessary.

The difficulties of achieving central coordination of social protection are illustrated by the example of Mozambique (Box 5.1).The obvious place to coordinate cash transfer types of social protection (including pensions) is the department of social welfare or its equivalent (in Mozambique, the National Directorate for Social Action – DNAS). Nevertheless this does not solve the problem of information sharing on vulnerability, nor how to avoid duplication or gaps in coverage caused by other line ministries pursuing their own social protection activities. A partial solution in Mozambique's case is found in SETSAN, a cross-sectoral secretariat that hosts a variety of different cross-institution social protection working groups or committees. However, SETSAN's location in the Ministry of Agriculture is a weakness and; overall, social protection is rather politically marginalized in the Mozambique case.

In the southern Africa region, two countries, Zambia and Malawi, have tackled central coordination in a formal way by adopting social protection

BOX 5.1:   COORDINATION AND COVERAGE IN MOZAMBIQUE

In Mozambique, a substantial range of social protection initiatives is in place, but institutional arrangements are confusing, and coverage is fairly limited. An initial distinction can be made between social security for formal sector employees (pensions, sickness, invalidity benefits) and social assistance to the destitute. Responsibility for social security comes under the Ministry of Labour, while responsibility for social assistance rests with the Ministry of Women and Social Action (MMAS). MMAS has two directorates, one for social action (DNAS) and one for women (DNM).

The National Directorate for Social Action (DNAS) is responsible for policy, coordination and oversight of social action, while a separate agency, the National Institute of Social Action (INAS), is responsible for social action programmes and implementation. The division of roles and reporting procedures between MMAS/DNAS and INAS is complicated. At province level INAS delegations report directly to INAS at central level, but are also supposed to interact with provincial directorates for women and social action that have a monitoring role. INAS depends on MMAS for political representation, for example to the Council of Ministers. Yet the largest INAS run programme, the *Programa de Subsidios de Alimentos* (PSA – see Case Study 2) is funded directly by the Ministry of Finance, and funds do not go through MMAS.

So far, apparently not too complicated; however, the package of competencies represented by MMAS, DNAS and INAS is only part of a diverse broader picture. The cross-sectoral Secretariat for Food Security and Nutrition (SETSAN) has a mandate to coordinate all actors (state and non-state) in actions aimed at ensuring food security. However, SETSAN has limited status and authority, being located under the National Directorate for Agriculture of the Ministry of Agriculture. Until recently, its main function has been gathering information on vulnerability to food insecurity in disaster-affected or disaster-prone districts of the country. In this capacity it links to the National Institute for Disaster Management also located in the Ministry of Agriculture.

SETSAN coordinates a number of cross-departmental working groups, including a Vulnerability Assessment Group and the Food, Nutritional Security and HIV/AIDS group (SANHA). It also hosts the National Council for the Fight against HIV/AIDS (CNCS). SANHA has overseen the development of a procedures manual (funded by CNCS) to help social protection initiatives identify vulnerability linked to HIV and AIDS. This manual was due to be piloted by INAS, thus representing a positive example of inter-institutional collaboration. In the meantime, the OVC mandate of CNCS was scheduled to move to the National Women's Directorate (DNM) of MMAS during 2007. A strong recent emphasis on medical delivery with respect to AIDS (ART) has created tension about functions between CNCS and the Ministry of Health.

Source: Waterhouse (2007)

frameworks and strategies. In both these instances, coordination occurs through a cross-sectoral steering committee supported by a parallel technical committee. In Zambia, the site of these initiatives is the Department for Social Welfare of the Ministry of Community Development and Social Security, itself a relatively peripheral ministry in the power hierarchies of the Zambia government. In Malawi, the National Social Protection Steering Committee and parallel Technical Committee are in the Ministry of Economic Planning and Development, where they come under the Department of Poverty Reduction and Social Protection created in 2007. In both cases, the principal focus of the coordination is social assistance, understood to be mainly about cash transfers to the destitute. This still leaves a wide variety of social transfers in other hands; nevertheless the scope for valuable exchanges of information on vulnerability and coverage is improved in these examples compared to the situation before the adoption of these frameworks.

In addition to these case studies, the PSNP in Ethiopia (Box 2.3) and the LEAP programme in Ghana (Box 5.2) both illustrate the significance of central coordination as a prerequisite for larger scale social transfers. The PSNP is a component part of a broader government strategy called the Food Security Programme located in the Ministry of Agriculture and Rural Development (MoARD) and managed by a specialist agency within the Ministry called the Food Security Coordination Bureau. Similarly, the LEAP programme in Ghana is a component of the government's National Social Protection Strategy overseen by Ghana's Ministry of Manpower, Youth and Employment, which also contains the country's Department of Social Welfare.

COORDINATION AT INTERMEDIATE AND SCHEME LEVELS

The coordination features of the 15 southern African social protection schemes are summarized in Table 5.1. This table indicates the source of funding of each scheme, as well as the principal agencies involved in its organization and implementation. The case studies are seen to fall into roughly five overlapping groups as far as coordination is concerned. These are described briefly as follows, and it can be noted that coordination patterns are closely associated with differences in scale and intention between social protection schemes:

A. *National programmes overseen by a single line ministry.* The pension scheme in Lesotho (Case Study 1), the national programme for the destitute in Mozambique (Case Study 2), the Input Subsidy Programme in Malawi (Case Study 11) and School Feeding in Lesotho (Case Study 8) correspond to this category. These require a prior commitment by central government towards recurrent funding (ministry of finance) as well as operational coordination appropriate to a national scale of delivery.

B. *Pilot projects designed for scaling up within a coordinated social protection strategy.* The single case study that corresponds to this category is the Social Cash Transfer pilots in Zambia (Case Study 5). These are designed to explore the implications of delivering cash transfers to the most vulnerable, within the context of a national Social Protection Strategy and under the coordination of the Department for Social Welfare.

C. *Projects of limited duration funded by donors and implemented by NGOs, UN agencies or government ministries, as well as local partners.* This set includes the Malawi DECT project (Case Study 4), the two Zimbabwe NGO-led projects (Case Studies 6 and 15), the Education Material Fairs (EMFs) and Input Trade Fairs (ITFs) in Mozambique (Case Studies 10 and 13), the WFP Food Assistance Programme in Mozambique (Case Study 7) and the Japan International Cooperation Agency (JICA)-funded farm inputs for child-headed households in Swaziland (Case Study 14). Schemes in this category tend to coordinate between stakeholders at an operational level, but are not part of a larger design formulated at a strategic level by government. The Mozambique ITFs represent a partial exception to the latter characterization because they are integrated into a broader Ministry of Agriculture strategy towards recovery from crop failures caused by floods or drought.

Table 5.1 Coordination in 15 southern African social protection schemes 2006–07

Case Study	Country	Social Protection Scheme	Coordination Parameters of Scheme
1	Lesotho	Old Age Pension	Ministry of Finance (funding): post office, Local Community Councils
2	Mozambique	Food Subsidy Programme	Ministry of Finance (funding): Ministry of Women and Social Affairs (MMAS), National Institute for Social Action (INAS)
3	Malawi	Public Works Programmes	World Bank, EU, others (funding): MASAF, DAs, NGOs
4	Malawi	Dowa Emergency Cash Transfer	DFID (funding): Concern Universal, MVAC, district level line ministry personnel, chiefs, headmen
5	Zambia	Social Cash Transfers	DFID (funding): CARE, MCDSS, DSW, Public Welfare Assistance Scheme (PWAS), PSWOs, DSWOs (department personnel), DWACs, ACCs, CWACs (stakeholder committees)
6	Zimbabwe	Urban Food Programme	DFID PRP (funding): Technical Learning and Coordination (TLC) committee, ActionAid International and local partners, private supermarkets
7	Mozambique	Food Assistance Programme	WFP/donors (funding): WFP, Ministry of Health (MINSAU), MMAS, NPA-OVC, SETSAN, provincial OVC committees, WFP district partners
8	Lesotho	School Feeding	GoL/WFP (funding): MOET, Food Management Unit, WFP, caterers
9	Swaziland	Neighbourhood Care Points OVC	UNICEF/other donors (funding): National Programme of Action (NPA) on OVC; NERCHA, WFP, several ministries, NGOs
10	Mozambique	Education Material Fairs	Donors (funding): SC-UK, district level Ministry of Education, MMAS, OVC committees
11	Malawi	Input Subsidy Programme	GoM (funding): Ministry of Agriculture (Logistical Unit), ADMARC, SFFRFM, districts, traditional authorities, village leaders and stakeholder committees
12	Zambia	Food Security Pack	Ministry of Finance (funding): joint oversight MCDSS/MACO; implemented by PAM with district partners overseen by DFSC; AFSCs/CWACs for beneficiary selection
13	Mozambique	Input Trade Fairs	Donors (funding): FAO, Ministry of Agriculture (HQ, province, district), consultation community leaders
14	Swaziland	Chiefs' Fields for OVC	GoS and JICA (funding): NERCHA, MOAC, chiefs (land allocation), *indlunkhulu* committees (beneficiary selection)
15	Zimbabwe	Small Livestock Transfers	DFID/PRP (funding): TLC, local partners

D. *National programmes with varying funding run semi-autonomously from government.* This category includes the Public Works Programmes (PWPs) in Malawi (Case Study 3) that are run by the semi-autonomous body, the Malawi Social Action Fund (MASAF); and the Food Security Pack (FSP) in Zambia overseen jointly by two parent ministries (MACO and MCDSS) and implemented by a national NGO called Programme against Malnutrition (PAM) (Case Study 12). It seems likely that projects of this type may be prone to governance problems, and their varying funding means that coverage and effectiveness vary from one year to the next.

E. *Intermediate level coordination around the social protection needs of a particular vulnerable group.* The example here is the National Plan of Action (NPA) for orphans and vulnerable children (OVC) in Swaziland. This coordinates resources and coverage for Neighbourhood Care Points (NCPs) (Case Study 9) and school fee waivers for OVC, under the umbrella of the National Emergency Response Council on HIV and AIDS (NERCHA). An additional OVC scheme, CFs (Case Study 14), comes under NERCHA but is not included in the NPA.

Cutting across this intermediate level classification of social protection case studies is the role of decentralized local government and traditional authority in coordinating social transfers at district level. For example, in Malawi the 2007 Social Protection Policy envisages District Assemblies (DAs) as coordinating all implementing partners in social protection at district level. In almost all social transfer implementation, local level officials, district or village committees, and chiefs play varying roles in coordinating, monitoring or legitimizing transfers that occur under their jurisdiction. However, as noted earlier, there are occasions when the multiplicity of such local stakeholders becomes dysfunctional to efficient implementation of social transfers.

COVERAGE

Basic data on the coverage achieved by the different projects and programmes included in the 15 southern Africa case studies is provided in Table 5.2. Coverage has several different dimensions that have a bearing on the outreach achieved by social protection programmes:

● *geographical coverage:* extent to which spatial coverage of an intended set of beneficiaries is achieved;

Table 5.2: Coverage of 15 southern Africa social protection schemes 2006–07

Case Study	Country	Social Protection Scheme	Notes on Scheme Coverage
1	Lesotho	Old Age Pension	National coverage, everyone aged 70+
2	Mozambique	Food Subsidy Programme	95 582 beneficiaries in 2006
3	Malawi	Public Works Programmes	National social safety net, with numerous short term and seasonal sub-projects; typical coverage 0.5 million beneficiaries, each receiving a maximum of US$16 for ten days' work.
4	Malawi	Dowa Emergency Cash Transfer	10 161 HHs in two extension planning areas (EPAs) of Dowa District; 65% coverage HHs in selected communities
5	Zambia	Social Cash Transfers	9627 planned beneficiaries (five schemes), 2150 confirmed beneficiaries (CARE projects)
6	Zimbabwe	Urban Food Programme	2000 HHs in five cities
7	Mozambique	Food Assistance Programme	26 689 beneficiaries in 2006, about 15% of HHs living with AIDS
8	Lesotho	School Feeding	All primary school children (100%)
9	Swaziland	Neighbourhood Care Points OVC	625 NCPs out of 2520 neighbourhoods (25%)
10	Mozambique	Education Material Fairs	3432 HHs in five communities in Zambezia Province 2006
11	Malawi	Input Subsidy Programme	National coverage, small farm HHs growing maize or tobacco, estimated coverage achieved about 60% of all farmers
12	Zambia	Food Security Pack	National coverage, but sharply declining numbers in recent years: estimated 220 000 unique recipients 2001–07, about 22% of an estimated 1 million eligible rural HHs
13	Mozambique	Input Trade Fairs	266 030 recipients over five years (2002–07), once-only transfer per recipient; about 8% of all rural HHs covered
14	Swaziland	Chiefs' Fields for OVC	Out of 360 chiefdoms, 339 had set aside 3-ha fields, and 320 were creating 0.5 ha HH farms, but area planted was 7% of intended area in 2006
15	Zimbabwe	Small Livestock Transfers	Overall coverage not known

- *group coverage:* extent to which full coverage of a designated social group is achieved;
- *predictability and duration of coverage:* extent to which vulnerable people who comply with the requisite targeting criteria can expect reliable and continuing social transfers.

Amongst the 15 southern Africa case studies, six represent an intention towards national coverage geographically or with respect to designated groups at risk. These vary, however, in the extent to which they achieve this coverage. Social pensions and School Feeding in Lesotho come closest to true national coverage, while the Input Subsidy Programme in Malawi also achieved nationwide outreach, if not necessarily owing to the precision of its implementation in that direction.

Others in this group less clearly achieve their intended national outreach. The Mozambique PSA has operated historically mostly in urban areas, and its limited resources mean that only a fraction of potentially eligible beneficiaries are reached by the scheme. The Zambia FSP notionally has national geographical coverage, but erratic funding has meant that only perhaps 20 per cent of intended beneficiaries have been reached over the life of the scheme. PWPs in Malawi respond to seasonal food insecurity and have tended to vary in national coverage depending on organization and funding.

The other nine case studies have limited coverage in their design. This may be due to their 'pilot' or lesson learning character (for example, Social Cash Transfers in Zambia and EMFs in Mozambique); or to intentional short term and targeted geographic response (for example, DECT in Malawi); or to a non-repeating formula (ITFs in Mozambique); or to limited annual budgets in the context of donor-led transfers (the Zimbabwe Protracted Relief Programme projects). The Swaziland *indlunkhulu* (chiefs' land allocation to OVC) projects are limited for a different reason, which is that the designated amount of land allocated nowhere near meets potential needs, even supposing that other requirements for the success of such schemes could be reliably met.

While the limited coverage of some schemes in the set of case studies can be attributed to the nature of the vulnerability addressed, in other cases poor coordination is also implicated. For example, the *indlunkhulu* projects in Swaziland are poorly coordinated with that country's National Plan of Action for OVC, resulting in multiple OVC farm or garden initiatives, overlapping responsibilities, and duplication of effort. Only two of the case studies directly involve dedicated state social transfer agencies – the pilot Social Cash Transfers in Zambia that come under the Department for Social Welfare and the PSA in Mozambique which is the flagship social assistance programme of INAS/MMAS (Box 5.1). Social pensions emerge from this discussion of coverage as having important positive attributes: their coverage is assured by the legal entitlement of anyone over the stated age threshold to claim the benefit on offer; their coordination is the practical matter of ensuring that the transfers reach their beneficiaries at stated time intervals, and this has been achieved well in the case of Lesotho owing to the success at harnessing the post office network for the task.

The LEAP programme in Ghana (see Box 5.2) provides an example of coverage in a poverty-targeted social cash transfer which also has several other interesting features. LEAP is funded by the Ghana government from expenditure savings resulting from HIPC debt relief. It aims to provide predictable cash transfers to the estimated 18 per cent of Ghanaians living in extreme poverty. It has a schedule for scaling up that should result in roughly 160 000 households (20 per cent of all extremely poor households) being reached by 2012, and the intention is to extend this coverage to all persistently hungry households thereafter, depending on budgetary resources being available to do this. There is some optimism that this will occur for two reasons: first, that the cost of the programme in its first phase has been estimated to correspond to less than 0.2 per cent of government expenditure; and, second, Ghana has expectations of oil production growth with associated positive effects on the strength of future government income.

LESSON LEARNING ABOUT COORDINATION AND COVERAGE

Coordination and coverage represent a large, multi-layered and rather complex area in social protection in Africa where approaches and solutions are likely to vary between countries. There are evident trade-offs between adding bureaucratic layers, effectiveness and the desirable scope of coordination. In principle, a national coordinating capability can be envisaged that would seek to bring all social transfers under a single guiding structure; however, it is not clear whether this is either feasible or desirable. Its feasibility is likely to be compromised by the interests of different line ministries in pursuing their own policy agendas, which may include significant social transfer components (as exemplified by school feeding programmes that are normally implemented by ministries of education). Its desirability is arguable owing to the risks such a monolithic structure could pose for diversity, change and innovation in social transfer provision.

For these reasons, it is unlikely that the apparently rather disorderly character of social protection in Africa (that is, the mosaic of numerous

BOX 5.2   LIVELIHOOD EMPOWERMENT AGAINST POVERTY, GHANA

The Livelihood Empowerment Against Poverty (LEAP) programme in Ghana was launched on 19 March 2008, initially providing 16 Ghana cedis cash transfer every two months to 2000 extremely poor and excluded households (the Ghana cedi was valued at about GH¢ 1.15 to the US dollar in 2008). LEAP is one amongst several social protection components of the National Social Protection Strategy overseen by Ghana's Ministry of Manpower, Youth and Employment, which also contains the country's Department of Social Welfare.

The problem addressed by LEAP is the 18.2 per cent of all Ghanaians who were found to be extremely poor in the most recent Ghana Living Standards Survey (GLSS5, conducted in 2005–06). Extreme poverty in Ghana, as in other countries, is defined by being unable to achieve minimum acceptable levels of nutrition, even when the entire household income is spent on food. It is estimated that roughly 880 000 households in Ghana live in extreme poverty, despite an overall good growth record for the economy since the year 2000 and a per capita income that surpassed US$600 per year in 2008. LEAP seeks to support the livelihoods of those excluded or left behind by this otherwise relatively successful economic performance.

LEAP has several interesting features from the viewpoint of the themes and comparisons of this book:

- cash transfers are conditional;
- they are paid every two months, throughout the year;
- a scaling up schedule is in place through to 2012;
- the programme is funded from the government budget;
- it requires poverty targeting, comprising a mixture of categorical and proxy indicators;
- delivery involves an innovative partnership between the Ghana Post Office and a supplier of electronic banking services called e-Care/M2M;
- it places emphasis on 'livelihood empowerment', meaning that a significant proportion of beneficiaries are expected, with the assistance of complementary services, to graduate.

LEAP is unusual amongst cash transfer schemes described in this book in incorporating conditionalities that go beyond mere engagement in physical labour (public works schemes) or age thresholds (social pension schemes). This reflects the influence of Brazilian experts in the design process (technical cooperation was provided by advisers familiar with the *Bolsa Familia* in Brazil). The conditionalities specified are as follows, and beneficiaries are given three to six months to comply with them:

a. sending children to school;
b. not allowing child labour;
c. enrolment of family members on the National Health Insurance Scheme;
d. birth registration of all children.

It is intended that LEAP should scale up rapidly as shown in the following table:

Year	Households	Districts
2009	15 000	50
2010	35 000	70
2011	115 000	100
2012	164 370	138

Along with scaling up it is intended that transfers should shift to monthly payments, and vary with household size, giving a range between a minimum of GH¢8 and a maximum of GH¢15 per month (US$85 to US$155 per year). It is worth noting that the coverage in 2012 represents about 20 per cent of the households classified as extremely poor in Ghana (or 3.5 per cent of all Ghana households). It is estimated that the cost of the programme in 2008–12 will represent only 0.1 to 0.2 per cent of total government expenditure.

At inception, the programme restricted its coverage to extremely poor households containing OVCs, older persons over 65 years, and people living with severe disabilities. However, these criteria are likely to be widened to include households containing caregivers more generally, and people living with HIV/AIDS. Overall, the emphasis is on extreme poverty in rural areas (farmers and fisher folk), old age, caregiving, lack of able-bodied labour, and OVCs.

In terms of similarities to, and differences from, other social transfer programmes discussed in this book, LEAP is distinctive particularly in its use of conditionalities for receiving payments. As with other large national schemes (FSP Mozambique, PSNP Ethiopia), the politics of LEAP turns much on debates about avoiding dependency and promoting graduation. LEAP seems to have gone further than other poverty-targeted programmes in being embedded in the government budget, with funds earmarked from HIPC debt relief savings. If LEAP reaches its intended 2012 beneficiary numbers it will be the third or fourth largest social protection scheme in sub-Saharan Africa.

Sources: Ghana (2007); Sultan & Schrofer (2008)

organizations pursuing many different social transfer objectives in relation to many different types of beneficiary) will ever be more than partially resolved by the advent of national social protection strategies and frameworks. This disorder is found in all countries worldwide, rich and poor alike, and reflects the great diversity of people in need due to a multiplicity of different causes, therefore giving moral legitimacy to the many different organizations with different mandates seeking to do what they can to help.

The experience of coordination and coverage in Africa suggests a number of principles and practicalities that can help guide the formulation of an effective approach to coordination, with positive features also for the adequate coverage of intended beneficiaries:

1. It makes sense to institute a national coordinating capability around a particular social protection objective (for example, ensuring food security for all) where multiple instruments are being utilized towards the same end (the Ethiopia PSNP described in Box 2.3 is a good example of this).
2. Nevertheless, not all social transfers addressing different needs necessarily fit within such a single coordination framework; therefore 'complete coordination' is likely to be something of a mirage and its pursuit could end up by stifling diversity and innovation.
3. The southern Africa case studies show that intermediate level coordination around a particular social group (for example, orphans and vulnerable children) or type of transfer (for example, social pensions) can work well.
4. For smaller scale social protection efforts, of the kind conducted by numerous different international and national NGOs, streamlining is

desirable regarding assignment of public sector partners to such endeavours: currently, in most countries, lack of clarity in this area results in much unnecessary involvement by multiple would-be stakeholders, and this particularly occurs at the district level of implementation of social protection projects.

5. A key attribute of successful coordination is the flow of pertinent information to decision takers and stakeholders, especially with regard to the geographical and social coverage of multiple social protection initiatives, and this points in the direction of having a single technical secretariat appropriately located within government with the capability to collect, process and disseminate data on social transfers and their outreach.

6. Donors could, of course, play an important role in the funding and technical support to such a technical secretariat, always bearing in mind that short term, intermittent and unpredictable funding for this type of capacity is just as inadvisable as it is for other worthwhile activities that donors support.

As exemplified by the national policies adopted in Ethiopia, Ghana, Malawi and Zambia in the period 2004–08, many countries in sub-Saharan Africa were moving towards greater coordination of social protection, especially with respect to larger scale implementation of poverty-targeted cash transfers. Nevertheless, the limits as well as the benefits of coordination need to be recognized. For certain types of social transfer, for example a social pension, coordination is built into the task of delivery, and what is perhaps needed most is independent oversight of good governance in delivery rather than extra layers of coordination bureaucracy. Likewise, coordination should not be pursued to the point where it stifles diversity and innovation in social transfers by instituting excessive control over the activities of multiple actors in social protection provision.

6. Cost-effectiveness

OVERVIEW

'Cost-effectiveness' is about the relationship between costs and effects. It is a measure of how cheaply specified objectives can be reached, or how far they can be reached at given cost. In principle, it provides a criterion for judging and choosing between alternative means of producing desired effects according to the value for money they offer.

The quest for cost-effectiveness has become something of a preoccupation amongst donors and governments funding social transfer programmes, and much of the rather polarized debate about the relative merits of different instruments, cash and food transfers especially, has been in cost-effectiveness terms. Choices about whether and how to target social transfers are judged on their relative cost-effectiveness, as are different methods of delivery.

Sponsors of social protection programmes, and the communities to whom they are accountable, have an obvious and legitimate interest in ensuring that programme outcomes justify money spent, and in whether these outcomes could be enhanced within budgetary constraints or achieved more cheaply in other ways. However, straightforward as it may seem at first sight when applied to social transfers, cost-effectiveness is open to different conceptual and empirical interpretations, and results of cost-effectiveness calculations can therefore be manipulated to serve particular policy advocacy interests. Perhaps the most important lesson of this chapter is that, before drawing any conclusions from findings about the cost-effectiveness of a social transfer scheme, it is necessary to scrutinize carefully what costs and effects are actually being referred to, whose findings these are, and how the data were collected and analysed. Unfortunately, for a number of reasons, reliable data on the cost-effectiveness of programmes is not nearly as widely collected, analysed or shared as it should be, so that in practice findings often remain inconclusive.

ANALYSING THE COST-EFFECTIVENESS OF SOCIAL TRANSFERS

Cost-effectiveness analysis differs from cost–benefit analysis in that whereas cost–benefit analysis attempts to assess financial or economic returns to an investment by attaching monetary values to all associated costs and benefits and comparing the two, cost-effectiveness analysis more straightforwardly specifies a project objective (or set of desired outcomes) and then analyses the cost of achieving it. Cost-effectiveness analysis is appropriate where effects cannot easily be reduced to monetary terms, even if they can be quantified. It is well suited to social transfer schemes, where the focus is most often on assessing value for money in attaining transfer objectives rather than on quantifying overall economic or financial returns to an investment. Like cost–benefit analysis, cost-effectiveness analysis can be used to compare alternative interventions with different costs and different effects, provided the effects can be expressed in the same units. However, unlike cost–benefit analysis, cost-effectiveness analysis findings are specific to the particular effects selected for the analysis, and are likely to differ between direct outputs of schemes (for example, amount of cash or farm inputs transferred) and indirect effects (for example, increased access to food or increased farm output).

Some initial distinctions regarding the reach of cost-effectiveness are helpful. At a minimum the analysis would seek to measure the cost per unit of the social transfer delivered, for example the unit cost of delivering US$10 per month cash to recipients, or of delivering a bag of maize flour. This rather limited exercise measures the cost-efficiency of delivery, but not necessarily the effectiveness in achieving programme objectives. The distinction is best understood by way of an illustration. If it costs US$2 in administrative and delivery costs to provide US$10 per month cash transfer, then the ratio of the transfer (US$10) to total outgoings (US$12) provides a cost-efficiency ratio of 0.83 (this is sometimes called the 'alpha ratio'). Alternatively, the reciprocal of the alpha ratio (US$1.20) tells us the total budget required to deliver US$1 worth of transfer to beneficiaries. The latter ratio is generally more readily understood, and is the preferred efficiency measure used in this chapter.

The efficiency ratio on its own tells us little about the effectiveness of the cash transfer in achieving a stated objective, for example, the food security of the beneficiary. For this, additional information is required, specifically in this instance the price of food, so that the quantity of food that can be purchased with the cash transfer can be calculated. Thus efficiency and effectiveness are distinct, as also are effectiveness and long run impacts (did the recipient family become and remain food self-sufficient as a consequence of participating in the programme?).

For cost-efficiency ratios to be thus calculated for physical transfers (for example, food or inputs), these need to be valued somehow. For example, the value of a food transfer to beneficiaries is often taken to be the procurement cost of the food incurred by the delivery agency. However, this has the flaw that, as procurement costs rise, the apparent efficiency of the transfer rises (if US$10 procurement cost of transfers doubles to US$20, with delivery costs remaining the same at US$2, then the cost-efficiency ratio defined above falls from US$1.20 to US$1.10). An evidently better method is to value a food transfer at the market price of food faced by the beneficiary, and compare this with total costs of providing the transfer including procurement, delivery, targeting and all other implementation costs.

This valuation of physical transfers at market prices (and, by extension, the valuation of cash by what it can buy) makes cost-efficiency ratios comparable across different transfer types, but also permits the analysis to go beyond cost-efficiency towards cost-effectiveness. For example, a cash transfer becomes less cost-effective when food prices are rising (since this reduces the amount of food the cash transfer can buy) and vice versa when food prices are falling. This approach to analysis can inform decisions about whether cash or food is most appropriate to transfer, especially when combined with examination of the simultaneous effect of food or cash transfers on local food markets, whereby in poorly integrated markets transfers could add impetus to price movements and so intensify cost-effectiveness differences between cash and food.

Cost-effectiveness analysis can be further extended in the direction of broader social transfer impacts. For example, a main objective of farm input transfers is to enable poorer farming households who would not otherwise be able to afford purchased inputs the means to increase their crop output. The above method of valuing transfers at local market prices would enable a cost-effectiveness comparison of an input transfer with a cash transfer which recipients use to purchase inputs on local markets. However, it would also be possible to assess cost-effectiveness in terms of the quantity or value of additional production which is expected to result or which actually resulted from the input transfer, and compare this with alternative options for boosting farm output, or alternative social transfer options altogether. As this example suggests, the more cost-effectiveness analysis focuses on broader impacts and the more it values effects in monetary terms, the closer it becomes to a standard cost–benefit analysis.

Cost-efficient delivery of transfers is necessary, but rarely sufficient, to ensure that a social transfer programme is cost-effective in terms of impacts. This depends on how direct the link is between the transfer and the intended impacts, and on other factors affecting impacts. For unconditional cash transfer programmes, the link is relatively direct: efficient delivery of cash might be assumed to lead automatically to cost-effective impacts, for example in terms of relief of extreme poverty, access to essential commodities (especially food), or avoidance of distress sales of assets. Yet even in this case, as we have seen, cost-effectiveness of impacts depends on the price levels of those commodities in local markets and how well those markets are linked with wider ones. For other programmes aimed at longer term or less direct impacts, such as improved uptake of health or education services, improved nutritional status, increased agricultural output or creation of community assets, cost-efficient transfers are even less a guarantee of cost-effective impacts. Furthermore, the link between the two is mediated by accuracy of targeting: transfers may be efficiently delivered to registered beneficiaries, but if there are large inclusion or exclusion errors in the targeting process then effective impacts on intended target groups will be correspondingly reduced. Table 6.1 summarizes factors that determine the cost-efficiency of transfer delivery and cost-effectiveness of transfer impacts for different programme types.

For cost-effectiveness analysis to be useful, information on both sides of the cost–effects comparison must be reasonably complete and reliable. For many social transfer schemes, there are severe information constraints on both counts. On the costs side, there is a often a lack of clarity about cost structures, with delivery agencies prone to understate costs, and particularly to ignore central overhead costs (salaries, buildings, etc.) and scheme start-up costs, and to report only those administrative costs directly associated with operating the social transfer project itself. On the effects side, market price data is often unavailable, and monitoring of impacts beyond delivery rarely undertaken. For example, a farm inputs transfer project may cease its monitoring with the delivery of 30 000 input packs to beneficiaries, and therefore neglect to collect data on the local market value of the packs at delivery time, or on the crop yields obtained at the end of the season in which delivery occurred.

COST-EFFECTIVENESS IN THE SOUTHERN AFRICA CASE STUDIES

Table 6.2 contains comparative data on cost-efficiency from the 15 southern African case studies in the second half of this book. As the foregoing discussion suggests, these figures must be treated with due circumspection. Ratios are often calculated from budget figures rather than actual outturns, costs are often understated especially in scaled up government programmes, and transfers are often valued using procurement cost rather than market value. The discussion that follows examines selected case

Table 6.1 Factors affecting cost-efficiency and cost-effectiveness

Transfer type	Cost-Efficiency of Transfers	Cost-Effectiveness of Transfers
Unconditional Cash Transfers	• cost of cash delivery per $1 transferred, including management, targeting, registration, delivery, M&E, etc. • exchange rates for externally funded schemes	• targeting effectiveness • price levels of essential goods and services in local markets, especially food • integrity of local markets
Conditional Cash Transfers	• as above, plus cost of conditional element (for example, additional health or education service provision)	• as above, plus service provision and impacts associated with conditional element (for example, improved health or educational achievement)
Food Aid	• overall cost of food delivery per $1 worth of food delivered, valued at point of delivery • market prices for food at point of delivery	• targeting effectiveness • market conditions affecting sale or consumption of food • health service provision and health hazards affecting nutritional uptake quality and uptake of education provision (school feeding)
Free Inputs or Input Subsidies	• cost of input delivery per $1 of inputs delivered, valued at point of delivery • market prices of inputs at point of delivery	• targeting effectiveness • market conditions affecting sale or farm use of inputs • growing conditions (weather, pests, etc.) • crop husbandry and storage • market conditions for output
Public Works	• cost of cash or in-kind payment per $1 of payment delivered, valued at point of delivery • market prices for in-kind commodities at point of delivery • cost of establishing and managing works projects	• targeting effectiveness • achievement of impacts of payment in cash or kind • value to local communities and maintenance of assets created

Table 6.2 Cost-efficiency in the southern Africa case studies

	Country	Social Protection Scheme	Cost-Efficiency* (expenditure per US$1 transfer)
1	Lesotho	Old Age Pension	1.02
2	Mozambique	Food Subsidy Programme	1.47 (2006), 1.55 (2007)
3	Malawi	Public Works Programmes	2.50 (early MASAF); 1.41, 1.75 (recent)
4	Malawi	Dowa Emergency Cash Transfer	1.32, 1.43 and 1.52 as maize price declined
5	Zambia	Social Cash Transfers	1.30 (Kazungula), 1.11 (Chipata) (budget)
6	Zimbabwe	Urban Food Programme	1.44 (overall ActionAid, not project alone)
7	Mozambique	Food Assistance Programme	not available
8	Lesotho	School Feeding	1.18 (WFP budget figure)
9	Swaziland	Neighbourhood Care Points OVC	not known, possibly relatively efficient
10	Mozambique	Education Material Fairs	1.20 (budget)
11	Malawi	Input Subsidy Programme	benefit–cost ratio estimated at 0.76–1.36 (2006/07)
12	Zambia	Food Security Pack	1.67 (rising because of declining coverage)
13	Mozambique	Input Trade Fairs	1.25–1.29
14	Swaziland	Chiefs' Fields for OVC	not known, likely to be high (inefficient)
15	Zimbabwe	Small Livestock Transfers	benefit–cost ratio estimated at 8.4 (2007)

Note: * These are often *ex ante* budget figures and often understate central overhead costs.

studies by transfer type in more detail, and with a view to cost-effectiveness as well as cost-efficiency considerations.

Cash Transfers

Cash transfers might be expected to be more uniformly cost-effective than transfers in kind, at least in direct effects. However, cost-efficiency ratios for the cash transfer case studies varied considerably. Pension programmes appear on the face of it to be the most cost-efficient. In Lesotho, the Ministry of Finance built only about US$0.5 million for administration costs into an annual pension budget of US$21 million in 2005/06, suggesting only US$1.02 total cost per US$1 received by beneficiaries. Even though this almost certainly understates central costs, the Lesotho OAP is likely to be cost-efficient due to its clever use of existing public infrastructure and personnel, in particular the postal service that undertakes distribution of the pension. A similar calculation for the Swaziland Old Age Grant suggests a US$1.11 total cost per US$1 transferred, which again appears very cost-efficient (Ellis, 2007a).

The other scaled up, government-run cash transfer is the Mozambique Food Subsidy Programme. This has an elaborate administrative structure for reaching its 100 000 beneficiary households across the country, involving large numbers of central and local level supervisory staff and police security cover. However the amount of the transfer has fallen from an originally planned one-third of the minimum monthly wage to between 4 and 6 per cent of that wage. Such a thinly spread transfer has inevitably impaired cost-efficiency. Although official guidelines state that operational costs should make up 15 per cent of total costs, in practice they appear to be much higher. Attribution of costs to the scheme are not completely clear, but budget figures and beneficiary numbers suggest that costs to deliver US$1 may have been as high as US$1.47 in 2006 and US$1.55 in 2007.

As far as the pilot scale NGO-implemented cash transfer case study programmes are concerned, the CARE-managed Kazungula and Chipata programmes in Zambia were at too early a stage for any *ex post* assessment of cost-effectiveness. Nevertheless budget and average transfer figures imply an envisaged US$1.30 and US$1.11 per US$1 transferred respectively, the higher cost for the Kazungula scheme reflecting its remote rural setting, whereas Chipata is an urban scheme. By comparison, data for the longer-established Gesellschaft für Technische Zusammenarbeit (GTZ)-managed pilot in less remote rural areas of Kalomo District suggest a cost of US$1.18–1.20 per US$1 transferred. In the DECT programme in Malawi, the innovation of varying the size of the cash transfer to reflect current maize prices while other costs remained constant meant that cost-efficiency varied correspondingly. As maize price halved during implementation, the total cost per US$1.00 transfer increased from US$1.32 to US$1.52. No government share of implementation costs is included in these cases, and there are uncertainties about attribution of technical assistance and training costs.

Broader measures of cost-effectiveness are lacking for most of the schemes. The Lesotho pension appears to score highly as a cost-effective means of reducing vulnerability among the over-70s and their extended families, who cover around a quarter of the country's population. As a means of reaching vulnerable people more generally, the scheme on its own would inevitably be less cost-effective, as significant groups of the vulnerable are excluded. In terms of protecting food entitlements for target households, the cost-effectiveness of all of the schemes except DECT will have been impaired by the general upward trend in retail food prices, only partly compensated for by adjustments in transfer amounts. Within its very limited geographical area, DECT was shown to be cost-effective in reaching its hunger and social objectives and testing design and delivery innovations, and in its impact on the local economy which was assessed with an impressive multiplier effect of 2.1 (that is, each US$1 transfer added around US$2 to the local economy).

Food Transfers

Food transfers are sometimes characterized as being inherently less cost-effective than cash transfers because of the additional logistical costs associated with internal transport, storage and handling of food which outweigh the extra security costs of distributing cash. However, if food is valued at procurement cost, and there are significant logistical costs involved in distribution to beneficiaries, then the value to recipients (and thus the cost-effectiveness of the transfer) may be misleadingly understated. This applies especially where relatively isolated local food markets are in deficit and prices are high compared with those prevailing at the point of procurement. These are precisely the conditions under which food transfers can also help to limit local food price rises to the benefit of all net purchasers locally, whereas cash could drive prices up further. Conversely, food transfers are likely to be less cost-effective than cash in non-deficit food markets, when their local market value may fall below costs of procurement and logistics, especially when procurement is from outside the region and landed costs are relatively high. If significant quantities are involved and markets are not well integrated, this is also when they can be expected to depress local market prices to the disadvantage of local producers. To compare the cost-effectiveness of food transfers with a cash alternative, it is therefore important that the food is valued at local market prices when and where it is distributed. Unfortunately this analysis is rarely carried out in practice, either *ex ante* or *ex post*, and was not applied in any of the food transfer case studies.

For the School Feeding Programme in Lesotho, available estimates of costs are *ex ante* costs that appear in WFP project documents. Based solely on comparison of expected procurement plus delivery costs with total WFP costs including management support, the programme appears cost-efficient at US$1.18 per US$1 of food transferred in 2004–07, though this is not a very useful statistic in itself for reasons given earlier. Reflecting a broader WFP move towards localizing procurement where market conditions allow, this programme has moved from trans-oceanic to regional to in-country food procurement, a move that is expected to have improved the overall cost-effectiveness of the food transfer over time. In terms of the programme objectives of improving primary school enrolment, retention, attendance and achievement rates, the commissioning of local caterers to provide food for future school feeding operations could well prove cost-effective provided food quality and quantity can be adequately monitored and maintained.

Farm Input Transfers

As with food transfers, an initial cost-effectiveness judgement to be made for input transfers is at the level of cost-efficiency, analysing the overall structure of all procurement and delivery costs per unit of each type of input delivered, and then proceeding to a comparison of costs with the value of the transfers at the point of delivery using equivalent local market prices. As the bulk of expenditure on input transfers tends to be for fertilizers, cost-efficiency assessment amounts to a comparison of scheme and non-scheme distribution chains involving large-scale domestic manufacturers or importers. Impact-oriented cost-effectiveness judgements can then be made in terms of broader objectives, such as those related to additional output and effects on input, labour and output markets and on rural livelihoods.

For most of our input transfer cases, information constraints preclude an adequate cost-effectiveness assessment. Swaziland's Chiefs' Fields have suffered from late inputs delivery, lack of community support and poor crop yields, and are unlikely to prove cost-effective in terms of their objectives of ensuring the long-term food security of orphans and vulnerable children. White & McCord's (2006) analysis of Zambia's Food Security Pack (FSP) programme for 2003/04 put the cost to deliver US$1 worth of inputs at current market prices at a fairly high US$1.67. Information on broader FSP impacts is lacking, but, with severe funding constraints and delays in delivery, cost-efficiency and broader cost-effectiveness are likely to have declined. Food and Agriculture Organization (FAO) support to Input Trade Fairs in Mozambique costs US$1.25–1.29 for each US$1 worth of input vouchers delivered, but this excludes unknown but apparently significant Ministry of Agriculture logistical support costs, and there is negligible monitoring of outcomes of these one-off events and no evidence of lasting impacts on beneficiary output or access to inputs.

Amongst the input transfer case studies, by far the largest and most extensively evaluated is the Input Subsidy Programme (ISP) operated by the Government of Malawi (at the time of writing in its third crop year 2007/08). At a total budgetary cost of US$91 million including a 25 per cent cost overrun and a donor contribution of just 10 per cent, the 2006/07 programme accounted for around half of the entire Ministry of Agriculture budget, and so its cost-effectiveness is of no small interest. In that year coupons were distributed for 175000 tons of subsidized fertilizer and 4500 tons of maize seed. Programme cost per ton of fertilizer distributed by parastatals (ADMARC and SFFRFM) and participating private traders amounted to US$490 (US$1.11 for each US$1 spent on procurement), of which 72 per cent (US$355) represented the government subsidy. An indication of the fertilizer value in local markets is given by equivalent private retail costs, which were also about US$490 per ton sold (Dorward *et al.*, 2008, p.27). Although parastatal costs were probably understated, and despite significant shortcomings in coupon distribution, this suggests that the transfer was implemented reasonably cost-efficiently.

Against the broader ISP objectives of improving smallholder productivity in food and cash crops, reducing food insecurity and hunger, promoting food self-sufficiency, developing private sector input markets and promoting wider growth and development, conclusions concerning cost-effectiveness are mixed but broadly positive. Account must be taken of displacement of private full-price fertilizer sales, so that only about 60 per cent of subsidized fertilizer was a true addition to overall use. Nevertheless, between 500000 and 900000 tons of additional maize production is attributed to the 2006/07 ISP, and the programme yielded significant household food security dividends through raising wage rates and lowering food prices. The benefit–cost ratio is put in the range 0.76 to 1.36 for that year, and 0.65 to 1.59 over the next five years, depending on assumptions about market displacement and yield response (Dorward *et al.*, 2008).

Public Works

In terms of transfer cost-efficiency, Public Works Programmes (PWPs) do not score highly, as the cost of organizing 'works' projects has to be added to that of delivering wages in cash or commodity form. Thus the norm for Malawi Social Action Fund (MASAF) projects under Phases I and II was to spend around US$2.50 for each US$1 of transfers. Again, cost-efficiency calculations for most Malawian PWPs considered in the case study were hampered by lack of scheme level data on actual transfer and overheads costs. For example, more recent evaluations imply that US$1 of transfer cost US$1.41 on the 2005 MASAF III PWP-CCT scheme and US$1.75 on the 2005/06 government/EU Special Programme for Relief and Investment in Needy Times (SPRINT) scheme, but this apparent difference in cost-efficiency appears to stem from different approaches to attributing overhead costs. Although in principle, unlike input transfers, PWPs provide a 'countercyclical' safety net by offering employment opportunities at times of stress when food prices are high, are 'self-targeting' and create useful community assets at the same time, they have consistently failed to demonstrate broader cost-effectiveness in these terms.

COST-EFFECTIVENESS AND TARGETING

The relationship between targeting and cost-effectiveness is worth reiterating at this point, since the connections between these two dimensions of social protection are rarely brought into the open very sharply. A targeting failure (for example, a high rate of exclusion of those who comply with the criteria for being programme beneficiaries) automatically reduces the cost-effectiveness of a social protection programme (since an important goal of intended coverage will not have been met). However, targeting is also a way of increasing cost-effectiveness by ensuring that scarce resources are directed only to those most in need of transfers, and choosing the most cost-efficient means of achieving this objective. In the Malawi DECT project (Case Study 4) it was found that, even with 70 per cent of households in the project area falling into the target group, the savings from targeting (as compared to providing universal coverage) outweighed the cost of the targeting process.

Nevertheless, targeting can be prone to another danger, as discussed in Chapter 9 and in Ellis (2008). The danger is that so little real difference in material circumstances separates targeted from non-targeted families in the community that the social transfer effectively makes its beneficiaries better off than non-beneficiaries. In effect, if only US$6 separates the mean household consumption of beneficiaries and non-beneficiaries, then a US$10 social transfer will propel some proportion of beneficiary households above the living standards of poorer non-beneficiary households, causing socially invidious changes in income distribution below the poverty line.

In the wider research literature on social protection, targeting has not yet demonstrated cost-effectiveness in terms of goals of reducing poverty or vulnerability, and 'policies that have the greatest impact on poverty are not necessarily the most narrowly, pro-poor, targeted ones' (Mkandawire, 2005, p.10). Aside from its potential to stigmatize and disempower recipients, as well as to tempt abuse of power ('elite capture'), targeting may in the end represent little more than cost-cutting dressed up as cost-efficiency. From this perspective, less rather than more targeting, set within a more universal approach to social policy, may in the end prove more cost-effective at reducing poverty and vulnerability.

POLICY LESSONS

A number of policy lessons emerge from this discussion about the difference between cost-efficiency and cost-effectiveness, the difficulty of measuring longer term impacts, and the inaccuracy of data on both the cost and the effectiveness side of the comparison:

1. The analysis of both *ex ante* and *ex post* cost-effectiveness of social transfer programmes should be central to social transfer design and decision making, because it addresses the key dimension of value for money in achieving social protection objectives.
2. However, the required data to do this accurately is often wilfully fudged (for example, failing to apportion overhead costs to schemes) or is not collected (for example, food prices at transfer sites, or yield data before and after an input transfer).
3. Longer term impact data on the lives and livelihoods of beneficiaries, requiring beneficiary tracking beyond the time frame of most social protection projects, has been rarely if ever been collected to date.
4. Cost-effectiveness analysis involves different levels and durations of comparisons between costs and outcomes, from the narrow cost-efficiency of delivery (how much it cost to achieve a US$1 transfer to beneficiaries), to the cost relative to achieving distinct programme objectives (such as food security), and longer term impacts on beneficiaries (such as the ability to do without transfers in the future).
5. For these measures to achieve their potential to guide the design of future social transfer policies, the required data collection needs to be built into programme operations.
6. Broadening the analysis to the level of impacts allows comparisons to

be made not just between different social transfer approaches, but also between social transfers and other policy options that share common objectives; ultimately, it is necessary to go beyond the narrow technical parameters of transfers to the broader economic, social and institutional goals that a society is hoping to achieve.

7. Market effects

INTRODUCTION

Social transfers interact with markets in two, fundamental, interdependent ways:

1. They have impacts on local markets, in particular markets for food, farm inputs, and labour.
2. They are themselves affected by market conditions, especially price levels of staple foods like maize and rice, and this influences the most appropriate design of transfers and their outcomes.

Taking each of these in turn, the impacts of social transfers on food, input and labour markets are rarely properly assessed. These impacts depend on the characteristics of supply and demand in each market; on how far food or input transfers add to consumption or substitute for commodities already traded; on the scale of transfers compared with corresponding volumes traded on local markets; on how well markets function or are integrated with markets further afield; and on how and where transferred commodities, food in particular, are procured.

The impacts of markets on social transfers are a more immediate challenge to scheme design. In general a main aim is to address vulnerability arising from changing market conditions, in particular by protecting food entitlements when food prices climb. Beneficiaries' transaction costs (time and transport especially) in accessing local markets are important and influence the choice between alternative forms of transfer. Ideally, transfers need to build in flexibility to vary their form and level in response to market conditions, though this complicates management and budgeting. Cash transfers are most effective when their level is linked on a monthly basis to prices of basic goods, especially food, whereas food transfers are most effective in protecting food entitlements when prices of staple foods climb in isolated, food deficit markets. Input transfers can have important redistributive effects in favour of poorer farmers, but fail to protect recipients in the event of unfavourable growing conditions (for example, rainfall failure). Public works schemes suffer from contradictory market influences which undermine their effectiveness.

In this chapter we explore these market interactions of social transfers in more detail, drawing especially on the case studies of the second half of the book, but also on other examples and the broader literature on this topic. The chapter proceeds by first examining evidence regarding the impacts of social protection on markets, distinguishing between the four main forms of social protection introduced in earlier chapters. It then considers the impact of markets on social transfers, and how this influences the appropriate design of social protection schemes. Finally, it identifies important policy lessons that proper acknowledgement of market interactions brings to social protection. The market interactions of the case studies are summarized in Table 7.1, and frequent reference to this table occurs throughout the chapter.

Impacts of Social Transfers on Markets

Some of the main primary and secondary market impacts that accompany different forms of social protection are summarized in Table 7.2. Market impacts occur wherever transfers either are in the form of cash or substitute for commodities that recipients would otherwise purchase, sell or exchange. Their magnitude can be expected to increase to the point where they deserve explicit programming attention when transfer amounts are significant in relation to corresponding volumes traded on local markets, and especially where those markets are isolated or fragmented. Market impacts may be a deliberate objective of scheme design or occur as side-effects of scheme implementation, and in either case outcomes depend on prevailing market conditions. For example, in a food deficit market food aid can help to constrain rising food prices, benefiting all net purchasers of food, while cash transfers aimed at helping recipients purchase food might have the perverse effect of driving food prices up still further. Conversely, in a non-deficit market, cash transfers can benefit communities by stimulating trade in food and other essential commodities, while food aid may depress food prices at the expense of surplus producers and traders, especially if not timely or well targeted. Direct transfers or subsidies of farm inputs are similarly likely to depress input prices and increase demand. Such effects will be more pronounced in remote areas where the costs of moving food in from or out to distant markets are high, or where there are other causes of market failure.

A complex array of secondary market effects is possible. Impacts on maize prices can induce price changes in alternative staples such as cassava, millet, sorghum or sweet potatoes. Input subsidies can displace unsubsidized supplies, with consequences for existing suppliers, and if they lead to increased farm production may cause prices to fall in output markets.

Table 7.1 Market interactions in the southern African case studies

Brief No.	Country	Scheme	Market Interactions
1	Lesotho	Old Age Pension	No evidence of inflationary effects. Cross-border and domestic markets well integrated. Local multiplier effect probably low. Grant value eroded by inflation.
2	Mozambique	Food Subsidy Programme	Scale too small for significant market impacts. Real value depends on maize prices; in 2007 the transfer was equivalent to only two days of household maize supply.
3	Malawi	Public Works Programmes	Food-for-work projects have some impacts on food markets, but for lean season transfer these effects are minimal. Cash-for-work transfers sensitive to maize price changes.
4	Malawi	Dowa Emergency Cash Transfer	Cash transfer levels reduced in response to maize price fall. Transfers stimulated local trade in food, other groceries, clothes, medicines. Local multiplier effect estimated at 2.1.
5	Zambia	Social Cash Transfers	Small scale pilots with no evidence of significant market impacts. Cash transfer levels raised in line with maize price increases.
6	Zimbabwe	Urban Food Programme	Scale too small for significant market impacts. Hyperinflation as rationale for physical deliveries then vouchers: inflation and exchange rate risks borne by AAI.
7	Mozambique	Food Assistance Programme	Food basket unaffected by prevailing prices; WFP bears cost of price rises. Scale too small for significant market impacts. WFP moving to local procurement.
8	Lesotho	School Feeding	Direction and magnitude of potential effects on food markets depend on how food sourced; local procurement supports prices. Protects school children and their families from food price fluctuations and need to sell assets.

9	Swaziland	Neighbourhood Care Points OVC	Significant market impacts of NCPs unlikely. Delivered food may protect beneficiaries from maize price rises.
10	Mozambique	Education Material Fairs	Temporary stimulation of local market supply for clothes and educational materials (average vendor sales of US$143). Little impact on wider scale.
11	Malawi	Input Subsidy Programme	Significant impacts on input and output markets. Net fertilizer use up by 34%, but serious displacement of private suppliers. Rise in *ganyu* labour rates. Maize output price declined to a recent history low of MK14/kg in June 2007.
12	Zambia	Food Security Pack	At original scale (200 000 farmers), input and output markets likely to be moderately affected. At present scale (20 000 farmers) significant market effects unlikely.
13	Mozambique	Input Trade Fairs	Stimulate local market supply for agricultural inputs, implements and other commodities in remote areas in the short term.
14	Swaziland	Chiefs' Fields for OVC	Do not compensate for inter-seasonal fluctuations in food production. Largely unsuccessful in terms of agricultural production, and market effects minimal.
15	Zimbabwe	Small Livestock Transfers	Add to demand for small livestock, supporting prices and trade opportunities. Market expansion through multiplication of stock. Build asset status and resilience of beneficiaries.

Table 7.2 Market impacts of social transfers

Transfer Type	Primary Market Effects	Secondary Market Effects
Cash Transfers	• Upward price pressures, especially food staples in isolated food deficit markets (locational and seasonal effects)	• Stimulate local economy and trade, especially in basic commodities and services • Limit distress sales of assets • Reduce labour supply; increase wages • Increase farm and non-farm investment
Food Aid	• Lowers food prices (especially seasonal effects), depending on procurement policies	• Lagged effects on food consumption and production decisions; possible disincentives if imported; possible incentives if locally procured • Income effect can reduce labour supply; increase wages
Input Subsidies	• Reduce input prices • Rationing at subsidized price, with market created for vouchers	• Increased production if growing conditions good (lowers input:output price ratio), with lagged effects on food consumption and production decisions • Reduced private sector input supply (if the state distributes subsidized inputs) • Immediate and lagged income effect can reduce labour supply, increase wages, increase farm and non-farm investment
Public Works	• Labour market effects (raises opportunity cost of labour) • Consumption smoothing during lean season	• Reduce supply of casual labour, increase wages (perhaps) • Reduced time spent on own-farm operations (if timing conflicts) • Improved market infrastructure (perhaps)

Transfers may increase the opportunity cost of labour, so that employers are obliged to raise wage rates to secure the labour they need. Food aid can also affect factor markets for purchased inputs, labour and finance by freeing up household labour and cash resources for investment in own-farm production. Cash transfers may stimulate rural markets for financial services, especially if they use similar delivery systems. There is concern that cash transfers on a national scale may induce general price inflation, although there is no firm evidence for this.

For commodity transfers procurement and delivery choices have further market implications. Food aid has historically been tied to procurement in and shipping by donor countries as a way of benefiting their domestic suppliers and serving foreign policy objectives. Recent moves towards procuring food aid in recipient countries or regions have not only reduced procurement costs but enabled those benefits to be secured by developing country producers and traders. However, care is then needed to ensure that vulnerability is not exacerbated by inadvertently creating food shortages and price hikes in areas of procurement. In the following paragraphs, these important market interactions of social transfers are explored further, drawing on the case studies listed in Table 7.1 as well as other examples.

Cash transfers
While cash transfers may result in upward pressure on prices of food and other commodities for which they are most used, this effect is likely only where several conditions jointly occur:

- transfers are on a large scale relative to purchasing power locally or nationally, *and*
- markets are relatively isolated (which makes commodity supply inelastic), *and*
- there is a local food deficit so that household food stocks are depleted and households are dependent on purchased food supplies (which makes demand for food inelastic).

Pilot cash transfer schemes such as those operating in Zambia in 2003–08 (Case Study 5) operate on an insufficient scale to inflate food prices. Mozambique's Food Subsidy Programme (PSA) covers all provinces and reaches over 100000 households, but these are mainly in urban areas, and transfer levels (US$2.70–5.40 per month) are extremely low. At this scale market impacts are minimal. More substantial transfers are provided by social pensions, and concerns are sometimes expressed about their possible inflationary effects. Lesotho's Old Age Pension provided US$29 in 2007 to all over-70s, around 72 000 in all. While total annual disbursement was substantial at about US$25 million, there is no evidence to suggest that this has been inflationary at either local or national levels. The pension is geographically dispersed and constitutes little more than 1 per cent of gross national income (GNI). Moreover, markets in Lesotho are well integrated with those of the surrounding and vastly larger market economy of South Africa. Since over 70 per cent of consumption expenditure goes on imported South African goods, any local multiplier effect of the OAP is likely to be low, even in remoter highland areas.

Under certain conditions a small scheme can have significant local market impacts. The DECT project in Malawi (Case Study 4) covered just two extension planning areas in Dowa District. However, it injected over US$1 million into this small area, covering 70 per cent of all households. Moreover, the project was implemented during the 'lean season' months in a food deficit area, and local markets are weakly integrated into the wider economy. On the other hand, maize was overall in plentiful supply that crop year (2006–07), and local traders felt that prices were more likely to fall than rise during the project period. In the event, prices did fall from January to March 2007 as farmers and traders sought to run down stocks held over from the previous year. Nevertheless, by boosting beneficiaries' purchasing power, DECT stimulated local trade in maize, bread and other groceries, health care services, clothes and other items, and increased trader numbers, creating an estimated local multiplier of 2.1 (Davies, 2007). In addition the scheme reduced the need for beneficiary households to undertake casual labour (*ganyu*) to earn cash for food and other necessities, freeing up more of their labour time for work on their own fields, and causing casual seasonal wage rates to rise (Devereux *et al.*, 2007).

Food transfers
Large-scale emergency food assistance, as well as boosting recipients' food consumption directly, can play a vital role in bringing down inflated food prices in deficit markets. Non-emergency food transfers can have several different objectives, but they raise the issue of possible negative impacts on local producers and traders through depressing normal price levels in non-deficit markets. This depends both on their scale and on how the food is procured.

For many smaller food transfer schemes, as exemplified by some of the southern Africa case studies, it is safe to conclude that transfers are too limited in scale or are too thinly spread to have discernible market impacts. However, School Feeding in Lesotho (Case Study 8) operates on a larger scale. The programme involves non-trivial volumes of food assistance, mainly maize meal, over an extended period. In recent years this has been a joint WFP–Government activity in support of free school meal provision under the government's Free Primary Education (FPE) policy. Although in the past school feeding involved overseas shipments landed in Durban, WFP's 2004–07 programme undertook to purchase food within the region. Since Lesotho normally imports more than half of its staple food requirements, this strategy was not expected to create local over-supply or undermine local producers.

The market context for school feeding in Lesotho can be contrasted with that in Malawi in May 2007 when, following a bumper maize harvest and a collapse in domestic maize prices, WFP approved a four-year US$60 million school feeding programme based on the importation of US-grown, US-shipped CSB at a cost two-and-a-half times greater than that of equivalent local purchases (Renton, 2007).

Input transfers
Again depending on scale, free or subsidized inputs for poor farmers can have significant effects in input, output and labour markets. The most direct impact is of course on the inputs themselves, lowering their price and increasing their demand. However, the net increase in purchases resulting from subsidizing inputs is never the same as the subsidized volume purchased, since some of the uptake represents a switch by farmers who would have purchased the inputs anyway, from the full price to the subsidized supplies. If greater input use results in higher output, then output market effects also occur, potentially causing prices to fall as supply increases. This in turn creates different income effects between surplus and deficit farmers, with gains in income from the higher production of surplus farmers being offset by falling market prices, while for deficit farmers their annual food gap narrows and they may be able to source supplies at lower prices than before. In the labour market, the improving food security position of deficit farmers will probably result in them offering less casual labour to other farmers than before, thus causing rural wages to rise.

Most of the input transfer case studies from southern Africa listed in Table 7.1 are far too small to have these market effects. However, the Malawi Input Subsidy Programme (ISP) (Case Study 11) is certainly sufficiently large to do so, covering 131 000 tons of subsidized fertilizer in 2005/06 and 173 000 tons in 2006/07, at a price roughly one-third of open market supplies. It has been estimated that the net increase in fertilizer use provoked by the scheme was 52 000 and 79 000 tons in each of those years respectively. On the output side, maize production rose from a five-year mean of 1.55 million tons (2001–05) to 2.72 million tons in 2005/06 and 3.22 million tons in 2006/07. These successive bumper harvests put strong downward pressures on maize prices. From a peak of over MK50 per kilogram in February 2006, the average retail maize price fell to under MK20 in May–August 2006, rising only moderately in the 2006 lean season, and falling to MK14 per kilogram in June 2007, a new low for recent history. Rising rural wages also ensued.

These inter-related but at least transparent market effects of an input subsidy are only part of a rather more intricate picture of true subsidy side-effects that are nevertheless critical for evaluating the eventual impacts of the scheme. First, if vouchers are used that entitle targeted holders to buy the fertilizer at government or retail depots at the subsidized price, a secondary market for the vouchers springs into existence. Some poor farmers sell the vouchers at a discount to their nominal value, preferring to raise cash than purchase the fertilizer. Other farmers may purchase vouchers even above their nominal value because this still enables them to acquire additional fertilizer well below the open market price. This secondary market encourages leakage of vouchers to non-target groups to occur when they are being distributed, since significant money can be made by having vouchers for sale. However, target groups still benefit from selling their vouchers, and the leakage is significantly less than occurs with an untargeted subsidy.

Second, a switch from previous private trade in full price inputs to government distribution of subsidized supplies (as occurred in Malawi) can all but destroy the private trade in inputs that may have taken many years to build up. Third, the effectiveness of an input subsidy as a means of reversing hunger and vulnerability is critically dependent on weather outcomes in successive crop years: when the climate is favourable input subsidies appear an excellent means to achieve rural poverty reduction goals; however, in the event of poor rainfall in the growing season they can prove a very expensive way of subsidizing crop failure.

Asset transfers
Asset transfers generally have less visible and more difficult-to-trace market effects than cash, food or input transfers, partly because the direct building of household assets is a relatively rare aim of social protection schemes. An example from the southern African case studies is the Small Livestock Transfers in Zimbabwe (Case Study 15), although here the effects are local rather than widespread owing to small scheme size. This scheme undertakes local purchases of small stock (chickens, guinea fowl, goats) for transfer to beneficiaries, thus helping to underpin their value in local markets, and organizes Livestock Trade Fairs with the same effect. Similar examples can be found in the Input Trade Fairs in Mozambique (Case Study 13), where some of the items traded for vouchers are durable assets (like hoes or machetes) rather than recurrent inputs (like seed and fertilizer).

Impacts of Markets on Social Transfers

The design of social transfer schemes needs to bear in mind not just the likely impact of proposed transfers on various markets as outlined in the preceding section, but also the impact that market trends and fluctuations have on the value of the transfer to beneficiaries. Here there is a considerable difference between market effects as applied to cash, food and input transfers.

For cash transfers, the critical consideration is the amount of food that can be purchased for the cash provided. This may influence design features such as varying the transfer amount according to household size. In most instances in Africa, it is the national maize price that is key, and its seasonal and annual instability causes uneven and often unpredictable changes in the purchasing power of the cash transfer amount that has been set. When the price of maize rises steeply, as it does when a shortage sets in, the real purchasing power of the transfer plummets, as also does the protection from hunger that it affords its recipients. In this sense, for fixed level cash transfers price risks are borne by the recipient rather than the provider.

For food transfers, an opposing set of considerations apply. A commitment to provide regular food transfers to a set of beneficiaries places price risks with the provider rather than the recipient. The provider must still purchase the food (unless it is made available under food aid terms) even if market prices for food are rising, causing purchasing costs to rise steeply. From the beneficiary perspective, food transfers can also overcome transaction cost problems, particularly in remote rural areas where markets may be more distant and less reliable.

Input transfers represent something of a hybrid with respect to these effects. Like food transfers, they release additional resources at household level that would otherwise have been spent on inputs. Poorer farm households normally unable to purchase fertilizer or approved seeds would not benefit from this effect, but may gain income from selling on the inputs to others. Outlay on subsidized inputs carries some risk, especially for poorer beneficiaries, since adverse climate conditions could result in lower-than-expected yields or crop failure. However, if favourable weather pertains, the gains realized by poor beneficiaries in terms of freedom from hunger and improving livelihoods can be substantial, as illustrated by the Malawi ISP in 2005/06 and 2006/07.

Various combinations and alternatives to these principal effects can be built into scheme design. Varying cash transfer levels in line with prevailing maize prices, as occurred in the DECT project (Case Study 4), shift the risk of price changes back from the beneficiary to the provider. This applies also to the issue of coupons valid for a fixed basket of food items and basic needs, as in the Urban Food Programme in Zimbabwe (Case Study 6), since it is the provider that must reimburse the retailer for items collected by the beneficiary against the coupon. Food and cash may be combined so that cash is provided after the harvest when food supplies are ample, and food is provided in the lean season when food prices are rising. A predecessor to the DECT project in Malawi, the Food and Cash Transfers (FACT) project, experimented with such a model (Devereux *et al.*, 2006a). Rural transfer recipients may find all three types of transfer useful at different points in the year, and quite a few small scale NGO schemes across Africa do indeed combine cash, food and inputs in different combinations for their recipients.

Most schemes which can vary transfer types and levels to stabilize their real value to beneficiaries are small scale, such as seasonal and location-specific projects (Case Study 4) or pilot cash transfer schemes (Case Study 5). This flexibility is substantially more difficult to secure at scale owing to the long lead times required to alter government budgetary allocations, and the inevitably politically charged character of policy change at national level. For example, it is rare anywhere in the world for categorical cash transfer benefits like social pensions or child support payments to be changed within a budget cycle, and they may remain unchanged for years depending on the state of government finances and the presence or absence of political leverage on the part of the beneficiary constituency.

LESSON LEARNING ABOUT MARKETS EFFECTS

This chapter has revealed that the market interactions of social transfers are both important and in practice rather complicated. They are important because, if they are ignored or misinterpreted, the very intention of social transfers to reduce vulnerability and hunger in the short or longer term may fail. They are rather complicated because beyond the immediate first round effects (such as the impact of food transfers on food prices) there can be secondary and obscure effects that may nevertheless play important roles in determining the eventual success of the transfer scheme or programme. Therefore market analysis, especially looking beyond the obvious, is a critical component of the design and implementation of any social transfer scheme.

The chapter has shown that market interactions work both ways: social transfer programmes can have impacts on food, input and labour markets, and it is important to think through these impacts carefully; however, markets also affect the goals and design of social transfer schemes, and nowhere is this more obvious than in the impact of food price changes on the real purchasing power of a cash transfer of given size. The significance of these two directions of impact varies considerably according to the scale of the social transfer scheme under consideration. In general, small schemes covering a limited locality or a tiny proportion of the total population have negligible impacts on wider markets, although they can nevertheless have observable local market effects, especially in remote or isolated places. By contrast, nationwide schemes reaching significant numbers of people can have broad effects in input, output and labour markets, as illustrated particularly clearly by the Malawi input subsidy scheme. Meanwhile, all schemes large or small are affected by the impact of market price changes on their own design and budgets, and on the real value of the transfer that they deliver to beneficiaries.

The case studies and experiences examined for this book suggest several lessons for appropriate types of transfer and the good design of social protection schemes where market interactions are concerned. These are set out as follows:

1. Cash transfers work best where food is relatively plentiful in local markets, or where local markets are well integrated with larger markets further afield, thus minimizing the risk that the scheme itself will cause food price inflation, and also providing conditions where large adverse movements in food prices are the exception rather than the norm.

2. In small cash transfer schemes, transfer amounts can be adjusted to changing food price levels (typically the price of maize); however, budgetary flexibility is necessary in order to put this into practice, and it is unclear how feasible such flexibility is for scaled up cash transfers dependent on public sector budgetary cycles.

3. Cash transfers have broadly pro-poor market impacts, stimulating the local economy, raising local wage rates, and creating a demand for financial services; however, these effects are less pronounced in small, open economies (such as Lesotho) owing to the propensity of recipients to spend on imported goods and services.

4. In circumstances where food deficits cause extreme seasonal food price inflation in poorly integrated markets, food assistance may be preferable to cash because the latter will simply push prices up further: a mixture of food and variable cash transfers, though administratively more demanding than just food or just cash, can combine the best of both and the drawbacks of neither.

5. Food transfers can have special roles when broader social or nutritional aims are being pursued such as keeping children in school (school feeding) or ensuring that AIDS patients on ART obtain the correct diet; in these instances cash transfers may just overcomplicate the realization of an intended social goal.

6. As a general principle in these instances, food transfers should rely on local procurement (thus supporting local food markets) rather than on food aid pipelines, as was highly prevalent in the past; however, this does increase the budgetary risk faced by the procuring agency.
7. Input subsidies and transfers can work well as a means of stimulating increased use of approved seeds and fertilizers and raising farm yields so that the food gap of vulnerable poor farmers is reduced, and most market impacts of such transfers work in favour of the poorest farmers.
8. Nevertheless, input subsidies have complex and far-reaching market effects, including erosion of the private input supply sector, potential excess output for the domestic market resulting in low output prices and expensive storage of surpluses, the emergence of a side-market in vouchers where these are used to limit subsidies to target groups, or an open-ended budgetary commitment to meet increased input demand at the subsidized prices where they are not.

In general, social transfers work best when they help to strengthen the functioning of markets, thus contributing to broader growth and development objectives, while limiting their adverse impacts on the poor. For cash transfers this occurs when there is not an immediate food shortage problem at the national or sub-regional level, so that expenditure of the transfers supports food prices and contributes to the integration of markets and the broadening of trade and exchange in the economy. Food transfers can play complementary roles in situations where immediate food shortage is the issue. The successful implementation of all social transfers will benefit from a well-organized and accessible flow of information on food price trends in local and national markets, so that adaptations to design and functioning can be made reasonably rapidly in the light of emerging trends.

8.   Asset protection and building

INTRODUCTION

Social protection programmes have several important, generally positive, impacts on household assets, either directly or indirectly. There are three main mechanisms. First, programmes that increase household income (in cash or in kind), or insure households against livelihood shocks, protect assets against 'distress disposal'. Second, many programmes aim explicitly to create assets at the individual level (for example, education and skills), the household level (for example livestock, farm tools) or the community level (for example, roads, village grain banks). Third, recipients of social transfers often choose to allocate some transfer income to purchases of productive assets or consumer goods. All of these effects can be observed in social protection schemes across Africa.

Just as social protection has impacts in terms of 'livelihood protection' and 'livelihood promotion', so the specific impacts on assets can be classified as either 'asset protection' or 'asset building'. Asset protection effects include the following:

a.   Cash or food transfers protect households against the need to sell assets to buy food.
b.   Social transfer beneficiaries can keep their children in school during episodes of livelihood stress, instead of withdrawing them to work or to save money.
c.   Social insurance mechanisms such as burial societies provide a buffer against the heavy and unavoidable costs imposed on poor families by the death of a family member.
d.   Projects supporting orphans and vulnerable children (OVC) protect the access of orphans to family land, which might otherwise be reallocated by local chiefs to other households.

Asset building effects can be sub-divided into impacts on each of the 'five capitals' from the sustainable livelihoods framework – natural, physical, human, financial and social capital (Scoones, 1998; Ellis, 2000):

a.   *Natural capital*: social transfer beneficiaries either purchase or are given livestock or land or tree seedlings.

b. *Physical capital*: at the household level, beneficiaries may utilize a transfer to purchase agricultural implements (hoes, machetes); at a community level public works programmes construct roads and other useful infrastructure.
c. *Human capital*: many social protection programmes explicitly support the improved education and health status of beneficiaries.
d. *Financial capital*: some transfers take the form of loans or provide access to financial services.
e. *Social capital*: some social protection schemes seek to build upon existing community support systems, while others create new community institutions around providing support to the most disadvantaged people in the community.

ASSET PROTECTION EFFECTS

Asset disposal is a common response by poor households to hunger and food insecurity, where 'asset disposal' includes selling domestic items (furniture, cooking utensils, housing materials), personal effects (clothing, jewellery), agricultural implements (farm tools, ploughs) and livestock (off-take first, then breeding stock), running down savings and mortgaging land. Household assets can also be depleted by taking on high-interest debt, withdrawing children from school (which undermines human capital formation), or begging neighbours for assistance (depleting social capital). In Swaziland 42 per cent of households interviewed in the 2006 national vulnerability assessment stated that disposing of assets was their primary mechanism for managing shocks (Swaziland Vulnerability Assessment Committee, 2006).

Asset disposal increases impoverishment and vulnerability, because this erodes asset buffers against future shocks and undermines productive capacity (especially if key productive assets are sold or mortgaged). So asset disposal, often misleadingly characterized as a 'coping strategy', is in fact an indicator of severe distress. Any intervention that protects poor households' assets against forced disposal also prevents further impoverishment and destitution. As shown in Table 8.1, quite a few of the social transfer case studies from southern Africa provide asset protection qualities along these lines.

By boosting disposable resources, social transfers protect poor and vulnerable households against the necessity to run down their savings and productive resources to meet their basic needs. Predictable transfers are an effective defence against unpredictable or occasional shocks, as this allows households to build up reserves and guarantees income for 'consumption smoothing' through a crisis period. However, the asset protection impacts of social protection programmes are less easy to attribute or quantify than asset building or asset accumulation, because it requires measuring something that did not happen (households did not sell assets, parents did not withdraw children from school, etc.). Asset protection can best be assessed by comparing beneficiaries' coping behaviour with that of a non-beneficiary control group.

In an emergency cash and food transfers project in Malawi, a 'coping strategy index' (CSI) was constructed that included asset sales. Monthly monitoring of beneficiaries and a control group confirmed that beneficiaries adopted fewer and less damaging coping strategies than control group households, many of whom sold household goods and key productive assets, and withdrew their children from school, to raise money for food during a severe drought. The asset erosion process of non-beneficiaries is shown in Figure 8.1. This shows how both sets of households started the 2006 hungry season in Malawi with a high CSI score, which continued to rise for the non-beneficiary control group, but fell significantly every month among beneficiaries. The receipt of monthly cash transfers effectively protected the assets of beneficiary households against 'distress sales' for survival.

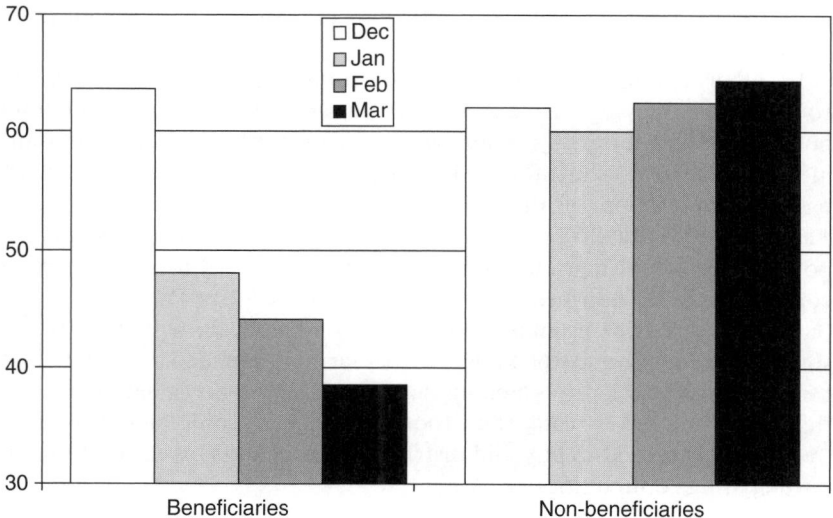

Source: adapted from Devereux, *et al.* (2006a, p. 40)

Figure 8.1 *'Coping strategy index' scores in Malawi, 2006 (female-headed households)*

ASSET BUILDING EFFECTS

Asset building effects involve direct as well as indirect effects, and varying scales from the individual to the household to the community. The discussion below disaggregates the types of assets built into the five livelihood 'capitals' listed earlier, and explores how assets are built amongst the 15 case study schemes (summarized in Table 8.1) as well as other examples.

Building Natural Assets

Asset transfer programmes, often involving livestock, are more popular in Asia than in Africa. Only one of the 15 southern African case studies increased household assets through direct transfers, and this was the Small Livestock Transfers Project in Zimbabwe. Beneficiaries received goats, chickens, guinea fowl or other small animals which they bred, and 'passed on' some of the offspring to other poor families, thereby expanding the coverage. Although the impacts of this programme have not yet been evaluated, anecdotal evidence suggests that the goat and poultry transfers have generated substantial income for beneficiaries. Transferring assets rather than cash seems logical, given Zimbabwe's hyperinflation, but there are also risks that livestock will die owing to poor husbandry or infectious diseases. However, evidence suggests that, on balance, the benefits outweigh these risks.

In other countries, predictable cash transfers, where recipients are confident of receiving a fixed amount of cash on a regular basis, can build household assets indirectly, by allowing beneficiaries to set aside small sums in savings until they can afford to buy assets and accumulate a modest asset base. An evaluation of the cash transfers project in Kalomo District, Zambia, found that 15 per cent of beneficiaries bought livestock (mostly poultry or goats) using some transfer income, compared to none among a control group of non-beneficiaries. The Food Security Pack in Zambia (Case Study 12) was originally conceived as a soft loan, with recovery of some harvested produce (60 kilograms per farmer) intended to stock village cereal and seed banks, thus creating significant community assets. However, this dimension never really took root and, instead, some of the produce 'recovered' was used to buy and distribute livestock (as breeding stock) to participating communities.

Building Physical Assets

Programmes that support agriculture allow farming households to acquire productive assets such as farm implements (in addition to agricultural

Table 8.1   Asset effects of 15 social transfer schemes in southern Africa

Assets Protected	Asset Protecting Impacts	Case Studies
Household Assets	Prevention of asset disposal for food	Old Age Pension (Lesotho) Dowa Emergency Cash Transfers (Malawi) Social Cash Transfers (Zambia) Urban Food Programme (Zimbabwe) School Feeding (Lesotho)

Assets Built	Asset Building Impacts	Case Studies
Natural Capital	Purchase of rights to land for farming	Dowa Emergency Cash Transfers (Malawi)
	Investment in farming (fertilizer, seed, tools)	Dowa Emergency Cash Transfers (Malawi) Urban Food Programme (Zimbabwe) Input Subsidy Programme (Malawi) Food Security Pack (Zambia) Input Trade Fairs (Mozambique) Chiefs' Fields for OVC (Swaziland)
	Purchase of livestock	Food Security Pack (Zambia)
	Transfers access to land for farming	Chiefs' Fields for OVC (Swaziland)
	Transfers small livestock for breeding	Small Livestock Transfers (Zimbabwe)
Physical Capital	Purchase of household assets	Old Age Pension (Lesotho) Dowa Emergency Cash Transfers (Malawi) Social Cash Transfers (Zambia)
	Construction of cereal and seed banks	Food Security Pack (Zambia)
	Construction of roads and infrastructure	Public Works Programme (Malawi)

Table 8.1 (continued)

Assets Built	Asset Building Impacts	Case Studies
Human Capital	Increased investment in children's education	Social Cash Transfers (Zambia) Old Age Pension (Lesotho) Education Fairs (Mozambique) School Feeding (Lesotho)
	Improved nutrition builds labour productivity	Food Assistance Programme (Mozambique)
	Improves children's nutrition, health, education and socialization	Neighbourhood Care Points for OVC (Swaziland)
Financial Capital	Use of smartcards and ATMs as delivery methods, leading to savings and loans	Dowa Emergency Cash Transfer (Malawi)
	Use of private banking system to deliver transfers	Social Cash Transfers – Chipata (Zambia)
Social Capital	Enhancing community responsibility to care for orphans and other vulnerable children	Chiefs' Fields for OVC (Swaziland) Neighbourhood Care Points for OVC (Swaziland)
	Community Welfare Assistance Committees (CWACs) or equivalent	Social Cash Transfers (Zambia) Food Security Pack (Zambia) Education Material Fairs (Mozambique)

inputs such as fertilizer and seeds). A case in point is Input Trade Fairs in Mozambique (Case Study 13), where farmers received coupons that could be exchanged for a range of items, including farm tools. This is an intended outcome of Input Trade Fairs. An unintended but positive side-effect of Zimbabwe's Urban Food Programme (Case Study 6) was that beneficiaries who grew and sold vegetables from their own gardens used some of the profits earned to purchase garden tools.

At the community or macro-level, Public Works Programmes aim to construct or rehabilitate physical infrastructure that is intended to raise household incomes. Examples include feeder roads to connect farmers with input and output markets, micro-dams for irrigation, or soil and water conservation to raise farm yields. Over 80 per cent of public works spending in Malawi has been on roads, but their quality is often questionable. This is a common complaint about physical assets constructed under labour-based employment schemes everywhere.

Building Human Assets

Several social protection programmes aim to build human capital as a direct impact. The Mozambique Food Assistance Programme targets individuals with AIDS on ART, with the objective of providing the nutritional support essential for them to respond properly to their medication. To the extent that this succeeds in bringing AIDS patients back to full physical strength, thus enabling them to resume productive labour, this is clearly a human capital building outcome. Other interventions such as Education Material Fairs in Mozambique and School Feeding in Lesotho focus on improving the educational status of vulnerable children, thereby building their human capital and enhancing their lifetime income-earning potential. In Swaziland, Neighbourhood Care Points pursue a broader social inclusion agenda, building the human capital of vulnerable children by addressing their 'nutrition, health, education, socialisation and life skills' (UNICEF Swaziland, 2006).

Other impacts on human capital formation are less direct. One of the most consistent findings across numerous social transfer programmes is that recipients invest some of this additional income in the education of their children or grandchildren. This is the case even where education is 'fee free' – many African governments have abolished primary school fees, to encourage enrolment – because there are various non-fee costs (uniforms, textbooks, transport) for which cash is needed. Interestingly, spending on education is strikingly high among recipients of social pensions (who are all over 60 and definitely not attending school!) because grandparents often take responsibility for caring for grandchildren.

Building Financial Assets

In many cases access to financial services is a by-product rather than a primary function of the social protection scheme. After all, any saving activity that results as a by-product of alleviating the hunger stress of households constitutes financial capital in one form or another. An intriguing consequence of Concern Worldwide's decision to subcontract Opportunity International Bank in Malawi (OIBM) to deliver cash transfers in Dowa District (Case Study 4) was a surge in demand by beneficiaries for the savings facilities potentially embodied in the smartcards delivered to beneficiaries. In response to this, Concern commissioned OIBM to continue providing mobile banking services for two years after the delivery of cash transfers ceased. Some DECT beneficiaries also used the smartcards issued to them to draw money from ATMs in nearby towns.

A different example from Zimbabwe (not included in the case studies) is a rural micro-finance programme in Zimbabwe called Kupfuma Ishungu that focuses exclusively on building financial assets (Box 8.1). This programme, still ongoing at the time of writing, is based on the establishment of savings and loans groups, of which there were 7600 in 2006, that accumulate savings and make small loans to their members. Because of hyperinflation in Zimbabwe the real value of cash erodes very rapidly, so loans tend to be converted into physical assets almost immediately. An innovative response to hyperinflation is called the 'asset-based saving innovation' in which group members buy assets instead of paying cash into the group savings fund, and share out these assets at the end of each cycle (see Box 8.1).

Building Social Assets

Many programmes that support orphans and other vulnerable children try to work with 'traditional' social norms and institutions that either provide this kind of informal support or used to do so in the past, thereby strengthening or rebuilding social capital at the community level. For example, the savings and loans groups just described in Zimbabwe are based on Rotating Savings and Credit Associations (ROSCAs), which that have been prevalent in many African societies for a very long time. The CFs scheme in Swaziland (Case Study 14) revives an ancient custom whereby village chiefs would set aside some communal land for use by poor and marginalized groups, such as the landless and those without adult labour power. Each chiefdom in the CFs project is expected to allocate a communal plot of 3 hectares and 26 individual plots of 0.5 hectares each to child-headed households. Experienced farmers are asked to contribute voluntary unpaid

BOX 8.1   ASSET ACQUISITION THROUGH
MICROFINANCE IN ZIMBABWE

Micro-finance is typically used to purchase productive assets or to invest in household farming and other micro-enterprises, and it is debatable whether micro-finance qualifies as social protection, strictly defined. However, Zimbabwe's Kupfuma Ishungu Rural Micro-Finance Programme differs from conventional micro-finance in several respects, in ways that have relevance to the theme of asset protection and asset building.

Micro-finance usually contributes to asset accumulation indirectly, through asset purchases made at the discretion of the borrower, either capital assets for conducting a business (for example, a sewing machine) or household assets acquired with the profits of the business (for example, a bicycle). In the Zimbabwe programme, asset accumulation by the mid-2000s had become a central feature, because the context of hyperinflation had prompted a switch from savings in the form of cash to savings in the form of assets. This 'asset-based saving innovation' meant that members of savings and loan groups bought assets instead of depositing cash in the group's account. This mirrored a trend within Zimbabwean society more broadly to hold wealth in the form of tangible assets, rather than cash the value of which was rapidly and consistently depreciating.

Assets Acquired	%
Household utensils	42
Livestock	31
Mixed assets	23
Property	6
Bedding	2

The most common category of assets purchased as savings was household utensils, not too surprisingly since most programme participants were women, with responsibility for cooking and maintaining the household's kitchen. This was followed by the small livestock that are reared by women rather than by men – poultry, rabbits, goats – followed by other 'productive' assets such as gardening implements, and 'consumption' assets such as bedding.

An evaluation found that members of Kupfuma Ishungu savings and loan groups had achieved significant improvements in well-being in terms of various indicators, including asset ownership. One concern, however, is that the inflationary economic environment was making programme participants risk-averse, as is evident from the predominance of consumer goods over productive assets in the list of assets purchased as asset-based savings.

Source: Ellis (2007b)

labour to farm these fields for their labour-constrained neighbours, and to transfer farming skills to older children who can participate in farming activities. The Neighbourhood Care Points for OVC (Case Study 9), also in Swaziland, aims to build a sense of community solidarity and collective responsibility for children affected by HIV and AIDS, by providing a range of support services with the help of local people. Finally, the Old Age Pension in Lesotho (Case Study 1) enhances the social status of older relatives, who were previously regarded as burdens on their families but have now become economic assets: 'there is some evidence that families may be encouraging their elderly members living alone to move closer and become part of the household' (Croome, *et al.,* 2007, p.5).

Another way that social responsibility towards the weakest members of society is built up by social protection schemes is through fostering welfare committees at community level. NGOs nowadays routinely facilitate the formation of such institutions in order to ensure community involvement and transparency in beneficiary selection. Where possible such committees are built on pre-existing community institutions, but in the absence (or disappearance) of such older institutions new ones are created for the purpose. In Zambia, the existence of such community level institutions has been formalized since the 1950s under the Public Welfare Assistance Scheme (PWAS) which operates through District Welfare Assistance Committees (DWACs) and village level Community Welfare Assistance Committees (CWACs). See Case Study 5 on the Zambia pilot Social Cash Transfers for details of how this structure works nowadays.

ISSUES ARISING

Although asset protection and asset building are unambiguously positive impacts of social protection programmes, it is important to focus on what the programme is trying to achieve. In certain circumstances, an observation that beneficiary households have accumulated assets could indicate failure rather than success, or perhaps a qualified rather than outright success.

As noted above, some social protection projects have asset building as an explicit objective. Amongst the southern African case studies, these include livestock transfers to poor households in Zimbabwe, public works that construct physical infrastructure in rural Malawi, and interventions that support the education of poor and vulnerable children in Lesotho, Mozambique and Swaziland. In these cases, if beneficiaries do not show evidence of asset accumulation or enhanced human capital, these programmes have failed in terms of this particular objective. Conversely, many other programmes aim simply to ensure that poor people have enough food to eat or enough cash to avoid impoverishing themselves even further, in short to protect assets rather than to build them.

The potential for household asset accumulation is limited in food aid or cash transfer programmes because of 'Engel's Law', which states that the proportion of total income spent on food falls as income rises. Put another way, a 'rule of thumb' definition of poverty is that poor people spend at least 70 per cent of their income on food, and most of the balance on meeting other basic needs. In fact, spending patterns among poor people tend to follow a predictable pattern, with priorities ranked roughly as follows: (i) food; (ii) groceries; (iii) utilities; (iv) health; (v) clothing; (vi) education; (vii) investment in family enterprises; (viii) assets. So if beneficiaries accumulate significant assets with transfer income this could suggest that mis-targeting has occurred i.e. people who received these transfers did not really need them.

Paradoxically, therefore, given the drive to find evidence of poverty reduction through cash transfer programmes, evidence of asset accumulation might signify a kind of failure, rather than a success. This is especially true of social transfers that are intended to protect subsistence food consumption, such as the emergency cash transfers for drought-affected farmers in Dowa District (Malawi) or cash transfers targeted at the poorest 10 per cent of households in Kalomo District (Zambia). Similarly, the Food Subsidy Programme (PSA) in Mozambique is targeted at destitute people who are typically labour-constrained and are not expected to graduate from requiring support; it follows that 'asset building does not really enter the PSA approach as currently implemented' (see Case Study 2).

Further examples come from the social pension programmes in Lesotho and Swaziland. These are regular cash grants to older citizens that are scaled to meet the basic needs of a single person – the beneficiary. As noted above, however, significant amounts of pension income are voluntarily diverted by recipients to the education of young children in their family or

in their care. This investment in human capital formation is often interpreted as a positive side-effect of social pension programmes, but another
more critical interpretation is possible, that cash grants to older citizens are
not large enough to meet the range of needs and demands that they face,
and that there are significant gaps in the social protection system which
mean that the priority needs of poor households (in this case, children's
education) are not being adequately addressed.

LESSON LEARNING ON ASSET IMPACTS OF SOCIAL PROTECTION

1. *Asset protection* should be a core objective of all social protection
    strategies, since poverty is defined by assetlessness, and vulnerability to
    livelihood shocks forces the poor to dispose of their few assets, impov-
    erishing themselves further. One model is to provide predictable social
    transfers that smooth consumption and minimize the adoption of
    damaging 'coping strategies'. A very different approach is social insur-
    ance, such as burial societies in many African countries which provide
    informal social insurance against shocks. Innovative approaches to
    asset protection should be explored that build on traditional commu-
    nity risk-pooling mechanisms, like burial societies and ROSCAs.
2. *Asset accumulation* through unconditional social transfers is unlikely to
    be achieved by small or one-off transfers of cash or food, as basic needs
    must be met first, and poor people spend most of their income on food.
    If promoting asset accumulation is an explicit objective of the pro-
    gramme, the size and duration of transfers must be increased.
    Predictable, guaranteed transfers (for example, pensions) allow bene-
    ficiaries to save towards asset purchases, and raise the proportion of
    transfer income that is spent on investment rather than consumption.
3. *Asset creation* through Public Works Programmes often under-
    achieves in practice, because construction is of poor quality and assets
    are rarely maintained after the programme ends. This raises a question
    about whether social transfers to poor people should be conditional on
    work at all. If hard labour is being used as a self-targeting device (which
    is ethically dubious, as, indeed, is paying low wages) and the outputs of
    that hard labour are of little value, there seems to be little justification
    for incorporating public asset creation as a programme objective.
4. *Asset transfers* should be considered more often than they are at present.
    There are positive lessons to learn from asset transfer programmes for
    the 'ultra-poor' in Bangladesh, and, since poor households are asset-
    constrained by definition, ameliorating these constraints can be an effec-

tive route out of poverty for economically active individuals. For the rural poor, livestock, farm implements, agricultural inputs and education materials for children can all contribute to asset building and sustainable poverty reduction.

5. *Asset impacts* are easier to predict than to measure, and many of our case studies follow a familiar pattern of making big claims for potential impacts at the programme inception or design stage, but failing to monitor or evaluate actual impacts at the implementation stage. Programmes that transfer assets directly (such as livestock) should monitor what happens to these animals and their offspring. Programmes that build assets indirectly (say by supporting children's education) should attempt to track these children's educational performance over time. This will require more complex and longer-term evaluation methodologies than simply reporting on programme outputs (how many goats were delivered to how many households, and so on), but there is no other way of assessing whether real impacts have been achieved.

In brief conclusion of this chapter there is one further point that needs to be made. Assets are important beyond their livelihood security attributes for individual poor and vulnerable families. Assets are the building blocks of rising economic activity and incomes, going from individuals and households, to communities and districts, and to the national economy. Successful and sustained asset accumulation at the household, community, district and national level is an essential feature of climbing out of poverty at those different levels of society and economy.

9. Lesson learning: strengths, weaknesses and the state of the art

GOOD PRACTICE PRINCIPLES IN SOCIAL PROTECTION

The purpose of this chapter is to pull together the strengths, weaknesses and lessons for future social protection practice in Africa that arise from the themes and examples of the preceding chapters as well as the 15 case studies contained in Part II of the book. Individual social transfer projects or programmes are typically formulated with clear intentions regarding the forms of deprivation they seek to address, as well as building what are understood to be good practices into scheme implementation. Since knowledge about best practice is widely disseminated through the donor and NGO community, as well as in government agencies, the implementation of social protection is in general on an improving trajectory throughout sub-Saharan Africa.

From the materials and case studies researched for this book, it is possible to discern a set of principles that add up to desirable attributes for social protection efforts overall. Of course, individual social transfer schemes do not always comply with all such attributes, but most case studies can be seen to attempt to comply with a majority of them. These cross-cutting desirable attributes can be codified as a set of Good Practice Principles that social protection practice in Africa should aim towards:

1. to protect recipients from hunger now, or in the future, while not enfeebling their capabilities to engage in productive livelihoods, nor relegating them socially to 'victim' status;
2. to increase empowerment through enabling individual or collective choice, whenever it is feasible to do so;
3. to strengthen rather than weaken community level cohesion and institutions;
4. to ensure inclusion of specific deprived social categories that are in danger of being socially excluded, such as orphans and vulnerable children (OVC);

5. to target intended beneficiaries successfully, and avoid as far as possible exclusion and inclusion errors;
6. to ensure cost-efficiency in delivery, and cost-effectiveness in achieving sustainable long term outcomes (especially for livelihood building social protection efforts);
7. to support rather than undermine local markets;
8. to ensure predictability and continuity in project or programme funding and coverage;
9. to establish rights to certain types of social transfer that are inviolable in law, and can be expected as a right by all citizens in the event that they find themselves in the circumstances delineated by the law;
10. to monitor outcomes, not just activities and outputs, so that proper evaluations can be conducted regarding sustained scheme impacts on the well-being and livelihoods of recipients.

The rising popularity of cash transfers as a social transfer method, discussed in many different places in this book, can be interpreted in the light of these Good Practice Principles. Cash transfers are widely thought to promote empowerment, choice, cost-efficiency, support to local markets, and potential for long term livelihood building; they also lend themselves more readily than other forms of transfer (food, inputs, assets) to predictability, continuity, and rights of receipt by specified categories of beneficiary. The type of social transfer where most of the desirable attributes seem to come together is a social pension, where subject to reaching the prescribed age threshold every individual can expect to be eligible in law to the transfer. A social pension also conforms to the notion of 'predictable funding for predictable needs' that we have seen strongly informed the direction in which social protection in Africa was moving in the mid- to late-2000s.

This chapter is structured as follows. First, it considers examples and patterns of strength in social protection practice that are identified from Africa-wide examples and southern Africa case studies. These strengths are of course quite closely associated with the Good Practice Principles that have just been identified. Second, this is followed by a synthesis of the flaws and weaknesses that stand out from reviewing many different social protection schemes, since as much can be learnt from mistakes and ineffective experiences as from the examples of good practice. Third, a number of points are collected together concerning social interactions and side-effects of social transfers, an area of social protection that is seldom brought to the fore, but which constitutes an important dimension that may help to clarify ideas around scaled up social protection in the future. Finally, key lessons learnt from the themes and case studies are drawn out, and some provisional conclusions about future social protection in Africa are put forward.

SELECTED STRENGTHS

Most social protection efforts in Africa do accomplish most of what they set out to do, and examples of only partial success or outright failure are the exception rather than the rule. There are instances where the relationship between resources provided and transfers realized might not stand up to too much detailed scrutiny, and this particularly applies to social action programmes and funds across the continent (such as the Malawi Social Action Fund, MASAF). However, in the absence of proper evidence these examples remain more as hearsay rather than properly documented occurrences. The NGO sector can be credited with not only usually achieving what it sets out to do, but also often doing so in an innovative and forward looking way that builds on past experience and actively pursues future improvements in implementation, although they are also responsible for promulgating pilot projects and short-term interventions that may contradict certain of the aforementioned Good Practice Principles, in particular the last three. The social protection examples examined for this book reveal patterns of strength that are useful for lesson learning, and these are examined under the following headings:

A. *Organization and coordination*. Many instances of thoughtful organization and good coordination between stakeholders can be found in social protection in Africa. Perhaps the most sophisticated examples of this are the relatively large-scale social transfer programmes in Ethiopia (Box 2.3), Kenya (Box 4.1) and Ghana (Box 5.2). Other examples are the Malawi Input Subsidy Programme, which overcomes significant logistical challenges in procurement, coupon distribution and fertilizer distribution on the big scale (Case Study 11), and the Protracted Relief Programme (PRP) in Zimbabwe which offers an interesting model of effective coordination, in which international and local NGOs conduct a variety of different social transfers with feedback and lesson learning occurring through a Technical Learning and Coordination committee (Case Studies 6 and 15).

It is notable that much of this coordination occurs at a 'meso' level below the strategic level of central government, but above the detailed organizational capability that is needed to deliver a single transfer to a defined group of beneficiaries. Effective central strategic coordination, guidance and monitoring remains lacking in most countries, although the National Social Protection Strategy in Ghana (Box 5.2), the Food Security Programme in Ethiopia (Box 2.3), and the frameworks put in place in Malawi and Zambia represent exceptions to this generalization.

B. *Choice and empowerment.* It is widely acknowledged that cash transfers provide recipients with choice over the use they make of the transfer, and are relatively empowering in comparison, say, to being given a food ration the composition of which is ordained by an external agency. The same holds true for the social pensions found in Botswana, Lesotho, Senegal and Swaziland amongst others. The design of trade fair projects (Input Trade Fairs, Education Material Fairs) incorporates the notion of empowerment through choice, since vouchers represent a cash value that can be exchanged for a wide variety of different items within the parameters of the fair (Case Studies 10 and 13).

C. *Building community cohesion.* The interaction of social transfers with social life in communities is potentially more problematic than many practitioners are prepared to concede (see 'Social Interactions', p. 130). Many social protection schemes set out to support or build community cohesion (sometimes referred to as 'social capital') as a subsidiary goal to the main transfer. However, some attempts to invoke traditional norms of community reciprocity have not worked well, either because the purported traditional practice was somewhat idealized (Case Study 14) or because contemporary stresses on everyone's livelihoods do not leave families with the scope to engage in former types of social reciprocity.

D. *Innovation.* Many social protection schemes contain examples of innovative thinking about modes of delivery of social transfers, making the best use of limited transfer resources, and building in incentives to longer term social goals in addition to short term protection against hunger. An outstanding example is the DECT project in Malawi (Case Study 4), which was risk-taking and innovative on at least four fronts: the smartcard/ATM method for making cash transfers, the designation of women as cardholders, the use of 'triangulated' wealth ranking as a targeting device, and linking monthly transfers to the price of food. In this project, the speed of acceptance of smartcards by mainly illiterate and innumerate beneficiaries suggests considerable potential for using new technologies (smartcards, mobile phones) for social transfers in the future. Several newer programmes (for example, Kenya HSNP and Ghana LEAP) are in the vanguard of electronic transfer technologies.

E.   *Pensions.* Social pensions have many strengths, and are therefore worth considering separately for these strong points. The pension is a right in law, or an entitlement, not a privilege that can be arbitrarily withdrawn. Pension incomes have been shown in numerous studies to reduce vulnerability in recipient households because payments tend to be treated by recipients as household income, and are spent to the benefit of all household members. For this reason, pensions are shown to increase the nutritional status and school attendance of children, and the food security and medical access of all members in pensioner households, not just the welfare of the pensioners themselves. Pensions have the significant strength of a single targeting criterion, eligibility being easily understood in all social settings. Pensions are also observed to have positive social impacts on the status, independence and dignity of older people.

F.   *Food transfers.* The case studies contain several examples of social transfers where food may be more appropriate than cash as a way of ensuring the desired impact of the transfer. This applies to the delivery of balanced food rations to AIDS patients undergoing ART, as well as to school feeding of primary school children. In both cases, it is the continuity of rather specific dietary provision that is critical, and cash transfers might not achieve this owing to fluctuations in availabilities and prices of ingredients.

SELECTED WEAKNESSES

Just as different examples and case studies reveal patterns of strengths that are useful for learning lessons about best practice in social protection, so also they reveal patterns of weakness that can be equally insightful in terms of the pitfalls to be avoided in social protection approach, design and implementation. A special category of weaknesses derive from social interactions of social transfers that are sufficiently distinctive and underestimated in social protection discussion to be considered in a separate section below. The following are the main individual or grouped weaknesses that are observable across numerous social protection schemes:

A.   *Unstable funding and lack of continuity.* This is a critical flaw that is nevertheless widely prevalent. The most severe example of it contained in this book is the Food Security Pack in Zambia (Case Study 12), which has had highly unstable annual funding and only received 30 per cent of the resources allocated to it in annual budget statements over a seven-year period (2000–07). Both funding instability and lack of continuity may occur due to poor decision making by donors, or, in one example due to a shortfall in food supplies required to make up food rations for AIDS patients (Case Study 7). Many small social transfer projects have limited duration that limits their claim to having long run beneficial impacts.

B. *Limited scope and imprint.* Many social protection schemes are tiny projects, part of a mosaic of NGO efforts to address the many different facets of chronic poverty and vulnerability, but with scarcely any evidence regarding cumulative or sustainable impacts. The recognized beneficial impacts of such projects are personal to the few beneficiaries concerned, and may or may not produce longer term results for improving the future well-being of those beneficiaries, their families or the communities in which they live. Common weaknesses are 'spreading too thin' (covering more communities but reaching few eligible beneficiaries in each), and short duration with lack of follow-up so that real impacts are not assessed.

C. *Motivation and incentives.* This aspect was elaborated in Chapter 4 in the context of the delivery of social transfers. There is an evident divergence between the motivational factors that guide NGO operations in social protection (including the risk of being sidelined in the competition for donor or government funding) and the incentive factors that pertain to civil servants or local government officials who are on the government payroll anyway, typically at very low salaries. Yet good performance by government personnel is essential for scaled up social transfers to work, and a lot more thought needs to be given to alternative incentive structures that would make this workable.

D. *Other flaws encountered.* A variety of other weaknesses were identified in the southern Africa social transfer case studies (Part II), typically associated with just one or a few projects rather than occurring across many of them. These are summarized briefly here as follows:

- *Undue complexity:* the Food Security Pack in Zambia was from the outset too ambitious in almost all respects – its coverage (all districts), its pack size and composition (grain, pulses, roots and fertilizer), and its multiple goals (ten goals covering such disparate aims as new cultivation methods, livelihood diversification and entrepreneurship).

- *Poor cost-effectiveness:* it is probable that trade fairs (Case Studies 10 and 13) are a rather costly way of delivering a certain type and level of transfer to beneficiaries, owing to the high gearing up costs around a series of one-off large events, the logistical costs of holding such events in remote rural areas, and the time and effort required to inform and persuade distributors and traders to turn up at the fairs.

- *Input timing problems*: where transfers involve farm inputs timing is critical – any slippage in organization and delivery means that inputs reach farmers too late to make a valuable contribution to the next season's crop, and this occurs in many input projects.
- *Lack of 'downstream' monitoring*: most schemes fall short when it comes to monitoring longer term impacts, as opposed to activities and delivery targets; for example, several input schemes fail to monitor harvests and yields in the seasons following the input transfer, and are thus unable to verify that they have made a measurable difference to farm outputs or livelihood outcomes.

SOCIAL INTERACTIONS

While implementers of most social transfer schemes examined for this book were acutely conscious of the social dimensions of their activities, and did their best to anticipate and incorporate, or work round, known pit-falls or sensitivities, nevertheless they are not always successful at doing this. Sometimes this is due to outsiders' misinterpretations of customs and cultural understandings around gifts and transfers, sometimes it is due to a certain amount of naivety about people's altruism, and sometimes it is due to underestimating the similarity of material circumstances that character-izes the majority of people in rural communities in low-income African countries (see Box 9.1)

The term 'social interactions' is used here to describe social and individ-ual behaviours that result from the advent of social transfers at community level, as revealed by numerous social protection examples. Some of these behaviours are plainly economic in character – social transfers represent an incentive to certain kinds of action or reaction. However, the emphasis here is on social processes and outcomes, for example reconfiguring household demographics in order to qualify for a targeted transfer. Social interactions evidently overlap with approaches to selecting beneficiaries, as well as political and institutional dimensions of social protection.

A. *'We are all poor here'*. A considerable proportion of social behaviour in relation to social transfers in Africa can be explained by reference to the perception of community members that 'we are all poor here'. This phrase recurs as a reaction to targeted beneficiary selection in numerous social protection contexts across all countries, and especially in remote rural areas. Several points arise in relation to this perception:

BOX 9.1:   'WE ARE ALL POOR HERE': ECONOMIC
DIFFERENCE AND SOCIAL
TRANSFERS

Social transfer practitioners are familiar with the social divisiveness that transfers can inadvertently create. One manifestation of
this divisiveness is the oft expressed opinion voiced in community
meetings, or by key informants, that 'we are all poor here'. This is
more often than not articulated by respondents as a plain state-
ment of fact, not as special pleading nor with undertones of vic-
timization. How accurate is this perception of ordinary people, and
what does it imply about social transfers to the poorest of the
poor?

Figure 9.1 provides a 'generic' income distribution for a poor sub-
Saharan African country with a large rural population. It is based
on nationally representative large scale household budget surveys
for Malawi (2004–05 Integrated Household Survey), Zambia
(2002–03 Living Conditions Monitoring Survey) and Ethiopia
(2004–05 Household Income, Consumption and Expenditure
Survey).[1] The data is presented as mean consumption per capita
per month in descending order of deciles, converted from national

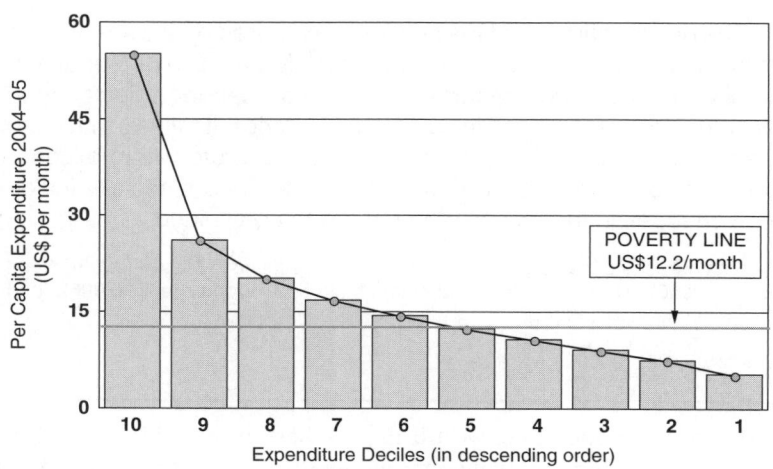

*Figure 9.1   Generic income distribution and poverty line based
on three countries (mean consumption per capita,
by decile, US$ per month)*

currencies to US dollars at the official exchange rates ruling at the time the surveys were conducted. The following interesting observations can be made:

- On average, US$1.8 per month separates each of the bottom six deciles of the income distribution (that is, covering 60 per cent of the population).
- The decile mean consumption per capita per month is US$5.4 for the first decile and US$14.4 for the sixth decile.
- It is only from the sixth decile upwards that differences between deciles begin to climb, gradually at first and then steeply towards the top of the distribution.
- These figures refer to national data. Rural data on its own shows even smaller differences in the bottom 70 per cent of the distribution, and less steep differences at the top of the distribution.
- A US$10 per month cash transfer to a five-person household in the bottom 10 per cent of the income distribution would bring their per capita income up to the level of the next decile.
- However, the same US$10 provided to successively smaller households quickly jumps recipients above adjacent consumption deciles: an individual receiving US$8, for example, would be catapulted to the sixth decile.

The data confirms that the sentiment captured by 'we are all poor here' accurately reflects the very small differences in personal and family circumstances separating more than half the population in very low-income settings in sub-Saharan Africa. It follows that cash transfers to the poorest of the poor must operate within exceedingly narrow parameters of economic difference if socially invidious changes in income distribution are to be avoided.

[1]   The published analyses of these surveys can be found in Malawi (2005); World Bank (2005); Devereux *et al.* (2006b); Malawi & World Bank (2006); and Woldehanna *et al.* (2008).

Source: Ellis (2008)

- the perception that 'we are all poor here' is rooted in the reality of minor differences in income and wealth status for most community members (Box 9.1);
- this is not to say that there is equality in African rural communities, but rather that the income distribution in most countries is

such that the genuinely 'better off' or rich tend to be quite a small proportion of the population, while most community members are struggling to keep their heads above water;

- in these social contexts, targeted transfers are potentially socially divisive especially if they involve multiple complex criteria to make refined distinctions between poor and destitute households;
- outsiders' perceptions about the most deserving poor may not correspond to community perceptions, or social norms and customs;
- reactions can vary from community solidarity (pooling physical transfers like fertilizer), to individual family strategies for inclusion (altering household demographic structure to fit targeting criteria), to connivance between selector and beneficiary to share transfers (where the selector may be a leader or a community committee);
- inclusion in a social transfer scheme may result in withdrawal of previous reciprocal support provided to that individual or household by family or community, thus adding less to the livelihood security status of the recipient than is indicated by the size or value of the transfer.

B. *Elite capture*. Another social behaviour that is rife around social transfers is so-called 'elite capture'. Elite capture appears in many different guises:

- beneficiary lists being stuffed with relatives and friends of chiefs or village leaders;
- leaders or community committees requiring a 'cut' of the social transfers in order to include beneficiaries on the list;
- substantial quantities of subsidized fertilizer coupons ending up in the hands of district officials, traditional leaders, police and the military (exemplified by the Input Subsidy Programme in Malawi);
- political interference in beneficiary lists to ensure that opposition voters do not stay on the list (mentioned for cash transfers in Zambia).

Leaving aside the self-targeting of food-for-work style social safety nets, social protection has evolved during the 2000s from top-down selection (by officials or NGO personnel), to stakeholder committees (often dominated by officials and traditional leaders), to community participatory selection (involving community-level verification of beneficiary lists). The stakeholder committee route has been particularly prone to elite capture, with local chiefs and other traditional leaders prone to orient lists to their own advantage. Community verification of beneficiary lists can successfully overcome elite capture, but it requires elaborate stages of verification to achieve this.

The phenomenon of elite capture tends to exacerbate social tensions arising from the 'we are all poor here' response to social transfers. Community members are aware of what is going on when their leaders siphon off resources, and the deserving poor get left out when a proportion of limited transfers are made to the better off or well connected. Nevertheless, social responses can be counter-intuitive and surprising. In some instances elite capture may be treated as socially acceptable, especially if the community believes it was the leadership that brought the social transfer to them in the first place.

C.   *Community reciprocity.* Some social protection sets out purposely to build on community reciprocity. An example provided in Part II of this book is the various initiatives for supporting OVC in Swaziland (Case Studies 9 and 14). Alas, the community reciprocity that is appealed to in such schemes is often a somewhat idealized representation of a past custom that has vanished, or has become vestigial owing to growing pressures on people's livelihoods, or as a result of the long term inroads of market relations.

Undue reliance on exaggerated notions of community solidarity can result in policy mistakes. For example, the notion is prevalent across Africa that communal school farms should contribute to school feeding programmes; however, they generally fail to do so, therefore wasting scarce resources that are allocated to them, and resulting in inaccurate estimates of the food delivery that is required in order to ensure that all primary school children get proper school meals.

In summary of these points, social transfers set out to protect the poorest and most vulnerable people from inadequate nutrition and basic needs. Clearly in a prospering society where people's standards of living are generally on an upward path, this objective can be met by targeting those left behind while the majority move forward. Moreover, in such a scenario, those moving forward are unlikely to feel resentful of those receiving help, since the level of such help will be significantly below their own material situation or what they are able to aspire to in the foreseeable future. Also, external support for the poorest community members removes the economic and moral pressure from wealthier community members to provide informal support, so the wealthy can also benefit materially from social transfers delivered to their poor neighbours.

However, especially in rural areas of Africa, such distinctions are hard to draw. Most community members consider that 'we are all poor here'. Moreover, opportunity is not rising at a rate (nor has it been doing so historically) for fractionally better off individuals to see an improvement in their circumstances coming into view round the corner. For this reason, social protection in Africa often involves seeking tiny variations in circumstance that ordinary people do not perceive as real differences in order to select a lucky few people as transfer recipients. This inevitably creates social tension and division, as well as personal strategies to work around the selection criteria that are proposed, or the organizational means of implementing them.

LESSON LEARNING FOR THE FUTURE

It is unlikely that the 'messiness' of social protection in Africa will ever be more than partially resolved by the much advocated advent of national social protection strategies and frameworks. This is because this 'messiness' is found in all countries worldwide, rich and poor, and it reflects the huge diversity of people in need due to a multiplicity of different causes, therefore giving moral legitimacy to the many different organizations with different mandates seeking to do what they can to help. Lesson learning in relation to this diversity is as fragmented and contingent as the sector itself, and ideas that improve practice in one set of circumstances may be irrelevant in another. Nevertheless, the Good Practice Principles identified in the introduction to this chapter can be considered a useful checklist applicable to most types of social protection.

However, putting this diversity to one side, much recent debate in social protection in Africa concerns the 'bigger picture' of how to achieve protection from hunger for large numbers of vulnerable people, and how best to move away from perpetual crisis management towards consistent and predictable delivery of such protection. It is this big picture that is addressed by the lesson learning points made here. The context is one of an upsurge of enthusiasm for cash transfers as a means for achieving the required consistency and predictability; the problem of scaling up to national level from successful cash transfer pilots; and many unresolved issues concerning funding, beneficiary selection, delivery methods and cost-efficient implementation overall. The examples of social protection examined for this book offer important lessons for this large-scale dimension of social protection, and these are set out as follows:

1. *Cash is not the only instrument.* While cash transfers can be seen to elicit powerful reasons in their favour (set out earlier in this chapter), it would be a mistake to neglect thereby the potential role of other transfers for achieving hunger reduction aims. Plenty of examples

demonstrate that subsidized farm inputs and food and asset transfers have their own places and strengths for tackling vulnerability to hunger. The Malawi Input Subsidy Programme surprised with both its political strength of purpose and its beneficial impact to date over three crop seasons (2005/06 to 2007/08) on food production and food access by the vulnerable due to low prices and less seasonal price instability. On the food transfer side, it is evident that certain social transfer types and goals (for example, school feeding or nutritional support to AIDS patients) are more efficiently and effectively accomplished by food than by cash, if for no other reason than that frequent adjustments to cash amounts to compensate for food price changes are administratively onerous, clumsy and costly in those cases. Although the evidence on impacts from livestock transfers in Zimbabwe is limited and so far inconclusive, asset transfer programmes in Bangladesh have achieved substantial positive impacts (Devereux & Coll-Black, 2007, p.25).

2. *Defects of multiple criteria targeting.* The use of proxy indicators and multiple criteria as means to target beneficiaries in social protection schemes is shown to possess several intrinsic weaknesses that even the best designed schemes struggle to overcome. The more complex the criteria, the more difficult it is for community members to grasp what it is that differentiates beneficiaries from all the other poor people in the community. This problem, alluded to above as the 'we are all poor here' reaction to social transfers, causes social divisiveness and friction in the process of selecting beneficiaries. It also causes social behaviours that seek to circumvent the criteria, such as altering the demographic structure of the household to fit the criteria and side deals between selectors and selected to share the benefits of being on the beneficiary list. While participatory processes of 'triangulation' at community level can go some way to resolving these problems, these are typically associated with small projects implemented by enthusiastic NGOs, and it is unproven and perhaps doubtful that they would work at national scale.

3. *Is categorical targeting the way forward?* The foregoing suggests that categorical targeting may offer a superior way forward for scaled up social transfers in Africa. In categorical targeting, beneficiaries belong to a social category defined by simple and easily understood criteria, such as people above 65 years of age, or children under 5, or pregnant women, or orphans (where an orphan is defined by just one or two clear criteria, though these criteria are often less clear cut than they might appear). Categorical targeting has several advantages at scale (that is, where coverage is intended to be the entire country). The number of potential beneficiaries can be estimated fairly accurately from demographic data. The transfer can be incorporated in the budgetary

process and become a predictable annual government expenditure. The transfer can be legislated as a right, so that all citizens falling into that category know that they are entitled to receive the benefit. It is less socially divisive than targeting by multiple criteria. For example, a social pension that everyone knows they will be entitled to receive in due course does not stir up the resentment that microscopic differentiation between families according to multiple proxy indicators causes.

4. *Innovation in delivery.* Where cash transfers are concerned there exists plenty of scope afforded by new technologies for delivering transfers efficiently to beneficiaries, and avoiding risks of leakage or loss of funds when cash is being moved. The HSNP in Kenya (Box 4.1), LEAP in Ghana (Box 5.2), and at much smaller scale DECT (Case Study 4) in Malawi represent the leading edge of experience in this area. Cellphone technologies also offer a potential route to cash delivery. Partnerships between public bodies or NGOs and the private sector (commercial banking and cellphone companies) are required in order to implement innovative forms of delivery. Aside from cost and security reasons for taking such methods seriously, potentially positive rural financial market side effects can arise, especially with smartcards that can provide an entry point to savings and credit in addition to the drawing down of regular transfers.

5. *The role of NGOs.* A considerable proportion of current NGO activity is focused on delivering transfers to destitute people using the multiple criteria approach to beneficiary selection. NGOs take their social protection activities seriously, and examples and case studies provided in this book demonstrate that they are often at the forefront of socially sensitive, innovative and cost-efficient delivery of social transfers. Useful partnerships between states and NGOs in scaled up social protection can be envisaged, going beyond the short duration, project-oriented, activities that are currently at the centre of such partnerships.

6. *The role of politics.* The focus of donors in social protection tends to revolve either around evidence about its ability to contribute to achieving Millennium Development Goals (often from pilot programmes which they initiate and support), or around moral principles concerning rights to social protection and freedom from extreme poverty and hunger, especially for vulnerable population groups such as children, mothers, those with chronic illness and disabilities, or older people. Politics tends to be viewed as a constraining or distorting force, driving patronage networks and elite capture, and preventing evidence from being heeded or benefits from reaching the neediest. Yet the case

studies provided in this book reveal that the programmes most likely to succeed in terms of government buy-in, implementation at scale, and fiscal sustainability are those that have electoral appeal. The vote-winning potential of programmes such as the Lesotho Old Age Pension, initiated by the Prime Minister through the Ministry of Finance (not the Social Welfare Ministry) in the run-up to the 2004 elections and increased in value as a 2007 election pledge; or Malawi's Input Subsidy Programme, which featured strongly in that country's 2004 electoral campaign, is not to be underestimated. Both programmes are government led, and in terms of scaled up delivery with national coverage they are arguably the most successful schemes deployed as examples in this book.

CONCLUSIONS: THE STATE OF THE ART

There are six key conclusions that arise from this lesson learning tour of social protection in Africa. First, variation and diversity of social protection practice is healthy and generates new ideas, so there is no need to move precipitously in the direction of monolithic structures of coordination or delivery. Second, in the headlong rush towards cash transfers, the validity and value of other types of transfer (food, inputs, assets) should not be neglected; there are many circumstances where these may turn out to be the preferred form of transfer, and individual cases should be taken on their merits rather than being brushed aside by the cash transfer juggernaut. Third, nevertheless cash transfers do possess many attractive qualities, especially for scaled up social protection aimed at national coverage. Fourth, new technology offers opportunities yet to be fully explored for the timely, secure and efficient delivery of cash transfers to beneficiaries. Fifth, predictability and continuity are absolutely key attributes of nearly all types of social protection, the only significant exception being seasonal transfers to overcome unpredictable seasonal food deficits. Sixth, political support is essential for any large-scale initiative with national coverage to work.

Finally, the power of pensions to act as a major vehicle for addressing vulnerability to hunger in Africa needs to be firmly on the future policy agenda. Social pensions correspond to all the positive attributes of categorical targeting noted earlier: entitlement as a right, a single simple criterion for eligibility (an age threshold), 'predictable funding for predictable needs', and potential to utilize innovative forms of delivery. Other positive points about pensions were made in the section on 'Selected Strengths' (p. 128), and do not need to be repeated here. In large very poor countries where documentary evidence on age is absent or inadequate, the initial registration of those eligible represents a substantial challenge, but this challenge is less onerous than attempting at scale to identify 'the destitute' through multiple proxy indicators. Once initial registration has occurred, and tested rules established for verification of eligibility, subsequent updating of beneficiary lists should be relatively low maintenance.

Social pensions would not, of course, provide a panacea for hunger and vulnerability in Africa. They exclude large numbers of hungry and vulnerable households and individuals which need to be catered for by other components of a coherent social protection strategy, and their livelihood promotion impacts are likely in most cases to be quite limited. The same may, however, turn out to be true for efforts to reach 'the most destitute 10 per cent', the majority of whom turn out to be older people when the selection is done anyway. Moreover, as emerges clearly from the case studies, reaching the destitute as a category is prone to complex identification difficulties as well as negative social side effects, and does not always provide the political leverage that governments need in order to move forward with the required authority and enthusiasm. As suggested in the last of the conclusions listed above, unless programmes are able to crystallize political support in the context of domestic political pressures and agendas they are unlikely to become embedded in the practice of government, and their long term durability will remain equivocal.

PART II

Case studies from southern Africa

10.   Introduction to the case studies

INTRODUCTION

This part of the book contains 15 social transfer case studies drawn from six countries of the southern African region in the period 2006–07. The six countries are Lesotho, Malawi, Mozambique, Swaziland, Zambia and Zimbabwe, and case studies were selected within and across them as the outcome of a stakeholder consultation that emphasized knowledge gaps and scope for lesson learning. The list of case studies including their countries, titles and acronyms appears in Table 10.1.

The chosen case studies provide a varied representation of social protection practice in southern Africa. Some are small scale and of limited duration, while others have national coverage and are permanently in place, secured by legislation and provided as a right to their recipients. Small scale projects are often innovative, and some were designed as pilots or experiments in cash transfers to vulnerable beneficiaries, with a view to their potential for scaling up in the future.

The authors are aware that case studies from southern Africa can hardly be regarded as representative of social protection in sub-Saharan Africa as a whole. It is for this reason that important examples from other sub-Saharan African countries are provided in the preceding chapters. Yet there are various reasons why these case studies can nevertheless offer lessons that are widely applicable across the continent. One reason is that this region more than any other experienced a prolonged era of periodic hunger crises between 2001 and 2006. This catapulted the region into the forefront of new initiatives designed to halt or reverse an apparent slide into chronic vulnerability. A second reason is that donors and international NGOs carry 'models' of what seems to work in social protection across national boundaries, so that lessons learned in west or eastern Africa are carried to southern Africa, as also such knowledge transfers occur in the reverse directions. A third reason is that no conceivable selection of just 15 case studies could be said to represent the full range of social protection practice in Africa no matter how many countries they were drawn from, so this selection is likely to do the job as well as any.

Table 10.1   Social transfer case studies, southern Africa 2006–07

Case Study	Country	Social Protection Scheme	Acronym[1]
1	Lesotho	Old Age Pension	OAP
2	Mozambique	Food Subsidy Programme	PSA[2]
3	Malawi	Public Works Programmes	PWPs
4	Malawi	Dowa Emergency Cash Transfer	DECT
5	Zambia	Social Cash Transfers	SCTs
6	Zimbabwe	Urban Food Programme	UFP
7	Mozambique	Food Assistance Programme	FAP
8	Lesotho	School Feeding	SF
9	Swaziland	Neighbourhood Care Points for OVC[3]	NCPs
10	Mozambique	Education Material Fairs	EMFs
11	Malawi	Input Subsidy Programme	ISP
12	Zambia	Food Security Pack	FSP
13	Mozambique	Input Trade Fairs	ITFs
14	Swaziland	Chiefs' Fields for OVC[3]	CFs
15	Zimbabwe	Small Livestock Transfers	SLTs

Notes:
1   These acronyms are often used as shorthand for the case studies.
2   Programa de Subsidios de Alimentos in Portuguese.
3   OVC = orphans and vulnerable children.

In the period during which the case studies were undertaken a great deal of interest by donors, NGOs and governments centred on cash transfers as an approach to securing minimum acceptable nutrition and basic needs for those most vulnerable to hunger in the region. For this reason, an important strand running through the case studies (but not present in all of them) comprises the scope and limitations of cash transfers, especially as contrasted to reliance on food aid not just in emergencies but as continuing support to the chronic extreme poor. As we have already encountered in previous chapters of this book, another way that this strand is expressed is in terms of the policy objective to replace ad hoc responses to crisis situations by 'predictable funding for predictable needs'. If only the chronically vulnerable were protected on a continuing basis from insufficient food consumption (and from having to sell assets in order to secure enough food), the argument goes, then emergency action would be required much less often, and indeed would only happen when unusually severe or widespread livelihood shocks occurred.

Table 10.2   Case studies clustered by scale and primary intention

Scale	Welfare Transfers			Livelihood Building Transfers		
Project or	4.	Malawi	DECT	13.	Mozambique	ITFs
Scheme	5.	Zambia	SCTs	14.	Swaziland	CFs
	6.	Zimbabwe	UFP	15.	Zimbabwe	SLTs
	7.	Mozambique	FAP			
	9.	Swaziland	NCPs			
	10.	Mozambique	EMFs			
National	1.	Lesotho	OAP	11.	Malawi	ISP
Programme	2.	Mozambique	PSA	12.	Zambia	FSP
	3.	Malawi	PWPs			
	8.	Lesotho	SF			

COVERAGE, SCALE AND INTENTION

The coverage of diverse social protection schemes in southern Africa is variable, giving social transfers both within countries and across the region a distinctly 'patchwork' character. Much social protection in the region seems accidental and anarchic: individual NGOs, UN agencies, quasi-state agencies, and public bodies undertake a diverse range of distinct social transfers to different social groups, according to criteria that are internal to each organization, or that follow the shifting priorities of funding agencies. In this respect southern Africa does not differ from other sub-regions of Africa. This accidental character of social protection means that both duplication (particular types of beneficiary being targeted by two or more different agencies) and exclusion (deserving individuals and families being missed entirely from all types of social transfer) in coverage can occur. The exceptions to this patchwork character are programmes with national coverage, exemplified by the social pension in Lesotho (Case Study 1) and the Input Subsidy Programme in Malawi (Case Study 11).

The coverage, scale and intentions of the case studies can be captured in part by clustering them by organizational scale (project or programme) and their principal objective as between providing social security or stimulating stronger livelihoods (see Table 10.2). In making this latter distinction, it is not intended to suggest that social welfare types of social protection cannot result in livelihood building; on the contrary, several of the case studies provide evidence of welfare transfers being utilized by recipients for livelihood building purposes. Nevertheless, there is an obvious difference in the underlying approach to ameliorating chronic vulnerability between, for example, a pension transfer (protecting the food consumption of older

Table 10.3   Case studies clustered by short term or long term intended impact

Mainly Transfer Focus			Long Term Outcome Intended			
1.	Lesotho	OAP	3.	Malawi	PWPs	Public assets created
2.	Mozambique	PSA	7.	Mozambique	FAP	AIDS patients into work
4.	Malawi	DECT	8.	Lesotho	SF	School attendance up
5.	Zambia	SCTs	9.	Swaziland	NCPs	OVC social inclusion
6.	Zimbabwe	UFP	10.	Mozambique	EMFs	School attendance up
			11.	Malawi	ISP	Farm output growth
			12.	Zambia	FSP	Crop yields and output up
			13.	Mozambique	ITFs	Farm output recovery
			14.	Swaziland	CFs	OVC farms for food
			15.	Zimbabwe	SLTs	HH livestock holdings up

people) and an input subsidy scheme (designed to increase the productivity and incomes of active small farmers).

A slightly different but overlapping way that intentions can be distinguished is between those projects or programmes where the transfer itself is the end result (for example, cash transfers to the destitute preventing hunger) and those where a longer term sustained impact is built into scheme design (for example, sustainable crop yield increases in the case of farm inputs, or sustained improvements in school attendance in the case of school feeding). As shown in Table 10.3, two-thirds of the case studies fall into the latter category (10 out of the 15 case studies). It is unfortunately true that many social transfer schemes do not undertake monitoring beyond the delivery of the transfers themselves, so that whether or not sustained outcomes are achieved is often not known.

VULNERABILITY

As implied by the clustering of Tables 10.2 and 10.3, different social protection schemes set out to provide support to different vulnerable groups or populations, over differing time periods, and some of them seek to ameliorate vulnerability without tackling its causes, while others seek to tackle the causes of vulnerability without offering an immediate improvement in access to food and basic needs. This means that a slightly different, but complementary, clustering of the case studies can be based on the alternative ways they approach vulnerability, in the two dimensions of groups or populations that are targeted, on the one hand, and causes compared to

Table 10.4   Clustering of case studies by vulnerability aims

Vulnerability Aims	Case Studies
A. Protecting the consumption of older persons	1
B. Protecting the consumption of the destitute	2, 5, 6
C. Protecting the consumption of those facing seasonal food deficits	3, 4
D. Encouraging farm input use for increased farm output	11, 12, 13
E. Breaking the intergenerational transmission of poverty	8, 9, 10
F. Ameliorating or reversing the impacts of AIDS	7, 9, 14
G. Reversing asset depletion caused by shocks	15

effects of vulnerability, on the other. This is done in Table 10.4, with related notes on the vulnerability approach of the different case studies provided as follows:

A.   *Protecting the consumption of older persons.* These are the explicit aims of social pension programmes, as exemplified by the Lesotho Old Age Pension (Case Study 1). In such programmes, the provision of a pension is seen as achieving a more widespread reduction in vulnerability than occurs just for the older people themselves. In particular, it is noted that grandparents often end up looking after AIDS orphans, so pension income can also mitigate the plight of a significant proportion of orphans and vulnerable children (OVC).

B.   *Protecting the consumption of the destitute.* Several of the social transfer case studies are schemes designed explicitly to reach the poorest and most vulnerable members of society, both rural and urban. The Food Subsidy Programme in Mozambique (Case Study 2) does this, as do the pilot Social Cash Transfer schemes in Zambia (Case Study 5) and the Urban Food Programme in Zimbabwe (Case Study 6). As emphasized throughout this book, a lot of interest centres on the notion that the destitute in African countries can be protected in the long term by cash transfers, and the Zambia pilots exemplify this focus.

C.   *Protecting the consumption of those facing seasonal food deficits.* Many rural dwellers in the southern African countries are particularly prone to insufficient access to food on a seasonal basis, in the lean season leading up to the next harvest. The Public Works Programmes (PWPs) in Malawi have had reduction of this type of vulnerability as their purpose for many years (Case Study 3), while the DECT scheme, also in Malawi, represented an alternative approach to the same problem conducted in a limited geographical area (Case Study 4).

D. *Encouraging farm input use for increased farm output.* This form of
    social protection sets out to tackle particular root causes of chronic vul-
    nerability (the low yields, outputs and incomes of poor small farmers)
    rather than their symptoms (Case Studies 11–13). There are differences
    between the case studies in this category. The Malawi ISP has nation-
    wide coverage of all small maize and tobacco producers, while the
    Zambia FSP is specifically designated towards poor small farmers who
    are unlikely to purchase fertilizer even at subsidized prices (in Zambia,
    a separate scheme covers fertilizer subsidies for those who can afford to
    pay). Meanwhile the Mozambique Input Trade Fairs have the limited
    scope of providing a recovery mechanism for farmers affected by
    drought or floods, and each individual beneficiary only has a one-time
    chance to take advantage of this social transfer.

E. *Breaking the intergenerational transmission of poverty.* Social protec-
    tion that prevents malnutrition in children and improves their chances
    of acquiring education and skills has intergenerational effects that will
    not be perceived until they grow up and are hopefully able to create
    better life chances than their parents. All social protection that suc-
    cessfully targets very poor families and provides a sufficient level of
    transfer to benefit the children in the household has this potential
    effect. Nevertheless, some forms of social protection specifically aim at
    this intergenerational goal. Amongst the case studies, School Feeding
    in Lesotho (Case Study 8), social transfers to OVC in Swaziland (Case
    Study 9), and Education Material Fairs in Mozambique (Case Study
    10) correspond to this type of social protection.

F. *Ameliorating or reversing the impacts of AIDS.* Several of the case
    study schemes are designed to address the nutritional and basic needs
    of families containing individuals with AIDS-related illnesses, or the
    social and consumption needs of children orphaned by AIDS. This
    category includes the Food Assistance Programme in Mozambique
    that provides food rations for families in which one or more members
    are receiving ART (Case Study 7), as well as the projects in Swaziland
    that address the well-being of OVC (Case Studies 9 and 14).

    While these case studies address AIDS and its deleterious impacts
    as their main focus, in truth a considerable proportion of all schemes
    in this set of case studies take into account AIDS impacts in the crite-
    ria that they establish for eligibility to scheme benefits. Thus house-
    holds lacking able-bodied labour owing to AIDS-related deaths,
    households containing OVC, and elderly looking after orphaned
    grandchildren are all circumstances that tend to enter the multiple cri-
    teria utilized by different agencies to target the most vulnerable people
    in society.

G. *Reversing asset depletion caused by shocks.* A feature of the dynamics of vulnerability that is well understood is that households that have experienced one or more shocks, and have depleted their assets to cope with those shocks (for example, in order to buy medicine or food), are often unable to rebuild their assets before the next crisis occurs, resulting in a spiral downwards into destitution. Some social transfer projects seek to reverse this sequence directly by providing assets or strengthening the capability of families to acquire assets. While many social transfer schemes have this as one amongst many hoped for outcomes, the transfer of livestock to small poor farmers (Case Study 15) explicitly has this as its main objective.

TARGETING APPROACHES

Many different scales and complexities of targeting are represented by the case studies examined in this part of the book. The most straightforward type is categorical targeting such as pensions, where a single criterion (an age threshold) determines whether or not someone falls within the category targeted. The most complicated types are those that approach identifying a beneficiary group (for example, destitute households containing no income earners) through a series of proxy indicators (for example, elderly widows caring for children under 10). The principal mechanisms for targeting found in this set of case studies may be distinguished from each other as shown in Table 10.5.

A. *Categorical targeting.* Applies in particular to pensions (Case Study 1) where the category is everyone over 70, although even in this case there are some exclusions (people obtaining civil service pensions). OVC are also a category targeted in several case studies (Case Studies 9 and 14).
B. *Proxy indicators.* The target group is destitute households. In one scheme this is specified as the poorest 10 per cent (Case Study 5).

Table 10.5   Clustering of case studies by targeting approaches

Targeting Approach	Case Studies
A. Categorical targeting	1, 9, 14
B. Proxy indicators	2, 4, 5, 6, 7, 10, 12, 13, 15
C. Multiple eligibility	12, 13
D. Geographic targeting	3, 4
E. Self-targeting	3

Various proxies for destitution are used, for example one meal per day, begging from neighbours, elderly, sick or disabled household heads, elderly looking after orphans, widows living alone, etc. Often it is the absence of income-earning capability (lack of able-bodied labour) that is the key attribute that various proxy indicators seek to pin down. Lack of land for cultivation may also apply. Many of the case studies in this set use proxy indicators of poverty and vulnerability as targeting criteria (Case Studies 2, 4, 5, 6, 7, 10, 12, 13 and 15).

C. *Multiple eligibility.* This often includes proxy indicators of poverty or vulnerability in association with one or two primary criteria for eligibility. Eligibility may be conferred by events, for example drought- or flood-affected farmers (Case Study 13), or by resources that the household must be able to deliver, for example ability to pay the subsidized price of fertilizer, access to land, or adequate labour for agricultural production. Multiple eligibility often takes the form of several stages or layers in the selection process: for example, access to land but under one hectare (primary eligibility criterion), elderly but with access to labour, female-headed households not in gainful employment, child-headed households, etc. (secondary proxy criteria) (Case Study 12).

D. *Geographic targeting.* This is usually associated with Vulnerability Assessment Mapping (VAM), which forecasts where hunger gaps are expected to occur (Case Studies 3 and 4). Geographical targeting rarely occurs on its own, except in emergency situations where the entire population of a particular area is found to be under acute stress. More typically, geographical location is a first criterion supplemented by eligibility or proxy indicator criteria. Small projects and pilots (Case Studies 5, 6, 10 and 15) by definition involve site selection as a first stage of targeting.

E. *Self-targeting.* In the case of Public Works Programmes (Case Study 3), this works by setting the benefit (food or cash) below the market wage rate and raising the cost of participation (heavy manual labour) to discourage the non-needy from turning up.

COORDINATION

The case studies in this series fall into roughly five overlapping groups as far as coordination is concerned. These are described briefly as follows, and Table 10.2 remains relevant as a reference point, since coordination patterns to some degree (but not wholly) correspond to the differences of scale and intention portrayed in that table:

A. *National programmes overseen by a single line ministry.* The pension scheme in Lesotho (Case Study 1), the national programme for the destitute in Mozambique (Case Study 2), the Input Subsidy Programme in Malawi (Case Study 11) and School Feeding in Lesotho (Case Study 8) correspond to this category. These require a prior commitment by central government towards recurrent funding (Ministry of Finance) as well as operational coordination appropriate to a national scale of delivery.

B. *Pilot projects designed for scaling up within a coordinated social protection strategy.* The single case study that corresponds to this rubric is the Social Cash Transfer pilots in Zambia (Case Study 5). These are designed to explore the implications of delivering cash transfers to the most vulnerable, within the context of the national Social Protection Strategy and under the coordination of the Department for Social Welfare.

C. *Projects of limited duration funded by donors and implemented by NGOs, UN agencies or government ministries, as well as local partners.* This set includes the Malawi DECT project (Case Study 4), the two Zimbabwe NGO-led projects (Case Studies 6 and 15), the ITF and EMF projects in Mozambique (Case Studies 10 and 13), the WFP Food Assistance Project in Mozambique (Case Study 7) and the JICA-funded farm inputs for child-headed households in Swaziland (a subproject in Case Study 14). Schemes in this category tend to coordinate between stakeholders at an operational level, but are not part of a larger design or oversight formulated at a strategic level by government. A partial exception is the Mozambique ITFs, which are integrated into the Ministry of Agriculture strategy towards recovery from crop failures.

D. *National programmes with varying funding run semi-autonomously from government.* This category includes the Public Works Programmes (PWPs) in Malawi (Case Study 3) that are run by the semi-autonomous body, the Malawi Social Action Fund (MASAF); and the Food Security Programme (FSP) in Zambia jointly overseen by two parent ministries (MACO and MCDSS) and implemented by a national NGO called Programme Against Malnutrition (PAM) (Case Study 12). It seems likely that projects of this type may be prone to governance problems, and their varying funding means that coverage and effectiveness vary from one year to the next.

E. *Coordination around the social protection needs of a particular vulnerable group.* The example here is the National Plan of Action (NPA) for orphans and vulnerable children (OVC) in Swaziland. This coordinates resources and coverage for Neighbourhood Care Points (NCPs) and school fee waivers for OVC under the umbrella of the National Emergency Response Council on HIV and AIDS (NERCHA). Nevertheless, CFs for OVC come under NERCHA but are not included in the NPA (Case Study 14).

ASSET PROTECTION AND BUILDING

Social transfers have various different asset protection and asset building effects. Cash or food transfers protect against the pressure to sell assets in order to buy food. Some social transfers have explicit asset building goals (for example, Small Livestock Transfers in Zimbabwe – Case Study 15), while others allow for potential asset protection or building by easing the pressure on poor people's exceedingly scarce resources.

Case studies can be distinguished to some extent according to the type of asset that they contribute towards building. These distinctions are not watertight, however, since cash or food transfers can release resources for other purposes that would otherwise have been spent on food, and cash is highly flexible between different uses. Indeed any increase in household resources potentially allows for asset accumulation by recipient households owing to substitution effects of this kind. A broad classification of the asset effects of different types of transfer is set out here as follows:

A. *Asset protection.* Assets are protected when social transfers enable households to avoid selling them in order to achieve minimum acceptable levels of food consumption. Cash and food transfers (Case Studies 1, 2, 3, 4, 5, 6, 7 and 8) have potential asset protection qualities of this kind.

B. *Human capital (health and education).* Some social transfers are concerned with improving the health, and therefore the productive capability, of recipients (Case Study 7), while others are concerned with raising the human capital of the next generation through education (Case Study 10) and still others with the social inclusion of OVC, including health and education aspects (Case Study 9).

C. *Land as an asset.* Land becomes a more valuable asset when its productivity rises, and therefore social transfers that aim to raise yields on farms through improved cultivation practices, more diverse cropping systems or greater input use at the same time improve land as an asset (Case Studies 11, 12, 13 and 14).

D. *Livestock as an asset.* The multiple purpose of livestock in livelihood systems is well known – a form of saving, a means of accumulation (through flock or herd growth, or trading up from small stock to big stock), a source of consumption and income (milk, eggs), and social reciprocity (transfers for ceremonies and feasts, etc.). In the absence of social protection, livestock often play a critical role in coping strategies that erode assets in order to maintain food consumption. One case study directly builds household livestock holdings as its goal (Case Study 15), while others contain varying potential for livestock acquisition from cash transfers or resources released by other transfers.

E.   *Physical and infrastructural assets.* One case study allows for acquisition of agricultural implements (Case Study 13), while Public Works Programmes are concerned with building physical infrastructure such as roads or irrigation channels (Case Study 3).

F.   *Building social capital.* Some projects appeal specifically to strengthening or reviving pre-existing social customs of care towards community members who have been hit by misfortune. This applies to CFs (Case Study 14) as well as other OVC initiatives in Swaziland. It is also mentioned as a subsidiary benefit in several other social transfer schemes in this series.

SUMMARY

The purpose of the case studies in this book is to enable the reader to pick out examples of social protection practice, and to see how they are organized and what evidently works well in them compared to what does not work quite so well. By setting out these case studies in the same framework of themes as the main chapters of the book, a consistent approach to assessing the strengths and weaknesses of any particular scheme is achieved. The great diversity represented by the case studies is a reflection of the diversity that can be found across Africa in social transfers, but also serves to emphasize that such diversity in itself creates a climate of forward thinking and innovation in social transfer delivery.

Case Study 1.   Old Age Pension, Lesotho

OVERVIEW

In the April 2004 budget speech for the 2004/05 financial year, the Government of Lesotho announced the introduction of a universal non-contributory pension for all citizens aged 70 and over. The pension came into force six months later in November 2004, set at a level of M150 (US$25) per month, and was formally legislated as an entitlement in the Old Age Pensions Act passed in January 2005. In taking this step, Lesotho became one of only seven sub-Saharan African countries to provide non-contributory pensions, the other six being Botswana, Mauritius, Namibia, Senegal, South Africa and Swaziland. In this group, Senegal and Lesotho are much poorer countries than the others, having per capita GNIs of US$700 and US$950 respectively in 2005.

The Old Age Pension (OAP) cost M126 million (US$21 million) in its first full fiscal year of operation, 2005–06. This corresponded to about 2.7 per cent of government expenditure. By May 2005, the pension was reaching 69 046 beneficiaries, or roughly 3.3 per cent of the total population. Owing to the lower life expectancy of men in Lesotho, as in most human populations, roughly 60 per cent of recipients are women and 40 per cent men. At the time of its introduction the pension amount was almost exactly equal to Lesotho's official national poverty line, set at M146 (US$24) in 2002. On its return to power after the 2007 general election, the government announced the pension would rise from M150 to M200 (US$29) a month, an increase in inflation-adjusted terms of about 20 per cent.

The Lesotho OAP is entirely funded out of domestic resources, with no technical or financial support from donors. In order to minimize delivery costs, the government chose to use the existing Post Office network as its principal institutional mode of delivery. Each month, the Ministry of Finance deposits the pension funds in the Post Office bank account at the Central Bank in the capital, Maseru. Post Office officials withdraw the money and distribute it to around 300 pay points throughout the country. In addition to post offices some of these pay points are in other public buildings such as chiefs' offices, schools and health centres.

Pensioners collect their cash by going to their designated local post office with a pension book, which includes a photograph for identification purposes. In cases where the pensioner sends someone else to collect the money on their behalf, a photograph of the delegate must be included in the pension book and a letter of verification produced, signed by the local chief. However, 85 per cent of pensioners collect the money for themselves, walking or taking a taxi to the pay point.

VULNERABILITY

A social pension addresses the vulnerability of older people in a society, and specifically their inability to generate income from productive activity due to physical incapacity. In societies with high HIV prevalence rates, older people are put under particular pressure by loss of income flows into households due to AIDS mortality in the next generation, the corresponding disappearance of support from their children that they might have expected in old age, and a rising burden of caring for orphaned grandchildren. Social pensions are thought to create broad vulnerability reduction effects across societies that adopt them owing to the tendency for older people to spend their pensions to the benefit of their extended families, and because cash in circulation is increased in poor and remote areas.

In Lesotho, the vulnerability of older people is compounded by (a) the third highest HIV prevalence rate in the world at 23.2 per cent of the adult population aged 15–49 (UNAIDS, 2006b), (b) a massive decline since the mid-1990s in a remittance economy at one time equivalent to 30–40 per cent of gross domestic product (GDP), and (c) (according to the latest available data from the 1990s) a poverty rate estimated at 60 per cent coupled with a Gini coefficient of 0.66, making Lesotho one of the most unequal sub-Saharan African countries.

TARGETING

The OAP is based on the age threshold criterion for eligibility. This is what is called a categorical social transfer, where the category comprises individuals over a certain age, in this instance 70. There is no means testing for the pension; however, it does have a few exclusions consisting of social groups covered by other public pensions (for example, civil servants and the armed forces).

Pensioners must be registered in order to receive their payment, and pension registration represented one of the most difficult challenges in introducing the scheme and ensuring its coverage of all eligible citizens. This is because many elderly people in Lesotho did not have documentation to prove their age, and relied on memories of particular historical events to locate their approximate birth date. As a result, registration was based on an officially recognized document that most citizens already possessed, which was their voter registration cards. These had been used in the 2002 general election and exhibited the name, date of birth and village of residence of the holder. These details had been certified by Independent Election Commission (IEC) registrars, who had collected them in personal interviews with each elector. OAP registration, also done on a village by village basis between May and November 2004, was mainly a matter of updating the IEC-certified data, and amending them where necessary, attested by local chiefs.

Note that eligibility is based on citizenship, not on residence. This means that Lesotho citizens living in South Africa are able to cross into Lesotho to register for, and collect, the pension. It also means that a few people manage to claim pensions both in South Africa and in Lesotho. A roughly 5 per cent net annual increase in the numbers of registered pensioners in its early years (about 3500 each year) probably reflected these cross-border movements.

COVERAGE

The OAP covers all Lesotho citizens of 70 years of age or older, an estimated 72 000 people in 2007. According to various sources, the pension was from its inception highly successful in its geographical outreach, and excluded few legitimate beneficiaries. The opposing problem may have occurred, in isolated instances, of individuals already receiving other transfers (see below) also attempting to claim the OAP.

The pension's age 70 threshold is an important policy debating point. Clearly this age was chosen by the government for reasons of political acceptability and fiscal affordability. Since once instituted a non-contributory pension cannot easily be withdrawn, the government will have erred on the cautious side in deciding this threshold. This does, however, mean that the 'spread' effect of the pension in terms of reducing vulnerability in the population overall is limited by the low proportion of families containing one or more persons over 70. In addition, the pension fails to address the difficulties of older people below 70 who in all likelihood will no longer be of working age or able to work at full capacity. It has been calculated that lowering the entry age to 65 would bring 49 000 more pensioners into the system and this would cost an additional M120 million (US$17 million) per year. While this may seem affordable (2.2 per cent of the recurrent budget), governments

always face considerable pressure to defend established budgetary allocations in the state sector, making large shifts across budget heads politically
difficult to accomplish.

COORDINATION

When the OAP was introduced, several long-running government-run
social transfers already existed. These were civil service pensions, African
Pioneer Corps pensions, and the public assistance programme, a small
scheme providing cash grants to the destitute. An intention of the 2005
Pensions Act was eventually to merge the public assistance programme and
the African Pioneer Corps pension into the OAP in order to unify such
transfers, excluding only civil service pensions.

COST-EFFECTIVENESS

The Ministry of Finance builds only around M3 million into the annual
OAP budget for administrative costs. This means in 2005–06 for example
that M123 million (US$20.5 million) out of M126 million (US$21.0
million) was allocated to the transfer itself, giving a ratio of US$1.02
required to deliver US$1.00 transfer value. This would make the Lesotho
Old Age Pension the most cost-efficient of all social transfers examined in
these case studies. On the other hand, the scheme makes extensive use of
existing public infrastructure and personnel (the postal services) that are
not costed into the administrative overheads of the scheme, and this may
not be replicable elsewhere.

MARKET EFFECTS

Some commentators have worried about the potential inflationary impact
of a categorical cash transfer scheme like a social pension. Such an impact
may be macroeconomic owing to the size of the cash injection into the
economy at large, or local in character owing to poorly functioning markets
in particular locations. Nevertheless, there is no evidence to suggest that the
Lesotho OAP has been inflationary at either local or national levels. This is
partly due to the small size of the pension in the macro economy as a whole,
and partly due to well-functioning markets in Lesotho as a small country
geographically embedded in a large market economy possessing excellent
transport and communications infrastructure (South Africa).

The market effects of cash transfers also include the impact of spending by recipients in stimulating economic activity in local and national economies (the 'multiplier' effect discussed in Case Study 4). In the case of Lesotho, the multiplier may be low owing to a high propensity even in remote rural areas to purchase goods imported from South Africa. Research on the expenditure behaviour of beneficiaries shows that the main use of the pension is on food purchases (around 70 per cent); however, the share of this spent on home-produced rather than imported supplies is not known. Other important expenditure categories are non-food groceries, household items (for example, blankets, clothes), services (health, education, transport, funeral societies), assets (chickens and pigs), livelihood activities (petty trading) and savings (Croome and Nyanguru, 2007).

ASSET BUILDING

The Lesotho Old Age Pension is not intended to result in asset building, all the more so since it targets citizens beyond working age. Nevertheless, both asset protection and asset building can occur from a pension, as happens also from other unconditional cash transfers. Asset protection occurs because households containing pension recipients are less likely to have to sell assets in the event of a personal or natural shock such as illness or crop failure. Asset building can occur because in practice cash transfers are spent in countless different ways by recipients, and these can include investment in tools, livestock and children's education.

STRENGTHS

The Lesotho Old Age Pension displays a number of important strengths, as a means of addressing chronic poverty and vulnerability in a very poor country:

  i.   The pension is an entitlement, not a privilege that can be arbitrarily withdrawn, and it reaches all citizens over the age of 70 in the country.
  ii. Pension incomes have been shown in numerous studies to reduce vulnerability in recipient households because payments tend to be treated by recipients as household income and are spent to the benefit of all household members.
  iii. For this reason, pensions are shown to increase the food security, nutritional status, school attendance of children, and medical access of members in pensioner households, and not just the welfare of the pensioners themselves.

iv. A social pension has the considerable strength of a single targeting criterion, helped in the Lesotho case by possession of voter registration cards by all citizens, giving details of place and date of birth.

v. Pensions are also observed to have positive social impacts on the status, independence and dignity of older people.

vi. In Lesotho, the overhead cost of delivering pensions has been minimized by utilizing the existing network of post offices.

WEAKNESSES

Of course it is to be expected that the Lesotho OAP has some weaknesses, although the main ones are policy aspects that are widely debated about utilizing pension payments as a vehicle for reducing chronic poverty and vulnerability, rather than problems specific to the Lesotho scheme:

i. Inevitably a lot of policy debate surrounds the threshold age of a pension, and we have seen earlier how the outreach of the Lesotho pension would increase considerably if this threshold was reduced to 65 rather than 70 years of age.

ii. A high age threshold like 70 causes a variety of implicit or explicit exclusions in terms of country-wide vulnerability reduction: people who are younger than 70 but too old to gain a living from productive employment are excluded; vulnerable households not containing someone over 70 are excluded; duration of pension entitlement in recipient households may be quite short owing to the relatively low remaining life expectancy of individuals over 70.

iii. In countries like Lesotho where HIV/AIDS has drastically reduced overall life expectancy at birth, a robust policy case could be made for the affordability of a lower rather than higher pension age threshold, with ripple effects throughout society in terms of protection against hunger and deprivation.

POLICY LESSONS

The Lesotho Old Age Pension demonstrates that even a very poor country can provide a predictable cash transfer to a defined category of the population, financed from the state's own tax revenue. This suggests that, if donors were prepared to take a longer term view on the funding of categorical social transfers, and arrive at partnership agreements with governments on cost sharing, many more such schemes could be initiated as legal entitlements instead of ad hoc arrangements. Pensions are particularly promising as a social transfer device providing predictable funding for predictable needs owing to their single targeting criterion (the age threshold of the entitlement), the empirical finding that pensions tend to be spent on the welfare of the whole family, the large number of orphans and vulnerable children who tend to be cared for by the elderly in countries with high HIV/AIDS prevalence rates, and the improved social status of the elderly that results.

Nevertheless there are two areas in which the Lesotho Old Age Pension may be difficult to replicate in other countries. The first is related to correct registration of beneficiaries, where the difficulties experienced at the margin in Lesotho (lack of birth records and so on) are likely to represent very serious challenges in larger and poorer countries like, for example, Zambia or Tanzania. The second is the ready use of the post office network for safe pay points for pension collection, suggesting a degree of accountability within the post office system in Lesotho that may hardly be present in other settings.

Case Study 2.   Food Subsidy Programme, Mozambique

OVERVIEW

The Food Subsidy Programme (in Portuguese, PSA – Programa de Subsidio de Alimentos) in Mozambique is a rare example in sub-Saharan Africa of a state-led social security programme with continuous funding over a long period. This case study is therefore a key one for informing the contemporary policy discussion about providing predictable funding for predictable needs, and scaling up cash transfer forms of social protection. The PSA began in 1990 during civil war conditions, but evolved to its current institutional form in 1997. The Programme provides a monthly cash transfer to people who are destitute and have no capacity to work, including older, disabled and chronically ill people (but not those living with HIV/AIDS and TB), and pregnant women who are malnourished (Taimo & Waterhouse, 2007a).

The PSA is implemented by the National Institute of Social Action (INAS), a semi-autonomous agency of the Ministry of Women and Social Action (MMAS). It is funded by the Mozambique government, and its recent budgets were Mtn164.2 million (US$6.3 million) in 2006 and Mtn188.6 million (US$7.3 million) in 2007. The value of the transfer to beneficiaries varies from Mtn70 (US$2.7) per month to a maximum of Mtn140 (US$5.4) per month depending on the number of dependants in the household. The number of beneficiaries was 96 600 in 2006, and had risen to 101 800 in March 2007.

At community level, INAS works through local volunteers, known as *Permanentes,* chosen by the community to act as its community agents. *Permanentes* are appointed only in communities with a minimum of 25 beneficiaries (urban areas) or 15 beneficiaries (rural areas). Each *Permanente* signs terms of agreement with INAS, and receives an incentive payment of Mtn300 per month. The *Permanente* is the link between INAS and the community and therefore should be someone who is available (that is, ready to carry out activities for INAS whenever asked), suitable, serious, honest and elected by the community. The *Permanente* has the tasks of informing the community about the PSA, actively participating in the identification of vulnerable people as potential beneficiaries, making home visits to beneficiaries, advising beneficiaries of payment dates, being present at payment posts on payment days and helping to check the payment list.

VULNERABILITY

The PSA explicitly targets the destitute, that is people who are unable to gain a living and feed themselves or their families. This social group is the most vulnerable in Mozambique in terms of negligible levels of assets and incomes, and the reasons that they are in this position include a wide variety of personal misfortunes in addition to underlying vulnerability factors in the society and economy at large. The PSA seeks to make a contribution (as it happens, a very small contribution) to the basic survival capability of its beneficiaries, and does not seek to address the causes of their vulnerability.

TARGETING

The programme documentation identifies the target social groups of the PSA as follows:

i.   the elderly – individuals of both sexes, aged 55 and over for women and 60 and over for men, who are recognized as being permanently unable to work and who live alone or are heads of destitute households;

ii. the disabled – individuals of both sexes, aged 18 and above, who are recognized as being permanently unable to work and who live alone or are heads of destitute households;

iii. the chronically sick – individuals of both sexes, aged 18 and above, who suffer from one of five chronic diseases recognized by the medical services (hypertension, diabetes, epilepsy, bronchial asthma and chronic renal insufficiency), are unable to work, and live alone or are heads of destitute households (it should be noted that neither tuberculosis nor HIV/AIDS is included in the list of chronic diseases, but some instances occur in practice of people living with HIV/AIDS who do receive the food subsidy);

iv. malnourished pregnant women – pregnant women with nutritional problems associated with social risk factors.

The PSA orientations and procedures manual poses this list slightly differently, in the form of the criteria that should be used to determine eligibility:

1. *age* – to be verified through presentation of an identity card, *bilhete de identidade* (BI);
2. *residence* – to be verified through a declaration issued by the local administrative structure;
3. *income* – applied when there are members of a household who are working or are receiving any type of pension; the monthly income per capita must not exceed Mtn70;
4. *clinical* – applied to the disabled, the chronically sick and malnourished pregnant women.

The orientations and procedures manual also lists the steps a person must follow to be admitted to the PSA, and these are:

- the candidate presents him- or herself to the *Permanente*;
- in coordination with the secretary of the *Bairro* or community leader of the settlement, the *Permanente* fills in a questionnaire form;
- presentation of the candidate to the medical unit for certification and analysis of his or her degree of disability or sickness, in the case of the disabled or chronically sick.

The delegation or sub-delegation of INAS should then:

- receive the forms from the *Permanente*, so that a decision may be taken on the case within 15 days;
- organize the individual case file, filling in the identification details of the beneficiary and attributing a reference number;
- make a home visit to confirm the candidate's socio-economic data;
- analyse the person's socio-economic situation; give an opinion in writing and a decision on the case supposedly within the 15 days foreseen in the manual;
- for candidates with a favourable decision, issue a beneficiary identity card.

This is a lengthy process which in reality takes months, and is one of the aspects most criticized by the *Permanentes* and by beneficiaries. The requirement to verify age through an identity card (BI) is a major constraint, since many – especially older – beneficiaries do not possess one and obtaining a BI can take months and implies a financial outlay that potential beneficiaries cannot make. INAS has tried to address this problem through a partnership with the Civil Identification Services and by accepting application receipts for a BI as adequate for PSA enrolment, before the

BI itself is issued. Even so, it is this aspect of the entry criteria which has caused most difficulty for older candidates, especially in the rural areas.

COVERAGE

PSA covers all provinces in Mozambique, but not all districts. Hitherto, the programme has been confined to urban areas, although INAS has recently started to expand coverage to selected rural areas. Of the 96 582 PSA beneficiaries in 2006, 89 819 (92 per cent) were older people (59 069 women and 30 750 men), 5606 were disabled, 933 were chronically sick, and 222 were female heads of households. Chimoio city in central Manica Province had the highest number of beneficiaries with 10 840, followed by Nampula city (northern, Nampula Province) with 8052 and Beira (central, Sofala Province) with 7264.

According to MMAS estimates, the older population (men over 60 and women over 55 years old) is approximately one million. Since the national poverty rate is 54.1 per cent, and typically older people as a group contain more poor people than those of working age, it is probable that there are around 600 000 older poor in Mozambique. Thus the 2006 level of PSA beneficiaries represents about 15 per cent of this number. Various other proportions could of course be examined, but the conclusion is that PSA reaches quite a small proportion of potential destitute beneficiaries in rural and urban areas of the country.

COORDINATION

INAS is an executive body charged with implementing MMAS policies, whilst MMAS has overall responsibility for coordinating 'social actions', mainly social assistance. This gives INAS direct or indirect access to decision-making as well as coordinating bodies and forums. The central level distinction of roles between MMAS and INAS is reproduced at province level, where MMAS provincial directorates have an overall coordinating brief, while INAS delegations solely manage the social transfer programmes under their jurisdiction, and their reporting obligations are directly to INAS headquarters.

In Mozambique 'social action' is included in the national Action Plan for the Reduction of Absolute Poverty (PARPA), the country's Poverty Reduction Strategy Paper. Donors and the government have set up a PARPA Working Group on Social Action headed by the MMAS Directorate of Planning and Studies. INAS participates in working meetings of the Technical Secretariat for Food and Nutritional Security (SETSAN), which aims to introduce food security as a cross-cutting issue in sector plans and also in the SETSAN Working Group on Food, Nutritional Security and HIV/AIDS (SANHA), which produced a procedures manual in 2007 providing guidelines on vulnerability targeting, including vulnerability related to HIV/AIDS.

While INAS runs a number of social protection programmes there is little cross-referral between them. For instance, a malnourished pregnant woman becomes ineligible for the food subsidy six months after giving birth, and could be transferred to the Social Benefit for Work programme; however, this is most unlikely to occur in practice since *Permanentes* who are tasked with such coordination are overwhelmed by dealing with single programmes like the PSA.

COST-EFFECTIVENESS

The value of the food subsidy was initially intended to correspond to one-third of the monthly minimum salary, currently Mtn1645 (US$63) in the formal sector and Mtn1126 (US$43) in agriculture. However, as implemented in recent years it has been considerably below that level, with the transfer amount for a single person corresponding to between 4 and 6 per cent of those two minimum wage rates per month. For beneficiaries, the transfer amount depends on the number of dependants in the household as shown in Table C2.1.

PSA operational and administrative costs are high in relation to the value of money disbursed. Officially these costs should represent 15 per cent of the INAS budget; yet in terms both of budgeting and of observation of implementation practices, they are clearly much higher than this. The cost-efficiency of PSA can be approximated by taking the budget figures for delivery of the programme in 2006 and 2007 and comparing these to the estimated annual value of the cash transfers, assuming that recipients on

Table C2.1   PSA transfers by number of dependants

Household Structure	Mtn	US$
Single person	70	2.7
1 dependant	100	3.8
2 dependants	120	4.6
3 dependants	130	5.0
4 or more dependants	140	5.4

average receive a monthly transfer of Mtn100 each. For 2006, the total budget was Mtn164.2 million (US$6.3 million) for an estimated cash transfer of Mtn116.4 million (US$4.5 million); thus US$1.41 was required to deliver US$1.00 benefit. For 2007, the total budget was Mtn188.6 million (US$7.3 million) for an estimated cash transfer of Mtn122.2 million (US$4.7 million), implying US$1.55 required to deliver US$1.00 benefit. These figures almost certainly exclude INAS permanent personnel and office costs, thus considerably underestimating the true cost of delivering the transfers.

Cost-effectiveness goes beyond cost-efficiency to ask how well a programme achieves its desired outcomes, in this instance providing adequate social support for destitute people. Here, the extremely low level of the transfer is a significant consideration. According to beneficiaries, the amount of the transfer they receive permits them to purchase about two days of their basic food needs. Therefore the transfer makes a minimal contribution to their survival capabilities, which must depend on other strategies. One of the reasons that beneficiaries turn up each month despite this meagre level of benefit is that if they fail to do so more than twice in succession their name is removed from the beneficiary list.

MARKET EFFECTS

The scale of the PSA as currently operating is not sufficient to have any significant effect on food prices, either nationally or in local, mainly urban, environments. Nor would seasonal or annual food price instability impact much on the programme, given that its transfer provides only about two days of provisions for the typical beneficiary household.

ASSET BUILDING

Asset building is not an explicit objective of the Food Subsidy Programme. Since the programme is targeted towards destitute people who are unlikely to graduate from requiring support, asset building does not really enter the PSA approach as currently implemented.

STRENGTHS

The Food Subsidy Programme in Mozambique has recognized strengths, which were confirmed by fieldwork undertaken in two districts in late 2006:

i. INAS and PSA represent an unusually long experience in the region of delivering cash transfers to destitute beneficiaries in urban areas in a big country.

ii. PSA is broadly successful in its targeting, although with delays in making decisions about individual beneficiaries due to rather cumbersome administrative procedures.

iii. INAS and PSA have excellent geographical coverage at province and urban levels, which can be, and are being, relatively easily expanded into districts and rural areas.

iv. The system of *Permanentes* who act as the interface between beneficiaries and the state is a real strength, since it provides beneficiaries with a supportive framework at the very local level to assist them with their access to benefits, while avoiding costs that would be incurred by having public sector employees in that role.

WEAKNESSES

PSA also, of course, has weaknesses, arising partly from being embedded in bureaucratic structures of the state, as well as from ambiguity in government policy towards social transfers of this kind:

i. INAS is dependent on annual allocations from the Ministry of Finance for the number of beneficiaries it can cover, and to date this has permitted only a small proportion of potential beneficiaries to be covered, mostly in urban areas.

ii. The administrative apparatus for delivering the PSA is somewhat top heavy, and administrative costs are high in relation to the value of the subsidy, although figures put on this are more of a back-of-the-envelope calculation than a strictly accurate accounting of such costs.

iii. The current value of the subsidy is so small as to have little impact on the lives of the vulnerable people who receive it, who must consequently fall back on marginal coping strategies, including begging, borrowing, street trading and appeals for other support from churches and so on.

iv. The PSA relies heavily on the goodwill of the *Permanentes*, who are remunerated at the trivial rate of Mtn300 (US$12.5) per month, and for whom any increase in caseload would need in the future to be treated as proper employment.

POLICY LESSONS

The Government of Mozambique appears to have an ambivalent view of social transfers, both recognizing the necessity for them in over-arching policy documents like the PARPA, and also being suspicious that they could create 'dependency' and result in a permanent drain on government resources. Nevertheless, an active debate about social transfers is occurring between some government agencies, donor organizations and NGOs, and it is possible that donors may commit to longer term support for expanding the coverage of the PSA or similar programmes. This would seem a positive way forward, since INAS and the PSA represent a capability already in place for scaled up cash transfers, and the only other examples of this capability in southern Africa are those countries that have pensions provision (South Africa, Swaziland, Lesotho).

Case Study 3.   Public Works Programmes, Malawi

OVERVIEW

Public works programmes (PWPs) in Malawi go back at least to 1995, when the Malawi Social Action Fund (MASAF) was created. MASAF is an ongoing programme, now in its third phase, which has attracted funding in the form of soft loans or grants to the tune of about US$250 million since it started (up to 2007). Nor is MASAF the only PWP sponsoring agency in Malawi, other large programmes in recent years having been funded by the EU through the Government of Malawi (GoM/EU), and by the Government of Malawi itself in the form of a Ministry of Transport and Public Works (MTPW) scheme. Over the years, many small scale PWP schemes operating for short durations in limited geographical areas have also been implemented by NGOs. Table C3.1 provides a list of large scale PWPs that have run in Malawi in the 2000s, as well as some details of their mode of operation.

The big PWP schemes such as those run by MASAF have been country-wide. They aim to underpin the livelihoods of the poor and vulnerable by providing employment during critical months of the year. Typical design features include using a low wage or food ration as a self-targeting mechanism, work on a public infrastructure project (mostly road construction or repair), work norms based on task rates, short duration of employment, and wide geographical coverage (except for smaller, NGO run projects). To give just one example, the MASAF CCT scheme (MASAF-CCT) that ran from September to November 2005 provided cash-for-work for two months to 504 012 individuals, on the basis of MK200 (US$1.6) per day (eight-hour task rate) up to a maximum of ten days (MK2000 or US$16 per person).

The organization of PWPs in Malawi varies by agency and scheme; nevertheless some important general shifts are apparent in this sector in the five years up to 2007. MASAF is a semi-autonomous agency of the Malawi government, set up specifically to manage social transfers funded by the World Bank. MASAF has a country-wide mandate to provide employment opportunities for poor and vulnerable people, but nevertheless has to make choices about the geographical areas on which to focus its efforts. In 2007,

Table C3.1 Large scale PWPs implemented in Malawi in the 2000s

Sponsoring Agency	Programme[1]	Partners[1]	Type of Project	Targeting Methods[1]	Implied Wage[2]
MASAF	PWP (1995–)	DAs	Core	• geographical targeting/VAM • self-targeting • administrative rationing	MK86
	PWP-CCT (2005)	DAs	Special	• geographical targeting/VAM • administrative rationing by local leaders	MK200
	ILTPWP (2003–04)	CARE/ DAs	Special	• selected districts in central region • community targeting	MK60
	ERDP (2002–05)	DAs	Special	• geographical targeting/VAM • administrative rationing by local leaders	MK86
GOM/EU	IGPWP (2005–)	PMU	Core	• geographical targeting/VAM • community targeting • rationing	MK113
	SPRINT (2005–06)	PMU/ DAs	Special	• geographical targeting/VAM • community targeting • rationing	MK113
	PWP-FSP (2002–04)	DAs	Special	• selected districts • rationing by local leaders	MK235
	PWP (2001–05)	PMU	Core	• central region districts • rationing by contractors and local leaders	MK85

| MTPW | SGPWP (2005–09) | DAs | Core | • national coverage
• administrative rationing by local leaders | MK200 |

Notes:

[1] DA: District Assembly; EDRP: Emergency Drought Relief Project; IGPWP: Income Generating Public Works Programme; ILTPWP: Improved Livelihoods Through Public Works Programme; MTPW: Ministry of Transport and Public Works; PMU: scheme's own project management unit; PWP-CCT: Public Works Programme-Conditional Cash Transfer; PWP-FSP: Public Works Programme-Food Security Programme; SGPWP: Special Government Public Works Programme; SPRINT: Special Programme for Relief and Investment in Needy Times; VAM: vulnerability assessment mapping.

[2] Figures for an eight-hour day, but participants often only allocated a four-hour task unit.

Source: Chirwa (2007)

MASAF was in its third phase (MASAF III). Earlier phases were top down in character with decisions taken at central level, a moderate degree of local consultation about appropriate projects, and heavy reliance on officials and leaders for advice about where to place emphasis at the local level. The principle of self-targeting in public infrastructure projects is inevitably administratively rather top heavy: the projects themselves must be identified, surveyed, costed for materials and labour, and managed on site from start to completion.

Since 2002, the emphasis in MASAF and other PWP schemes has been on shifting management responsibility to DAs, under decentralized local government. For example, a MASAF programme running since November 2003 is called Local Authority Managed Projects (LAMPs). In this, MASAF provides finance to selected DAs, which are then responsible for running projects that have been decided upon at the district level. DAs remain accountable to MASAF for the funds disbursed. LAMPs have tended to select more diverse public projects than the typical PWP emphasis on roads, with forestry, flood control, irrigation schemes, dam rehabilitation and land conservation featuring in project lists. A further change in emphasis has been towards supplementing or replacing the self-targeting principle by community-based targeting, often done on the basis of wealth ranking methods. Nevertheless, community-based targeting has been selectively used by DAs, and its application varies from one district to another.

VULNERABILITY

Malawi is a country in which chronic vulnerability is widespread and seasonal food deficits either locally or on a broader scale are commonplace. Many factors are implicated in this state of affairs; however, poverty (52.4 per cent of the population) and ultra-poverty (22.4 per cent of the population) are the most immediate ones. In the 2005 Integrated Household Survey (IHS2), ultra-poverty was defined as not having sufficient income even to meet minimum acceptable food consumption per capita. Most of the ultra-poor live in rural areas and eke out a livelihood from tiny plots of land, growing mainly maize for survival.

Public works programmes address vulnerability by providing social safety nets when and where people are considered to be most prone to insufficient access to food. They therefore have a strong seasonal attribute, since most food gaps at household level occur in the lean season when the next year's maize crop is growing but is not yet harvested.

TARGETING

The core targeting method for PWPs in Malawi, as elsewhere, is self-targeting. This has the well-known advantage of costing much less to implement than other targeting methods. Self-targeting works by setting the level of transfer (wage rate or food ration) below the reservation wage of non-poor and non-vulnerable individuals. Sometimes the PWP wage rate is set by reference to, and below, the formal sector minimum wage set by government. In Malawi, the government minimum wage from 1 March 2003 was MK76.50 (US 60 cents) in rural areas for an eight-hour working day. However, in practice few PWPs have offered wages as low as this, a selection of programmes run between 2003 and 2007 revealing daily equivalent rates varying between MK60 and MK235, with MK200 being utilized in two large programmes run by MASAF and the Ministry of Transport since 2005 (Table C3.1). A complicating factor in making comparisons is that PWPs do not always offer a full day's work, but rather a task unit of four hours. For example, several MASAF core programmes have had a wage rate of MK43 for a four-hour task unit, which seems to equate to MK86 per day, above the minimum wage; however, only one task unit per day has been available in practice to those who offer themselves for work on projects run under those programmes.

A common occurrence in Malawi PWPs has been for more people to offer themselves for employment than can be found work within individual project budgets. This is especially so when livelihoods are under stress owing to crop failures and depleted household food stocks. In these instances, self-targeting is overlaid by rationing as a selection procedure. Rationing may sometimes be anarchic, that is, there is a scramble that occurs on 'a first come first served' basis, or may be done by local leaders on site who directly choose those who will be permitted to work. In either case, the self-targeting principle is breached and projects become prone to high inclusion and exclusion errors. One reason for this is a tendency to use household or individual characteristics that are uncorrelated to vulnerability when rationing is used as a targeting method.

While being the dominant targeting principle in PWPs, self-targeting is not their only beneficiary selection criterion. MASAF, for example, has tended to have a strong secondary criterion of targeting female-headed households and vulnerable women, and some PWPs have offered work only to women. More recently, community targeting has become popular as a beneficiary selection method for PWPs, with varying interpretations of what this should consist of, for example selection by village elders and headmen, or community wealth ranking as a selection method. The more participatory the selection process, the more time intensive it is in terms of facilitation and community meetings, so there are significant cost trade-offs to be considered.

At a more aggregate level, PWPs require some element of geographical targeting. In Malawi, initial selection of priority districts has tended to be guided by Vulnerability Assessment Mapping exercises (VAMs). These have improved in accuracy over the years, so that current Malawi Vulnerability Assessment Committee (MVAC) forecasts provide broadly accurate indications of parts of the country most likely to encounter serious food deficits in the hungry season. While in the past exact project locations were dominated by central MASAF decisions, under the MASAF III decentralized approach these decisions within districts are made by the DAs.

COVERAGE

Since its inception, MASAF has had the mandate to provide a national social safety net for vulnerable groups. This national coverage is modified by vulnerability assessment considerations, as discussed above, with programme and project budgets spatially distributed according to predictions and perceptions about places most in need. Other large PWP schemes have often had more limited geographical coverage. For example, the GoM/EU programme mentioned earlier had two sub-programmes entitled respectively Income Generating Public Works (IGPWP) and Special Programme for Relief and Investment in Needy Times (SPRINT). These operated in five of Malawi's 28 districts that had been identified at the time as likely to represent priority locations for safety net support.

COORDINATION

Within MASAF a high degree of coordination of PWPs is achieved through its own organizational structure, and the partnerships that it has entered into occasionally with NGOs and more recently with DAs. MASAF's utilization of vulnerability assessment data for geographical targeting has also been an important coordinating factor. However, the extent of broader coordination between MASAF PWPs and other large and small PWP initiatives seems likely to have been rather haphazard over the years. Duplication of PWP effort in particular places (or closely adjacent places) is a well-known occurrence in Malawi. In the future, this problem may be resolved by the adoption by the Malawi government of a National Social Protection Policy and Programme, currently under development.

COST-EFFECTIVENESS

As with most other types of social transfer, it is difficult to obtain accurate data on the cost of delivering PWPs, since the costs assigned to individual projects typically exclude the sometimes substantial administrative overhead costs of the implementing agency. In the earlier years of MASAF (MASAF I and II) the guideline was that 40 per cent of the budget should be paid out as transfers to beneficiaries. This seems very low compared to other social transfer schemes (implying that US$2.50 is required to deliver US$1 transfer), but is perhaps realistic in recognizing the additional cost of implementing works projects as well as the overhead cost of having a national PWP delivery capability.

More precise figures on the cost-efficiency of individual PWPs can be obtained from project evaluations, although always subject to caveats concerning unattributed administrative overheads. For example, the MASAF-implemented PWP-CCT programme mentioned earlier ran from October to December 2005, had a total cost of US$11.3 million, and reached 504 012 beneficiaries. The cost per beneficiary was US$22.50 and the transfer amount per beneficiary US$16.00, implying management and operating costs of US$6.50 per beneficiary. Thus the average cost per US$1.00 benefit was US$1.41.

In another example, the GoM/EU SPRINT programme operated from December 2005 to September 2006 and had a total cost of US$863 400 for 21 216 beneficiaries in five districts. The cost per beneficiary was US$40.70 and the transfer amount per beneficiary US$23.30, implying average management and operating costs of US$17.40 per beneficiary. In this case the average cost per US$1.00 benefit was US$1.75.

In comparing these two PWPs that undertook similar activities, albeit for different durations, the attribution of overhead costs is crucial. The SPRINT programme was relatively expensive because its costs included technical assistance and capital equipment such as vehicles that were purchased new for the project. Meanwhile, the PWP-CCT would not have included existing MASAF infrastructure and equipment in its costs, and it relied heavily in its implementation on the time and resources of district officials. In terms of effectiveness (outcomes), as against just cost-efficiency, organizational slippages in both programmes meant that not all beneficiaries received their cash transfers in a timely manner. For SPRINT this problem was more serious than for CCT, with many SPRINT beneficiaries not getting the opportunity to work and get paid until after the critical hunger season had passed.

MARKET EFFECTS

PWPs have market effects because they either put food into markets (in the case of food-for-work schemes) or put cash into circulation (in the case of cash-for-work, which is far more prevalent nowadays). They also intervene directly in the labour market by providing short term employment opportunities. Most PWPs, and especially the large national or multi-district ones, are strictly limited in duration or in the maximum amount that can be earned by any individual beneficiary. They typically seek to help families overcome food deficits in the hungry season, which in Malawi lasts from around November/December until the start of the next harvest in late March/April. It is doubtful that the cash injected by PWPs thinly across geographical space has much influence on food prices or inflation. On the other hand, in the event of rising maize prices due to other causes (an emerging overall shortage in the market), the purchasing power of cash earned in PWPs can decline steeply, considerably reducing the protective element that schemes seek to confer on their participants.

ASSET BUILDING

PWPs help build public or community assets, and this is often cited as a strength in their favour. Nevertheless, in Malawi there has been a tremendous bias towards road building or repair (over 80 per cent of PWP expenditures have been on roads), and doubts surround the construction quality, ownership and true additionality of the infrastructure that is thus created. More recent PWPs have tried to diversify into other community assets such as soil conservation and irrigation works.

STRENGTHS

From the late 1980s, several attributes of PWPs have made them a popular form of social transfer:

  i. The principle of self-targeting was viewed favourably, especially in reducing the cost of beneficiary selection.
 ii. The notion of work in exchange for social support is attractive to some ways of thinking about 'the deserving poor' and avoidance of dependency.
iii. The creation of socially useful public or community infrastructure was considered an additional benefit.

iv. The community development approach of PWPs gives local people a voice in development issues affecting them, in addition to the building of project management capacity.
v. The decentralized management of PWPs has helped in consolidating devolution and decentralization in Malawi.

WEAKNESSES

PWPs have a number of well-known flaws as a means of delivering social protection to poor and vulnerable populations, which apply in Malawi as elsewhere:

i. By definition, participants must be capable of hard physical work, which excludes some of the most significant vulnerable groups – the old, the ill, the disabled, or women looking after orphans and vulnerable children.
ii. There is a risk that their occurrence in the hungry season, which is also the cultivation season for the next year's crop, diverts labour away from the best cultivation practices.
iii. PWP projects are costly to set up and execute, since skilled personnel are needed to design and manage them if they are going to produce useful infrastructure.
iv. They are costly for other reasons too – maintaining a national capacity to respond to scattered and unpredictable geographical food deficits, as MASAF has done, is very expensive, and gearing up and winding down seasonally intermittent projects is also costly.
v. For vulnerable people facing inadequate access to food for a few months in the hungry season, timing is crucial, yet PWPs are prone to logistical delays meaning that they sometimes miss the critical months.
vi. When dependent on local power brokers to select beneficiaries (which often occurs when 'self-targeting' is rationed), inclusion and exclusion errors are rife; however, accurate community targeting is skill- and time-intensive in its own right.
vii. Large country-wide PWPs are almost certainly prone to significant leakages in resources, although little work has been done on this and evidence therefore tends to be more anecdotal than substantiated fact.
viii. The positive impact of assets created by PWPs on the economy and on local livelihoods remains unproven; PWPs tend to remain uncoordinated, with mainstream development programmes not properly 'owned' or maintained by either sectoral government departments or local communities.

POLICY LESSONS

The provision of short term employment on PWPs can assist those affected by seasonal vulnerability following community-wide shocks such as crop failure, provided they involve timely, well-managed projects and an index-linked wage rate combined with effective targeting – but for this purpose transfers of cash or food may well prove to be more cost-effective unless projects also efficiently create assets which are highly valued by local communities and help reduce future vulnerability. For chronic poverty, PWPs are unlikely to be an appropriate response unless they in addition guarantee longer term, flexible employment, well linked to other livelihood building initiatives and broader development programmes. These requirements have not yet been substantially met on Malawian PWPs (McCord, 2008), but are recognized to some extent in the government's efforts to develop a national Social Protection Policy (Malawi, 2007), which envisages a role for PWPs both in protecting assets and in promoting productive livelihoods.

It is also true that the wider debate about how best to support the livelihoods of chronically vulnerable people has moved on from PWPs, and so too have technologies that can be used for effecting transfers. The search now is for means of delivering stable transfers to social categories that can be readily identified, thus moving away from the ever shifting terrain of short term and fragmentary safety net provision. However, this is still a discussion in progress, yet to find its eventual shape, so a role for PWPs is likely to persist for a few more years, albeit with diminishing importance in social transfers overall.

Case Study 4.   Dowa Emergency Cash Transfer, Malawi

OVERVIEW

The DECT was an innovative project that provided monthly cash transfers to beneficiary households, banded according to the size of the household and adjusted monthly in line with the price of maize. The international NGO Concern Worldwide linked up with a commercial bank, the Opportunity International Bank Malawi, to trial the delivery of cash transfers through smartcards, utilizing mobile ATMs to visit rural areas at pre-determined times and places. As extra security, a fingerprint reader was incorporated into the card issuing process, so that future cash draw-downs would be against a fingerprint as well as the smartcard. The DECT was designed to address a localized, seasonal food deficit identified in the northern part of Dowa District in Malawi in the lean season of 2006–07.

The DECT ran from December 2006 to April 2007, a five-month duration leading up to the harvest period of the next season's crop. Project beneficiaries numbered 10 161 households in total, although some of these did not receive the first monthly payment (8 384 households received payments in December 2006). The baseline amount of the transfer varied from MK370 (US$2.64) per month for a one-person household to a maximum of MK3700 (US$26.40) for a household of ten or more. However, transfer amounts were adjusted downwards as maize prices fell during the season, reflecting the release of stored supplies on to the market ahead of the 2007 maize harvest. An additional innovation of DECT was to provide the smartcards to women rather than men in beneficiary households.

VULNERABILITY

Some basic data about poverty and vulnerability in Malawi are provided in Case Study 3. DECT responded to evidence of a localized severe incidence of food deprivation, meaning that households were eating less than enough for daily maintenance (typically, one meal or less a day) or were having to rely on inferior and wild foods in order to survive. After a good national maize harvest in 2005–06, fewer families than usual country-wide were in such dire straits in the hungry season of 2006, but northern Dowa District was identified as one location where local drought and poor maize harvests had precipitated a food crisis during this period.

TARGETING

DECT was targeted at families with a food deficit or 'missing food entitlement', in a geographical area identified as highly prone to food deficit by the Malawi Vulnerability Assessment Committee (MVAC), using the household economy approach.[1] Owing to uncertainty about the exact number of households in the target area, Concern undertook its own census by bringing together group village headmen and extension agents and asking them for the number of households under their jurisdiction. This yielded an estimate of 15 600 households in the 260 villages in the target area.

Selection of beneficiaries was a multi-stage process best described as 'community triangulation' of the beneficiary list. This comprised, first, conducting community wealth ranking in the designated villages, in which households were divided between the three categories of poor, middle and well off according to well-being criteria put forward by community informants themselves. Second, after an interval, communities were revisited and told about the proposed humanitarian intervention (although not about its cash character), and the community was split into three groups (leaders and elites, men, and women) to discuss the accuracy of utilizing the list of poor households from the wealth ranking as the beneficiary list for transfers. Third, the three groups had to reach agreement on an acceptable single list after adding or subtracting households, and this final list was then signed by the chief as a fair representation of those most in need.

Like other social transfer schemes targeted at vulnerable people, DECT experienced some manipulation of targeting procedures, including would-be recipients changing household composition to suit the targeting criteria (for example, increasing the apparent size of the household to obtain higher transfers), and chiefs and village leaders getting relatives and friends on to the beneficiary list. However, the community triangulation approach overcame these in most instances.

COVERAGE

DECT focused on just two extension planning areas (EPAs) in the northern part of Dowa District in central Malawi. Within these EPAs, the project sought to achieve complete coverage of households facing severe food deficits in the hungry season of 2006–07. This corresponded to about 65 per cent of all households in the target communities. The original beneficiary list arising from the first stage of community ranking stood at 8142 households, while subsequent recalibration to take into account cross-community differences in food insecurity brought this number up to a final figure of 10 161 households.

COORDINATION

DECT involved coordination between several agencies for its formulation and implementation. First, MVAC findings were used to identify a location exhibiting severe impending food deficits, and DFID was approached for funding to address this food gap. Second, fact-finding and beneficiary selection visits involved close collaboration between Concern staff and officials from line ministries (especially extension officers of the Ministry of Agriculture), as well as with the chief, village headmen and villagers themselves in Traditional Authority Chakhaza in north Dowa District. Third, collaboration between Concern and OIBM broke new ground for coordination between an NGO and a private financial institution.

COST-EFFECTIVENESS

The overall cost of DECT was US$1.4 million for a period of six months from November 2006 to April 2007. While the final division of this budget between overhead costs and transfers is not known, Concern undertook several calculations to assess how maize price variations affected its cost-efficiency. These showed that cost-efficiency would go down as the maize price fell, since the consequent decline in the level of the cash transfer would result in transfers being a smaller proportion of total cost. More specifically, a fall in the maize price from MK40 to MK30 and MK20 per kilogram would result in a rise in the total cost per US$1.00 transfer from US$1.32 to US$1.43 to US$1.52 respectively.

In addition to cost-efficiency, cost-effectiveness assesses the relative success of a project in meeting its stated goals. Evidence summarized in later sections of this case study demonstrates that the primary objective of ensuring the food security of beneficiary families in the hungry season was met, and a number of subsidiary goals to do with innovative aspects of the cash transfer were also broadly accomplished.

Table C4.1   Cash transfer amounts by month in the DECT, 2006–07

HH Size	Monthly Cash Transfer (MK)				
	Dec.	Jan.	Feb.	Mar.	Apr.
1	370	355	250	300	300
2	740	710	500	600	600
3	110	1065	750	900	900
4	1480	1420	1000	1200	1200
5	1850	1775	1250	1500	1500
6	2220	2130	1500	1800	1800
7	2590	2485	1750	2100	2100
8	2960	2840	2000	2400	2400
9	3330	3195	2250	2700	2700
10 or more	3700	3550	2500	3000	3000

Note: The exchange rate in this period was MK140 = US$1.

MARKET EFFECTS

One of the concerns about cash transfers is that they might provoke local inflation, especially in remote places where consumer goods are in short supply or food supplies are tight. In the case of DECT, the best advice available to stakeholders was that Malawi had plentiful food overall owing to an unusually good crop season in 2005–06. Nevertheless, Concern took several steps to protect the project against rises in food and other prices. Typical seasonal rises in the maize price were built into the project budget, a private sector liaison officer was appointed by Concern, and traders in the locality were informed about the opportunity represented by the DECT transfers.

In the event, maize prices fell from January to March 2007, as farmers and traders country-wide sought to run down stocks held over from the previous season's harvest. This was unexpected, and in accordance with the project's design it caused the value of the transfers to be adjusted downwards in January and February 2007. This declining payment was unpopular with beneficiaries, and was considered by them to have greater adverse effects on small compared to large households. In the event, Concern then slightly raised the payment for the final two months of the scheme (see Table C4.1).

Concern monitored the expenditure patterns of its beneficiaries on a monthly basis between December 2006 and April 2007. On average 61 per cent of the cash transfer was spent on maize and 71 per cent spent on food and essential groceries in total. The other significant individual category of expenditure was on medicines and health care, at 5 per cent of the transfer.

BOX C4.1 SOCIAL IMPACTS OF THE CASH TRANSFER

The social effects of DECT were monitored from within the project, and were also explored in a small field study undertaken in seven villages in January 2007 involving three focus groups, discussions with seven key informants, and interviews with 20 beneficiaries (Mvula, 2007). Findings are summarized briefly as follows:

- Adaptation to the smartcard was surprisingly rapid in communities with no access to banks and no prior experience of electronic technologies.
- Issuing smartcards to women had an empowering effect for them, even those in the typical male-headed household context, where it gave women just a little more social leverage than before over household expenditure priorities.
- In general men adapted with equanimity to the implied change in their control over womenfolk, although a few complaints of loss of male status were voiced, and there may have been behind-the-scenes disputes (kept hidden since Concern had made it clear that domestic conflict would result in ejection from the beneficiary list).
- Some limited sharing with non-beneficiary kin and neighbours occurred, typically with children rather than adults.
- The cash transfer helped with medical costs in some instances, and proper meals encouraged improved school attendance by children.
- Far fewer community members engaged in *ganyu* (casual work on bigger farms) than normal, with the social effect of families staying together all season, and being better able to care for the sick, elderly and children.
- Most beneficiary families were able to move from one to two meals per day, and did not have to resort to eating 'green maize' (that is, unripe maize not ready for harvest), and stealing also declined.
- Cases were reported of village heads asking for a cut from each beneficiary in the range of MK10–20 at each cash transfer, and this was not denied by the heads involved, instead being justified by reference to the amount of their time that they had to spend organizing beneficiaries at the distribution points.

Concern used these expenditure patterns to follow up second and third round effects of the cash transfer, that is, the effects on traders and producers of items purchased with the money. These data were then used to calculate the 'multiplier' effect of the transfer – the extent to which it caused a multiple increase in economic activity in the local economy. The result was a multiplier of around 2.0, meaning that for every US$1 of the transfer US$2 additional local economic activity was created (Davies, 2007).

ASSET BUILDING

Asset building was not an explicit goal of DECT; nevertheless, helping to ensure the adequate nutrition of beneficiary families may be considered as a form of asset protection with regard to human capital. In addition, there were scattered instances of beneficiaries saving their transfers or purchasing productive assets, such as chickens, with them. It is probable that more such behaviour would occur with cash transfer schemes of longer duration.

STRENGTHS

DECT displayed significant strengths as a cash transfer scheme, within the parameters of its limited duration, geographical coverage and number of beneficiaries:

i.   DECT was risk-taking and innovative on at least four fronts: the smartcard/ATM concept, the designation of women as cardholders, the use of wealth ranking as a beneficiary selection tool, and linking the monthly transfer payment to the price of food.

ii. The transfer of cash rather than food to beneficiaries gave them the ability to make expenditure choices according to their own priorities, and was therefore empowering for them.

iii. In DECT, this positive attribute was expressed in the empowerment of women as the holders of the smartcards and direct recipients of the cash at distribution points.

iv. Coordination between stakeholders in the DECT seems to have worked well in general, with some operational misunderstandings between Concern and OIBM being understandable in view of no previous experience by either party of such collaboration.

v.   The speed of acceptance of smartcards by mainly illiterate and innumerate beneficiaries suggests considerable potential for using new technologies for social transfers in the future (see Box C4.2).

BOX C4.2 ACCEPTABILITY OF THE SMARTCARD TO BENEFICIARIES

'The card is the thing that has our money. It is safe because nobody is allowed to draw money apart from the owner. . .' (widow, mother of four)

'To be honest with you, the card is good and safe. Nobody can steal this money from me. In addition to this, I heard that the card can be used at a later date, after the project has ended. . .' (61-year-old, married, mother of six)

'. . .The card is convenient. If one misses payment now, they can withdraw the money in the next month or one can follow the bank field workers at another centre where cash can be collected . . .' (focus group discussion)

---

vi. Evidence collected by DECT suggested that even in remote rural areas cash transfers could have a local economic multiplier effect of around 2.0, meaning that, for every US$1 transferred, US$2 of local economic activity is generated.

WEAKNESSES

DECT did display some weaknesses, although some of these are to do with its replicability to larger scale, rather than defects in its implementation as a small scale humanitarian project:

i. While the community triangulation of beneficiary lists was highly commendable, it was too elaborate as an approach to scaled up cash transfers, taking too much time (for both delivery agencies and local communities).
ii. There is an evident trade-off between the cost of achieving accuracy (including the social cost to communities of going through potentially invidious and divisive selection processes) and the inclusion and exclusion errors that result from less rigorous approaches to selection.
iii. Interestingly, many beneficiaries themselves, as well as community

  leaders, suggested that, if more than 50 per cent of the households in a community were considered in need of assistance, then a universal benefit would be more appropriate than a targeted one, for these social and economic reasons.

iv. Many social transfer schemes, and this arose in DECT in a fairly mild form (village heads asking for a cut from the transfer), have not come to grips with issues of incentive and remuneration of those non-project personnel that are involved in the delivery of the benefit.

v. The diminishing value of the transfer as the maize price declined was confusing for beneficiaries, suggesting a need for improved price forecasting as well as perhaps setting a minimum level of transfer taking non-food expenditure into account.

POLICY LESSONS

The DECT was an innovative humanitarian transfer project in a very poor country, combining the use of smartcard technology with women as recipients of cash transfers, and community-led beneficiary selection. At the policy level, the project demonstrated the feasibility of using new technologies, in this case smartcards and mobile banking, to make transfers to beneficiaries, even when recipients are low in literacy and numeracy. It also showed that such technologies could have positive effects for rural livelihoods going beyond the immediate transfer, owing to rural financial market effects (savings and investment) that even in a short project like DECT could be seen to start occurring as beneficiaries became more accustomed to their use. Finally, the project showed that cash transfers can stimulate local market effects in remote rural areas, manifested by increased trader activity and sales of food, farm inputs and consumer goods, with potentially significant multiplier effects in the local economy.

NOTE

1. The 'household economy approach' is a livelihoods-based framework for analysing the way people obtain food, non-food goods and services, and how they might respond to changes in their external environment. For a practitioners' guide to the approach see http://www.wahenga.net/index.php/views/in_focus_view_hea.

Case Study 5. Social Cash Transfers, Zambia

OVERVIEW

In 2007, Zambia had five social cash transfer pilot schemes running in Kalomo, Monze and Kazungula Districts in Southern Province, and Chipata and Katete Districts in Eastern Province. The longest established of these was the Kalomo Pilot Cash Transfer Scheme, which has run since 2004 in Kalomo District, initially providing transfers to 1027 destitute beneficiaries in 143 villages and five township sections. The Kalomo scheme had been taken as a model for other pilot cash transfers, each intended to test different aspects of cash transfer delivery and to enable lessons to be learnt for scaling up cash transfers in the future.

Technical assistance for these schemes was provided by GTZ (Kalomo and Monze) and CARE International under a DFID-funded partnership agreement (Kazungula, Chipata and Katete). The focus of this case study is on two out of the three CARE supported schemes, Kazungula (rural southern) and Chipata (urban eastern); however, these examples are placed within the broader context of the set of pilots as a group.

The Kazungula cash transfer scheme sought to test the feasibility of unconditional cash transfers in a remote, sparsely populated and agriculturally marginal rural area. From August 2005 to March 2007, this scheme provided 554 destitute and incapacitated households with ZMK30000 (US$7.5) per month (if they had no children) or ZMK40000 (US$10) per month (if they had children). In April 2007, these amounts were raised to ZMK40000 and ZMK50000 respectively (CARE Zambia, 2007).

The Chipata cash transfer scheme was designed to examine the modalities of delivering cash transfers to destitute households in urban areas. The scheme provided 1011 destitute families in the Chipata urban area with ZMK40000 (US$10) per month (if they had no children) or ZMK50000 (US$12.5) per month (if they had children). In addition, the Chipata scheme paid for each child enrolled in school grades 1 to 7 (primary school) a bonus of ZMK10000 (US$2.5) per month, and a bonus of ZMK20000 (US$5) for children in grades 8 to 12.

The transfer amounts in these schemes were set at a level permitting the purchase of a 50-kilogram bag of maize per beneficiary family per month, given prevailing maize prices. This was considered sufficient to increase the food consumption of a typical beneficiary household from one to two meals per day, and permitted minimal scope for discretionary expenditures. The transfer was not designed to lift beneficiary households out of poverty, but rather to lift them '[from] critical poverty that is life threatening to moderate poverty' (Zambia, 2006, p.5).

Social cash transfers in Zambia are implemented by the Public Welfare Assistance Scheme (PWAS) of the Ministry of Community Development and Social Services (MCDSS). PWAS operates at district level through the District Social Welfare Office under the guidance of a District Welfare Assistance Committee (DWAC). At lower levels there are Area Coordination Committees (ACCs) covering several communities, and Community Welfare Assistance Committees (CWACs). In terms of personnel and decision making, DWACs, ACCs and CWACs are stakeholder committees of the PWAS system, while government officials are the Provincial Social Welfare Officer (PSWO) and the District Social Welfare Officer (DSWO). These officers come under the Department of Social Welfare, which is one of two main departments of the MCDSS (Mulumbi, 2007).

In Kazungula District, selected beneficiaries were from 25 CWACs (an average of 22 beneficiaries per CWAC) in four ACCs, and were paid their monthly cash transfers by 17 Pay Point Managers (PPMs). In Chipata, beneficiaries were from the three ACCs of Msanga with 15 CWACs and 566 beneficiaries, Dilika with 9 CWACs and 403 beneficiaries, and Kanjala with 4 CWACs and 100 beneficiaries. In Chipata, around half the beneficiaries were paid through personal accounts opened in their individual names at the Finance Bank. The rest were paid by PPMs, or by the DSWO, who performed the functions of a PPM in some instances.

VULNERABILITY

Zambia is an exceptionally poor country. Living standards surveys conducted throughout the 1990s and 2000s have indicated overall poverty rates at around 70 per cent, with rural poverty at 80 per cent and urban poverty at 50 per cent. Such very high poverty figures suggest populations under extreme livelihood stress, such that poverty itself is a cause of high vulnerability to food shortages. Also implicated is the HIV prevalence rate (estimated in 2005 at 17.0 per cent of the adult population aged 15–49), poor economic performance, and local, national and regional rainfall failures.

The Kalomo Scheme in Zambia pioneered the notion that the destitute make up about 10 per cent of the country's population. This figure constituted the proportion of households found in the 2004 Living Conditions Monitoring Survey to have a per capita food consumption under 1400 kilocalories per day, and in addition lacked able-bodied labour. This category of households is sometimes referred to in the social protection literature as the 'non-viable' poor.

TARGETING

The intended beneficiaries of the Kazungula and Chipata cash transfer schemes were destitute households, corresponding to 10 per cent of all households living in the catchment area of a CWAC. The 10 per cent rule seems operationally useful because it solves the problem of identifying cutoff points with respect to absolute numbers of beneficiaries; however, difficult decisions still have to be made about who falls into the 10 per cent grouping and who is excluded.

According to the PWAS manual of operations, destitute households are identified by eating only one meal per day, begging from neighbours, having malnourished children, having very poor shelter and clothing, and being unable to afford medicines. Such households are typically elderly-, sick- or disabled-headed households, households caring for large numbers of children, and female-headed households. These attributes convert into a set of three criteria that households must meet in order to qualify:

- *extremely needy* (hunger, undernourishment, begging, in danger of starvation);
- *incapacitated* (no able-bodied person of working age; however, if one household person is fit for work and the dependency ratio is more than 3, this would qualify);
- *no valuable assets* (for example, cattle, functioning TV or fridge), and no regular support from relatives.

The targeting process was undertaken by CWACs. Each CWAC divided the number of households in their area by 10 to arrive at the total number of households that could be included in the scheme. However, PWAS guidelines stated that, if fewer households qualified, the CWAC should not add non-qualifying households to the list; conversely, CWACs should list all households that met the criteria even if their number went above the 10 per cent rule. In the event, during 2005–08 few CWACs departed much from the 10 per cent rule, with a variation of 9–11 per cent being the norm.

Having made a list of extremely needy households, CWACs compiled the list on a prescribed form and then ranked the individuals by priority of the severity of their destitution. To ensure the ranking was transparent, a public meeting was held where the list of potential beneficiaries was presented to the community for corroboration, and disagreements could be aired and resolved.

COVERAGE

As already indicated, the five social cash transfer schemes were in the nature of pilots rather than fully fledged schemes. The pilots were much too small by themselves to make much difference to overall poverty and vulnerability in Zambia, but they did of course have important local impacts in the places and for the time periods of their implementation. They were intended as lesson learning towards identifying what works best in cash transfers, with a view to incorporating best practice into scaled up cash transfers in the future. The planned coverage of the five pilots is shown in Table C5.1, together with information on the particular lesson learning opportunities that each represented in the 2007–08 period.

COORDINATION

Zambia has a Social Protection Strategy that is built into the National Development Plan for 2006–10 as a chapter on social protection. The strategy states the government's intention to harmonize, prioritize and improve upon existing and new approaches to social protection. The strategy is given practical effect in the formation of a Sector Advisory Group on Social Protection, comprising stakeholders from key ministries, civil society, donors, NGOs and other cooperating partners. The group is chaired by the Ministry of Community Development and Social Services, the lead ministry in the area of social protection. It has created five Technical Working Groups (TWGs) to work on different facets of social protection in Zambia, covering low-capacity households, social assistance, women and children, disability and advocacy. That on social assistance, chaired by the Department of Social Welfare, coordinates all social assistance interventions in Zambia.

Table C5.1   Cash transfer pilots in Zambia and their lesson learning features

District	HH Nos	TA Agency*	Special Features
Kalomo	3300	GTZ	PWAS, capacity building, scaling up
Monze	3300	GTZ	the above, plus soft conditionality
Kazungula	654	CARE	alternative payment methods
Chipata	1100	CARE	urban transfers, school allowance
Katete	**3000	CARE	age-based transfers (age 60 plus)
TOTAL:	11 354		

Notes:
* Refers to the organization providing technical assistance to the MCDSS.
** Individual beneficiaries rather than households.

Source: adapted and updated from Zambia (2007, Table 5, p.14)

COST-EFFECTIVENESS

Since the Kazungula and Chipata cash transfer schemes were works-in-progress in mid-2007, it was too early to examine the eventual overall costs of the schemes and their relationship to the transfer value to beneficiaries. According to budget figures, the administrative costs of the Kazungula scheme were projected to be ZMK132 million (US$31 579) per year, or US$32 per beneficiary household per year. Meanwhile, on the assumption that an average beneficiary receives ZMK35000 per month, the annual transfer value would be about US$105 per beneficiary. This implies a total expenditure per beneficiary of US$137, such that a total cost of US$1.30 is required in order to deliver US$1.00 of benefits. For the Chipata urban cash transfer scheme, the best that is known is that administrative costs were planned to be as low as 10 per cent of total costs; therefore a total cost of US$1.11 is needed to deliver US$1.00 of benefits. Data for previous phases of the Kalomo scheme suggest overhead costs in the range of 15–17 per cent of total budgets, and this translates into US$1.18–1.20 required to deliver US$1.00 transfer value. None of the overhead costs mentioned here include the government share of implementation costs.

MARKET EFFECTS

One of the concerns about cash transfers is that they may have an inflationary effect on food prices, especially in remote areas where markets do not function very well and there are high transport costs involved in bringing new supplies into an area. Such concerns evidently do not apply to pilot schemes that do not inject significant amounts of additional cash into local economies. The converse problem of a price rise in the national staple food eroding the ability of the transfer to protect recipients from food security failures may, however, apply. In the Zambia pilot cash transfers, monthly amounts were increased in April 2007 for this reason.

ASSET BUILDING

Asset building is not an explicit objective of pilot cash transfer schemes; however, as noted in relation to other cash transfer case studies, a proportion of beneficiaries in such schemes are observed to spend part of their transfer on asset building (savings or education or livestock) rather than on direct consumption.

STRENGTHS

The Zambia social cash transfer schemes have the following observable strengths:

  i. They are implemented through the formal structures of the Government of Zambia, and are therefore building familiarity with the concept of cash transfers at central level, as well as building experience in their implementation at district and local levels.
 ii. They represent important attempts to seek best practice in social transfer delivery and to learn lessons from mistakes as well as to build on good features of design.
iii. The Chipata scheme represents a first in terms of cash transfers to urban beneficiaries in Zambia, and is among only a few examples of urban cash transfers in the southern African region.
 iv. The Chipata scheme incorporates the innovative idea of a special incentive to school attendance for households with school age children.
  v. Innovative forms of delivery were beginning to be trialled in late 2007, including the outsourcing of payments to NGOs or the private sector in Kazungula, and the use of smartcards in Chipata.

WEAKNESSES

Naturally, these pilot cash transfer schemes also exhibit certain weaknesses, some to do with the readiness of government, especially at district level, to take on board social transfers to the neediest, and some being more generic problems that are widely encountered in social transfers in the region:

i.   In Zambia, as in most countries of the region, social protection is a policy response largely driven by donors and NGOs, and government 'buy-in' is not unambiguously assured; for this reason there was some risk that the impetus created by the five pilot social cash transfer schemes would lose momentum as they moved into their final phase.
ii. Social transfers run by government and its agencies require high motivation for successful implementation, and the pilot schemes revealed potential problems that might occur on this score, from DWSOs and other district level personnel requesting remuneration for their efforts, and CWAC members (who are voluntary) also beginning to talk about recompense for their work; a significant factor here is that CWAC members may see themselves as little different in income or wealth from those they are reviewing as potential candidates for the beneficiary list.

POLICY LESSONS

The small scale pilot cash transfer schemes in Zambia provided valuable lessons about the administrative feasibility, safety of cash in transit, accuracy of beneficiary targeting, and expenditure patterns out of transfers by recipients. Nevertheless, these pilots had something of a 'hothouse' character about them: they received reliable funding (from donors), special attention from supporting agencies (like GTZ or CARE), and intense overall interest from the aid community. The performance arising from these special conditions may be difficult to replicate in the context of broader implementation by the state.

A particular problem that arose in the Zambia pilots was the incentive to effective performance of the government officers and stakeholder committees that are essential for cash transfer success. Some schemes provided special incentives to CWACs (for example, providing each of them with bicycles in the Kalomo scheme), and there were motivation issues associated with DSWOs and pay point managers. In small and intensively monitored pilots such problems can be kept small and peripheral to scheme success; however, they may loom considerably larger in scaled up, state-led social cash transfers, where systemic patterns of political patronage may come into play.

Case Study 6. Urban Food Programme, Zimbabwe

OVERVIEW

The Urban Food Programme (UFP) in Zimbabwe is a food delivery and food voucher programme implemented by AAI that also includes other activities, namely low input gardens, and capacity building and training with local partners. The programme comes under the umbrella of DFID Zimbabwe's Protracted Relief Programme (PRP). The purpose of PRP is to stabilize food security and protect the livelihoods of vulnerable households in Zimbabwe, particularly those affected by HIV/AIDS. PRP is implemented by 12 NGOs (of which AAI is one) and their local partners.

In the UFP, AAI has pioneered the use of food vouchers as a means of ensuring stable food and grocery supplies to recipients in conditions of hyperinflation, steeply deteriorating exchange rates, and macroeconomic instability. In 2007, the food voucher was worth £9.00 sterling (US$18) per month. The voucher provides beneficiaries with a basket of commodities designed to fulfil nutritional as well as non-food basic needs (see Box C6.1). The CSB nutritional supplement is delivered directly to beneficiaries by AAI partners; it is not collected at retailers with the other voucher items. At its peak the UFP reached 3145 beneficiaries; however, erosion of the real value of its external resources, due to exchange rate and inflation effects, meant that by 2007 it was only able to reach 2000 beneficiaries.

Initially AAI started with food deliveries, but then shifted towards food vouchers that could be redeemed by recipients at local supermarkets. This switch reflected the comparative advantage of different institutions in procuring food and groceries in an unstable macro environment. AAI established a partnership with the OK supermarket chain in March 2005, covering the redemption of Harare vouchers, and extended this to TM supermarkets in March 2006, covering vouchers for Bulawayo, Gweru and Chitungwisa. The choice of supermarket is determined entirely by its location relative to the living places of beneficiaries.

AAI liaise closely with the retailers to ensure that the supermarkets stock adequate supplies for the redemption of vouchers on beneficiaries' stipulated shopping days. Owing to the prevailing economic situation, shortages

---

BOX C6.1   COMPOSITION OF THE FOOD VOUCHER

20 kg maize meal
1 kg beans
375 ml peanut butter
2 bars laundry soap
4 tablets carbolic soap
750 ml cooking oil
12.5 kg CSB porridge

---

do occur and the retailer either provides a substitute or shifts the shopping days in order to enable it to source the required items. The relationship between AAI and the retailers is cooperative. AAI meets the cost of producing the vouchers, as well as the personnel and administration overheads of the scheme. The supermarkets are given 1 per cent of the value of the voucher as a handling fee for their administrative costs. OK supermarkets produce the vouchers themselves, while TM supermarkets outsource the printing of the voucher.

AAI works with ten implementing partners (see Table C6.1), all legal entities, a mixture of NGOs, such as the Child Protection Society, and community-based organizations, such as New Dawn of Hope. AAI's choices of operating locations were partly determined by the existence of community-based organizations that provide home-based care and AIDS services. The implementing partners work with community groups and resident associations. These groups provide the entry point to the beneficiaries. They are voluntary organizations and form committees, often comprising school heads, retired teachers, nurses, police and officials from the Department of Social Services.

The implementing partners work with community volunteers who interact with beneficiaries on a daily basis. About 90 per cent of these volunteers are HIV positive and hope to get some assistance when they get sick; most are themselves poor and vulnerable and their turnover is high because of death and becoming bedridden. Besides providing money allowances, some partner NGOs provide food packs, uniforms and bicycles. However, these benefits are not standardized and can be a source of disharmony when different organizations are working in similar areas and some give more incentives to their volunteers.

Table C6.1   *AAI locations, implementing partners and beneficiaries, 2007*

Town	Suburb	Partner	No. of HHs
Harare	Mufakose	New Dawn of Hope	150
Harare	Budiriro, Glen View	Chiedza Children's Home	300
Harare	Highfields, Mabvuku, Tafara	Aids Counselling Trust	300
Harare and Chitungwisa	Mabvuku, Tafara	Island Hospice	30
Harare	Kambuzuma, Glen Norah, Highfields	Child Protection Society	300
Harare	Mabvuku, Tafara	Mavambo Trust	100
Bulawayo	Magwegwe, Lobengula, Nketa, Nkhlumane, Belaview, Goodhope, Hope Fountain	Matabeleland AIDS Council	335
Bulawayo	Robert Sinyoka, Methodist Village, Pumula South	Christian Health Care Services	225
Gweru and Chitungwisa	Mukoba	Padare Men's Forum	100
Gweru	Mukoba, Senga, Mambo, Mutapa	Midlands AIDS Service Organisation	160
Total			2000

Source: Manjengwa & Mukamuri (2007, Table 1, p.14)

VULNERABILITY

By 2007, the Zimbabwe economy had been in deepening crisis for five or more years. The outward manifestations were hyperinflation (estimated to have reached 6600 per cent in mid-2007) and a rapidly depreciating external value of the domestic currency. Hyperinflation affects most severely those whose income and assets do not adjust upwards in value as fast as the rate of inflation, and the poorest and most vulnerable members of society are always the hardest hit.

Almost all macroeconomic data about Zimbabwe have to be treated with a great deal of caution, since accurate measurement is practically impossible when events are moving so fast. According to official UN data, Zimbabwe GDP fell by more that half, from US$7.4 billion to US$3.4 billion between 2000 and 2005, while per capita GNI declined by 25 per cent from US$460 to US$350. The discrepancy between these two rates of decline is explained by remittance income from outside the country underpinning the income levels of a great number of Zimbabweans. It is estimated that, out of a total population of 13 million in 2005, roughly 3 million Zimbabweans are living outside their country.

Rapid economic decline increases the proportion of the population in poverty, as well as their vulnerability to food entitlement failure. Additional factors are rainfall failures, causing production failures and food security stress in rural areas, and AIDS, causing loss of able-bodied labour, chronic illness, and medical and funeral costs, more prevalently in urban than in rural areas. Zimbabwe currently has an overall estimated HIV prevalence rate of 20.1 per cent in adults aged 15–49 years. This has apparently come down from higher previous levels, although quality of reported data may be an issue. At any rate some 1.7 million Zimbabweans are thought to be living with HIV (2005 estimates) and there are believed to be 1.1 million AIDS orphans (UNAIDS, 2006a).

TARGETING

According to AAI programme documents, the criteria for selection of beneficiary households are those obtaining less than US$1 per day from all sources, plus one or more of the following:

- a home-based care client who is chronically ill;
- families caring for a large number of orphans and vulnerable children (high dependency ratio);
- single-parent-headed households due to death of a spouse from chronic illness;
- households with no able-bodied adult;
- overall: priority is given to bedridden home-based care clients.

In the UFP, selection is mainly carried out by implementing partners (Table C6.1). These are largely HIV/AIDS service organizations, which identify and assess potential beneficiary households. There is also self-selection where potential beneficiaries can approach the implementing partners and are placed on a waiting list. Clinics and the Zimbabwe government's Social Welfare Department also sometimes refer beneficiaries. AAI and implementing partners then jointly verify these potential beneficiaries through follow-up visits. Spot checks are conducted monthly on 10 per cent of both selected and beneficiary households to identify targeting errors.

AAI has tended to take a flexible approach to targeting, as the symptoms of AIDS-related deprivation are multiple and constantly changing. Those helped by the scheme have included the bedridden with no sources of income, old people with cross-infections, orphans and grandmothers. The food voucher is particularly useful to those on ART as proof of obtaining adequate nutrition, which is a prerequisite for being registered for treatment. The home-based care organizations have a waiting list, and it is estimated that AAI can reach only about 10 per cent of those who fit its criteria in the urban areas where they operate. Thus exclusion is substantial, not owing to administrative incompetence, but due to limited budgets in a non-universal transfer context.

COVERAGE

Table C6.1 shows the coverage of AAI implementing partners across suburbs in the main urban areas of Zimbabwe. AAI started in the cities of Harare and Bulawayo and then moved into Gweru and Chitungwisa towns. A drawback of this expansion was the risk of spreading beneficial impacts too thinly, especially when the total number of beneficiaries that could be funded declined. However, one positive reason for spreading out beneficiaries was to avoid overstretching any particular supermarket. An advantage of having implementing partners across many suburbs is that it helped AAI manage urban transport limitations, which are often a problem in reaching needy urban households.

COORDINATION

The UFP delivered by AAI and its partners is part of the DFID-funded Protracted Relief Programme (PRP) in Zimbabwe. The PRP provided £30 million sterling over the three years 2004–07 to improve the food security of more than 1.6 million of the poorest and most vulnerable people in Zimbabwe. The PRP works with a consortium of NGOs that include ActionAid, CARE, Oxfam, Save the Children UK and several others. The activities of these DFID partners are coordinated through a body called the Technical Learning and Coordination Unit (TLC) to which all PRP partner-NGOs belong, managed by a consultancy company (GRM International) under contract to DFID. The TLC plays multiple coordinating roles, assisting NGOs with their proposals and action plans, providing guidance on targeting and implementation, and stimulating cross-project lesson learning between projects.

COST-EFFECTIVENESS

Cost-effectiveness data on AAI were not available for 2007, presumably owing to the massive accounting difficulties occasioned by the acceleration in the rate of inflation (see Figure C6.1). Nevertheless, an earlier study by Samson & Mac Quene (2006, p.20) provided cost-efficiency data for several of the projects coming under the PRP umbrella, covering the period from their inception in 2004 or 2005 up to March 2006. In that era, both exchange rate and inflation effects were more moderate than in the post-March 2006 period. According to these data, AAI was perhaps the most efficient of the five PRP schemes examined, requiring US$1.44 to deliver US$1.00 benefit to direct beneficiaries (cash value of transfer) and US$1.30 to deliver US$1.00 total benefit (including nutrition gardens, capacity building, etc.).

MARKET EFFECTS

The critical market difficulty in the Zimbabwe context is the impact of inflation and exchange rate changes on the feasibility of keeping a constant real exchange value for beneficiary transfers. AAI has responded to these challenges, first by delivering physical packs to recipients and then by developing the voucher system. The vouchers proved less expensive to deliver for AAI, and were more popular with recipients, who were able to enter shops to receive the items specified on their voucher from the shopkeepers. In instances of market failure in specified items, that is, their physical disappearance from urban supply chains, then the voucher fails to deliver its full list of items, or substitutions are made.

The voucher system switches the risk of rapidly changing prices from the beneficiary to the delivery agency. The cooperating supermarkets charge AAI for the bundle of supplies at the prices then ruling in their stores. AAI must convert budgets denominated in sterling into Zimbabwe dollars that are then sufficient to meet its obligations to the beneficiaries via the supermarkets. AAI uses the Crown Agents to negotiate an exchange rate with the Zimbabwe authorities that is higher than the official rate but is still some way below the unofficial rate that more accurately reflects domestic market price movements, so some loss of potential benefit occurs at this point. The accelerating rate of inflation means that AAI often has to pay cooperating supermarkets higher amounts than estimated, and further loss in the real purchasing power of a given budget occurs at this point.

To give some idea of the difficulties confronting AAI and retailers, Figure C6.1 shows how the value of the food voucher in Zimbabwe dollars

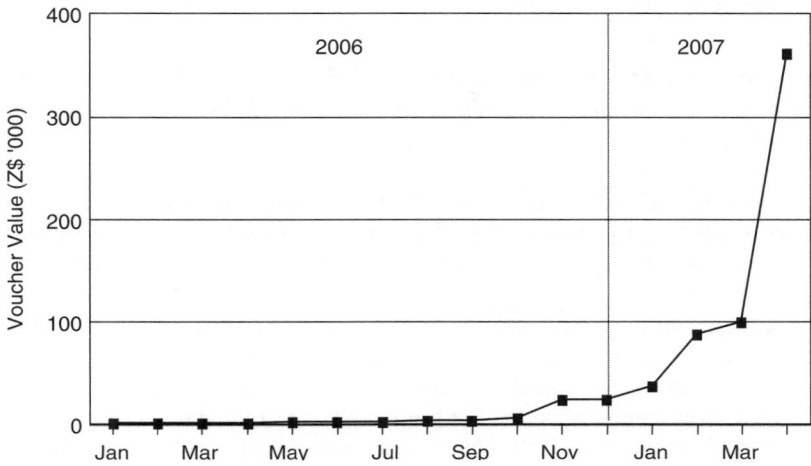

Source: Manjengwa & Mukamuri (2007, Table 1, p. 14)

*Figure C6.1   The rise in the Zimbabwe dollar value of a £9.00 food
voucher (Jan. 2006 to Apr. 2007)*

varied between January 2006 and April 2007. In this period the external
value stayed the same at £9.00 sterling, while the Zimbabwe dollar value
moved from Z$1592 to Z$362 200, a rise of more than 200 times in 16
months. Moreover, this rise accelerated steeply in the last four to five
months of the period, making price coordination between retailers and
AAI increasingly difficult to accomplish.

ASSET BUILDING

The destitute who are the beneficiaries of this programme have few assets to
start with. The most such a programme can hope to achieve is protection of
any existing assets. The monthly food voucher provides some asset protection. The best-case scenario is that selling products from the low input
gardens could lead to some asset building, albeit at a very small scale. Some
assets, such as garden tools, may be gained through the low input gardens,
but the majority of garden assets, such as wheelbarrows, are community
owned. The gardens are of different sizes, with household gardens ranging
from a few containers to about ten square metres. Even with containers and
small plots, foodstuffs such as green vegetables, carrots, beans, onions, toma-
toes and pumpkins can be produced to supplement the diet. The larger community or institutional gardens provide training opportunities and seed.

STRENGTHS

The Urban Food Programme implemented by ActionAid International in Zimbabwe has a number of strengths that are worth bringing together at this point:

i. There is wide agreement from available sources (including the independent review conducted by Samson and Mac Quene in 2006) that AAI has done a good job in difficult circumstances in its urban social transfers in Zimbabwe.
ii. AAI has pioneered a food voucher scheme as a way of overcoming the problem of rapid changes in the prices of basic goods in a situation of hyperinflation; the food voucher switches the risk of price changes away from beneficiaries to the implementing organization (AAI).
iii. A food voucher is not the same as direct food delivery to recipients, as occurs with WFP food aid; a food voucher inserts itself into the food and grocery retail system and helps to support that system, while food delivery tends to come from outside and may disrupt normal market functioning.
iv. AAI achieved a successful partnership with two private supermarket chains for the implementation of the voucher scheme, even in conditions where the supermarkets themselves were dealing with unpredictable price policy rulings from government.

WEAKNESSES

In the Zimbabwe context it is difficult to isolate weaknesses in scheme design or implementation from the extreme circumstances within which any social transfer scheme has to operate. Some comments can, however, be made about scope and sustainability:

i. The Urban Food Programme has been of limited scope, and has spread itself thinly across five urban centres, and several suburbs within each of those centres. This is not the fault of AAI, which seems to be doing its best in exceptionally difficult circumstances, but nevertheless the 'imprint' of such efforts tends to be tiny in relation to the overall scale of the problem addressed.
ii. Like other components of the Protracted Relief Programme, the Urban Food Programme faced uncertainty from early 2007 over whether DFID funding would extend beyond the scheduled end of the PRP in mid-2007. In the event a new PRP phase was agreed in August

2007, along with an extension of Phase 1 so that some activities could continue while Phase 2 was being prepared. In the context of Zimbabwe's deepening political and macroeconomic crisis, subsequent delays in the contracting of a management consultant for Phase 2 meant that as of mid-2008 Phase 2 was not expected to begin before late 2008.

iii. While altogether benefiting over 1.5 million people nationwide (2 million envisaged during Phase 2), the PRP is nevertheless a patchwork of NGO initiatives which operates in isolation from central government in Zimbabwe, and cannot hope to be more than a very partial substitute for a properly functioning state apparatus for social protection. Uncertainty remains over how the PRP will articulate with the latter once normal donor–government relations resume, during an era of macroeconomic recovery in which urban as well as rural poverty and vulnerability are likely to persist.

POLICY LESSONS

AAI's Urban Food Programme in Zimbabwe reveals in an usually sharp way circumstances in which cash transfers may not be the appropriate mechanism for delivering social transfers to destitute people and their families. In conditions of rapidly rising prices of food and other basic needs, monthly or quarterly cash transfers may not be able to adjust quickly enough to prevent beneficiaries from incurring a steep fall in the value of their benefit. Even with recent innovations in electronic cash delivery systems, a Zimbabwe-style situation necessitating payments to be adjusted instantaneously to the times when recipients purchase their supplies would be difficult to accommodate. In the absence of this degree of technical capability, the food voucher scheme implemented by AAI in urban areas of Zimbabwe is an effective and tested alternative in protecting beneficiaries from adverse price movements, providing the burden of adjustment can be borne by either the implementing or the funding agency of the transfer scheme. Once hyperinflation is brought under control, cash transfers may become a more flexible and cost-effective option for protecting the food entitlements of Zimbabwe's urban poor. Attention should be given now to strategies for supporting programmes of a future government in addressing this need.

Case Study 7. Food Assistance Programme, Mozambique

OVERVIEW

The Food Assistance Programme (FAP) is a World Food Programme (WFP) sponsored social transfer scheme, designed to provide nutritional support for families living with AIDS. The scheme aims to improve the health and nutritional status of patients in ART, in home-based care and registered in the programme for Prevention of Mother-to-Child Transmission (PMTCT) of HIV. The scheme recognizes the fundamental role of diet in strengthening the immune system of AIDS patients. This is so especially for those beginning ART, for whom proper nutrition plays a critical role in determining the success of the drug regime in returning patients to fitness levels that enable them to re-engage in productive activities. For the individual patient or household beneficiary, the scheme allows transfers up to a strict maximum duration of six months (Taimo & Waterhouse, 2007b).

FAP is organized by WFP in conjunction with the Ministry of Health (MINSAU) in Mozambique and local level partners that may be NGOs, government agencies or religious organizations. The scheme began in 2006, and in that year provided food transfers to 26 689 beneficiaries, utilizing 40 different partner organizations in 46 districts. Of this total number of beneficiaries, 18 684 were in home-based care, 4980 were others beginning ART, and 3025 were women registered in the vertical transmission (PMTCT) programme (see Table C7.1). The designated food basket per month comprised 36 kilograms cereal, 18 kilograms of a CSB supplement, 6 kilograms of beans or peas, and vegetable oil. This food basket is intended to provide 2100 kilocalories per day per person for a typical household containing one AIDS patient and four other household members. In 2007, the intended total number of beneficiaries increased to 35 000.

WFP organizes the distribution of food baskets through partner organizations, which must fulfil certain competency and ethical criteria; for example, NGOs must have been trained in and utilize the manual for home-based care produced by MINSAU. In addition, all partner organizations of WFP must fulfil the following requirements:

Table C7.1   People on ART obtaining food assistance in 2006

Numbers Covered	Home-Based Care	Other ART	PMTCT	Total
Patients*	18 684	4 980	3 025	26 689
Districts	37	22	18	46
Partners	39	12	6	40

Note: * Food is provided for patients and their households. The food basket is based on the assumption of an average household size of five persons, including the patient.

- at least three full-time staff members involved in management, logistics and monitoring;
- an office, basic telecommunications, computers, storage and transport;
- sufficient funds in order to share delivery costs with WFP;
- capability to assist at least 80–100 beneficiaries;
- a bank account in the name of the organization;
- capacity to prepare reports on activities carried out;
- experience in assisting people affected by HIV/AIDS.

These criteria tend to rule out smaller and local charitable organizations while favouring international NGOs and religious organizations. Nevertheless, exceptions are sometimes permitted, such as a privately run Catholic orphanage in Manhica District that receives WFP support through the District Health Services despite assisting fewer than the stipulated minimum number of beneficiaries. Many of the partner organizations rely on volunteers to undertake home visits, and a significant proportion of these volunteers are themselves living with HIV/AIDS and may be on ART.

VULNERABILITY

The specific vulnerability addressed by this programme is chronic sickness and mortality arising from infection with HIV, resulting in lack of able-bodied labour in the household to undertake productive activity and secure sufficient food and basic needs. Mozambique is among the ten countries in the world with the highest rate of HIV infection, with the prevalence amongst adults aged 15–49 years estimated to have increased from 8.2 to 16.2 per cent between 1998 and 2004. In 2003, roughly 1.5 million Mozambicans were living with HIV and AIDS, of whom 58 per cent were women. Among women in the age group 15–24, the prevalence is three times greater than among men in the same age range.

TARGETING

FAP would appear to be straightforward for targeting. After all, the beneficiaries are AIDS patients requiring home-based care and embarking on regular ART, and are therefore a narrowly defined vulnerable group. Nevertheless targeting even in this instance still requires fulfilment of several layers of criteria. These layers comprise:

- *Organizational criteria:* as noted above, partner organizations must have a minimum outreach of 80 patients, as well as fulfilling various administrative requirements.
- *Medical criteria:* patients must be certified by a medical practitioner as requiring and being able to benefit from ART, including testing for CD4 count and having a BMI of 16 or under.
- *Vulnerability criteria:* the scheme aims to target the most vulnerable in socio-economic terms amongst those designated to receive home-based care and ART, involving considerations such as loss of able-bodied labour for productive activity, lack of alternative income sources, households where the carer is elderly or widowed, poor housing conditions, and so on.

Inevitably use of multiple vulnerability criteria means that subjective judgements are made by those compiling beneficiary lists. There is some inclusion error (patients who would be able to purchase the food and nutritional supplement from their own resources) and, correspondingly, some exclusion error (genuinely desperate individuals or households that fail to get on the list). In the case of home-based care, volunteers are in a potentially ambivalent position, as some of them are HIV infected and just as poor as those to whom they provide a care service. It is inevitable that some volunteers get on to beneficiary lists, and perhaps justifiable that they should do so, but this does mean a conflict of interest between their roles as contributors to the beneficiary selection process and as recipients themselves of transfers. In addition, there is lack of clarity concerning the eligibility of households to more than one food basket, when several household members have been accepted for ART.

COVERAGE

FAP reached 26 689 beneficiaries located in 46 districts in the central and southern regions of Mozambique in 2006 (see Table C7.1). This then reached 35 000 in 2007. According to the government, 38 000 individuals were obtaining ART in December 2006, with plans to increase this to 55 000 people by the end of 2007. The FAP coverage of ART patients seems to have been roughly 70 per cent in 2006, falling to 64 per cent in 2007. In the meantime, UNAIDS estimated in 2006 that 235 000 people in Mozambique were medically eligible and urgently needing ART in order to avoid preventable mortality. Thus the projected coverage of the Food Assistance Programme in 2007 represented less than 15 per cent of those potentially eligible to receive ART in the country at large. The vertical-break medication to prevent mother-to-child HIV transmission is estimated to reach less than 7 per cent of HIV-positive pregnant women.

COORDINATION

Coordination of FAP takes place at three levels. First, at central level, WFP participates in a group of stakeholders coordinated by the Ministry of Health. In this group, the different clinical stages of ART and the need for dietary supplements in each of them are discussed, as well as the clinical and socio-economic criteria for entry to the Programme. With regard to orphans and vulnerable children (OVC), the WFP and the Ministry of Women and Social Action (MMAS) have signed a memorandum of understanding to enable organizations working with OVC to access food assistance. WFP participates in technical committees for OVC created at central, provincial and district levels in the context of the National Plan of Action for Orphans and Vulnerable Children. With regard to food security and HIV/AIDS, the Technical Secretariat for Food and Nutritional Security (SETSAN) includes a working group called SANHA charged with looking at this topic, which has produced a manual to assist voluntary organizations decide on appropriate courses of action for helping food insecure families living with HIV and AIDS.

Second, at provincial level, technical committees have recently been established by government to coordinate assistance to OVC. WFP is represented in such committees, if at all, by partner organizations, an example being International Relief and Development in Inhambane Province. Some provinces also have home-based care coordinating committees such as the Forum for Home-Based Care in Inhambane Province which brings together NGOs, donor agencies and the Provincial Directorate of Health in taking forward HIV/AIDS prevention and mitigation policies.

The third level of coordination by FAP is that of delivery of food basket transfers through partners at the district level. There is evidence of lack of coordination between WFP partners in the district, with the result that lesson learning regarding best practice does not get transferred between partners, and nor is there any cross-reporting of experience and outcomes. However, there is some coordination between WFP partner organizations and the Ministry of Health in respect of training in home-based care.

COST-EFFECTIVENESS

No evidence is available regarding the cost-efficiency or sustainable outcomes of the Food Assistance Programme in Mozambique. It is apparent that WFP is able to defray some of the costs of delivery to its partner organizations, which are expected to raise funds in their own right and not to rely wholly on their contracts with WFP for operating resources. WFP does not make available the operational costs associated with conducting an individual scheme like FAP. Nor is there any follow-up between WFP or its partners on the nutritional or vulnerability status of beneficiaries once the three- to six-month period of transfers has come to an end. There is nothing unique to WFP in this regard, as remarkably few agencies monitor their beneficiaries beyond the termination date of the period of transfers to them.

MARKET EFFECTS

An advantage of food delivery for beneficiaries needing to meet strict nutritional requirements is that the nutritional content of the food basket is independent of the market prices of ingredients. This is a significant positive feature and it places the financial burden of adverse changes in market prices upon the sponsoring agency, in this case WFP. In the case of FAP, the aggregate amount of food delivered is unlikely to have any perceptible impact on market prices either locally or nationally. WFP is moving towards applying the principle of local procurement to its food aid operations; however, it is not known how much of FAP draws on local as compared to external food supplies.

ASSET BUILDING

Asset building is not an explicit objective of FAP. Nevertheless, the improved health of individuals who benefit from nutritional support taken together with the return to physical activity of those on ART implies a significant impact on the level of human capital in beneficiary households. Labour as an asset is enabled to return to productive activity, and this is therefore a definite asset-building outcome of the scheme.

STRENGTHS

The Food Assistance Programme in Mozambique has recognized strengths, which were confirmed by fieldwork undertaken in two districts in late 2006:

i.   The improved nutrition made possible by the programme has visibly beneficial effects on recipients.
ii. This impact is especially significant for children, who recuperate rapidly and spectacularly after starting ART while supported with proper meals.
iii. In addition, sick and bedridden adults recuperate, and in the majority of cases are once more able to contribute to household incomes.
iv. In several districts the FAP is complemented by nutritional education included in the home-based care training provided to volunteers by the Ministry of Health.

WEAKNESSES

The FAP also has some identifiable weaknesses, although some of these might be regarded as acceptable costs or slippages that are of relatively minor importance relative to the impacts of the programme:

i. Once a programme of transfers is initiated, continuity is perhaps one of the most important rules to which it should adhere – a stop–go transfer scheme has negative effects on the well-being of beneficiaries, as well as causing stress and costs amongst volunteers and delivery organizations. Yet in 2006–07 WFP did not secure enough food supplies to maintain its flow of food baskets to beneficiaries, and the size of rations was reduced (the basket was reduced to 25 kilograms maize or rice, 10 kilograms CSB and 6 kilograms beans or peas), as well as a three-month gap occurring at one point between deliveries, the latter having a particularly adverse impact on those still in their first few months of ART.
ii. The food basket is generally made available at clinics for beneficiaries to collect, and WFP argues (perhaps fairly) that this is the only feasible way of distributing a physical transfer to such a large and scattered set of recipients; yet travel to the collection point and carriage of the goods do entail significant costs for beneficiaries, depending on how far they are from collection points and their access to able-bodied labour – these costs are typically paid to helpers in kind out of the package itself, thus diminishing the eventual ration available to the recipient household (in

one case reported in connection with this case study, beneficiaries spent Mtn160 per month in transport and carriage charges).

iii.   Despite the use of firm medical criteria to identify beneficiaries in this instance, targeting remains a problem; in community situations where virtually everyone regards him- or herself as poor, proxy indicators (such as widowhood, looking after orphans, etc.) that attempt to draw refined lines around vulnerable social groups do not work very well, with the result that final beneficiary lists are not as objectively compiled as sponsoring agencies would like to think.

iv.   The six-month cut-off point for assistance is arguable as an approach to social protection, especially where beneficiaries are mainly drawn from amongst the most vulnerable and destitute members of society; even the medical reasoning around the six months (in relation to supporting the physiological adaptation to the ART regime) is crudely drawn, with longer periods of adjustment to the drugs being required by some patients.

POLICY LESSONS

The Food Assistance Programme addresses an identified and legitimate need in relation to policy responses to AIDS, which is to fulfil the nutritional requirements for successful drug therapy that enables people living with AIDS to regain sufficient good health in order to contribute once more to the livelihoods of their families. In the case of pregnant women, good nutrition is also needed to ensure the effectiveness of drugs that prevent mother-to-child transmission of HIV. However, like so many social protection programmes in the southern African region, the Food Assistance Programme is somewhat ad hoc and accidental in character: its scope is determined more by WFP food pipelines and donor resource commitments than by the size of the problem it sets out to address; and the duration of its commitment to individual beneficiaries is relatively short in relation to the dire circumstances in which many of them will continue to live when their transfers stop.

This raises important strategic issues about short term against long term commitments by donors, governments and NGOs to provide support to AIDS patients. The expense of providing ART seems difficult to justify if recipient patients and their households are then left with a high probability of future food deprivation that will undo the benefits that have been realized. As with many short term social transfers, the FAP illustrates that the beneficial outcome of immediate good intentions may be seriously undermined by failure to address long term chronic vulnerability.

Case Study 8.   School Feeding, Lesotho

OVERVIEW

School feeding as a social transfer has a long history in Lesotho. It can be traced back to at least 1961 when Save the Children UK (SC-UK) began to provide meals for ten schools in the country's lowlands. In 1965, the World Food Programme (WFP) began to provide the ingredients for meals to primary schools in the highlands, and in 1966, after Lesotho's independence, WFP began sourcing food from abroad for distribution to schools across the country by the Government of Lesotho (GoL) and SC-UK. This is also when the government's Food Management Unit was created, which ever since has had chief responsibility for distributing food to schools.

Between 1966 and 1990, the WFP school feeding programme covered all schools in the country. However, decisions were then taken to phase out WFP feeding in the lowlands and foothills regions and replace it with the School Self-Reliance Project (SSRP), based on providing schools with farm inputs in order to encourage them to grow their own supplies for school meals. In 1999, Lesotho adopted a Free Primary Education (FPE) policy and as part of this decided to phase in country-wide primary school meals once again, covering one additional grade each year, beginning with grade 1 primary and eventually covering grades 1–7 by 2007.

In this phase, sourcing of food was shared by GoL and WFP, with WFP continuing to be mainly responsible for supplying highland schools, while GoL has supplied schools in the lowlands and foothills according to the FPE roll-out programme by grade. This intended plan was interrupted in 2002–03 when a hunger emergency was declared and WFP was requested to supply all children in the lowlands and foothills with food under a regional emergency operation. WFP had a four-year project lasting from the beginning of 2004 to the end of 2007 complementing the GoL-FPE feeding programme, with a gradual phasing out of WFP's involvement envisaged (although subject to continuing joint review).

Under GoL-FPE, school feeding is contracted out to caterers at school level, who procure the required ingredients and provide labour for a fixed fee of M2.30 (US$0.33) per child per day. Caterers are typically local women who prepare the food off site and bring it into the school. Each

Table C8.1   Prescribed weekly menu for school feeding under FPE

Day	Menu	Quantities per Child
Monday	Maize porridge (*papa*) and green vegetables (*moroho*)	150g *papa* 100g vegetables
Tuesday	Bread and pulse soup, e.g. beans	¼ loaf 250ml soup
Wednesday	*Papa* and green vegetables and boiled egg	150g *papa* 100g vegetables, 1 egg
Thursday	Maize (*samp*) mixed with beans (ratio 5:1)	150g *samp*
Friday	*Papa* with processed or pasteurized or UHT milk	150g *papa* 250ml milk

Source: Chaka *et al.* (2007)

caterer provides meals for between 100 and 150 school children. Caterers must follow a weekly menu prescribed by the Ministry of Education and Training (MOET), and they must adhere to the stipulated menu through-out the duration of the contract. This menu is described in Table C8.1.

WFP school feeding operates differently. WFP procures food, typically adds mineral and vitamin supplements to flour, or fortifies maize with soya, and delivers these fortified supplies to local distribution points, from which they are distributed to schools by the Food Management Unit. In the past, a considerable proportion of WFP procurement has been external to the region, with WFP being responsible for transport costs to Lesotho. More recently, however, WFP has focused on local procurement, either in Lesotho or in South Africa. At school level, cooks under the WFP scheme are paid M0.90 (US$0.13) per child per day, since they are only required to supply their own salt, sugar and fuel. Meals are prepared at the school kitchen or premises using the WFP food supplies. Under both schemes, a positive side-effect of school feeding is the employment and income generated for school caterers.

There are several different components to WFP school feeding in Lesotho. The biggest component is the provision of school lunches. The menu for each child comprises 150 grams maize, 40 grams pulses and 20 grams vegetable oil. The maize flour and the vegetable oil are fortified with micronutrients, and in some cases the maize flour is additionally enriched with soya to increase the protein content of the meal. In addition, WFP provides take-home rations for orphans and herd-boys that comprise 25 kilograms of fortified maize meal delivered to families once a month through schools, and requiring evidence of regular school attendance.

Finally, WFP provides fortified maize meal to community members and parents who participate in collective school projects such as maintenance of schools or work on school farms.

VULNERABILITY

Lesotho is a country characterized by deepening poverty and rising vulnerability, and a highly unequal income distribution. The poverty rate in the country as cited in recent documents is estimated at 68 per cent, and half of this proportion is considered destitute. A number of factors are responsible for the worsening personal circumstances of many Basotho; however, among these, four stand out in particular:

i.   rising prevalence of HIV (third highest rate in the world at 23.2 per cent of the adult population aged 15–49);
ii. decline in remittance income (in the 1980s Lesotho was one of the most remittance-dependent economies in the world, corresponding to 48 per cent of GDP);
iii. decline in agriculture (cereal production contributed to 80 per cent of national grain needs in the early 1980s; this had fallen to 50 per cent by the 1990s, and to 30 per cent by the early 2000s);
iv. changes in trade regimes: a collapse in markets for a textile industry built up from 2000 on the basis of favourable access to the US market under the African Growth and Opportunity Act.

School feeding seeks to reverse rising vulnerability by helping to break the intergenerational transmission of poverty and vulnerability (World Food Programme, 2006). Persistent hunger keeps children out of school, results in high drop-out rates, and diminishes their ability to learn. As articulated by the Lesotho Ministry of Education and Training (MOET), school feeding has the following objectives (Lesotho, 2007):

- to alleviate short term hunger among school pupils and contribute to their nourishment;
- to attract orphaned and other vulnerable children to attend school by providing the needed meals during school days;
- to sustain learning among all pupils by maximizing school attendance and raising their attention span during classes;
- to inculcate good eating habits among children from an early age;
- to mitigate the effects of HIV and AIDS among affected children by providing meals to vulnerable children.

TARGETING

School feeding in Lesotho has shifted uneasily around the de facto situation that it has practically been a right for many years, and especially so for primary school children. In the highlands, children have received school meals from WFP more or less continuously since independence. To the extent that there has been targeting, it is towards primary schools and the highlands. However, efforts to shift schools in the lowlands and foothills towards self-provisioning from their own farms and gardens have not really worked for staple foods, and have often been overtaken by broader events such as crop failures across the country.

While targeting does not apply to school lunches for primary school children, who under FPE now receive school meals as a right, it does apply to take-home rations which are part of the ongoing WFP school feeding project (2004–07). Take-home rations are targeted to orphans and herd-boys in the highlands region, rising from 2500 in 2004 to 10 000 in 2007. This component was implemented by partner NGOs that were responsible for devising appropriate beneficiary selection mechanisms in collaboration with schools and the Ministry of Health and Social Welfare.

The targeting of herd-boys in the highlands of Lesotho results from the observation over many years that boys drop out of school more than girls, and that the chief reason for this in highland areas is that they are required by their families to look after cattle, goats and sheep. The provision of a monthly take-home ration for them conditional on school attendance provides an incentive for their families to keep them in school, in effect taking the form of a conditional social transfer. Similar reasoning applies to orphans, who are often otherwise prevented by their guardians from attending school so that they can help with household chores. There are an estimated 97 000 orphans in Lesotho.

COVERAGE

The coverage of school feeding is universal for primary school children, as envisaged by FPE. The chief policy issue is not about the extent of overall coverage, but about how that coverage is to be achieved between the GoL-FPE system, WFP procurement, and self-provisioning by schools under the SSRP. Under its 2004–07 project, WFP was to be phased out of school feeding, first in the lowlands and foothills where the government was to have taken over entirely by the beginning of 2006, and later in the highlands where by the end of 2007 WFP was supposed to be supporting schools in only a handful of highly vulnerable districts. Nevertheless, the strategy of phasing out WFP involvement in school feeding is an elusive and moveable target, with frequent reversals when it is found that WFP is in fact needed in order to ensure that children's access to food at school is secure. A follow-on WFP project for 2008–2010 focuses mainly on highland schools, with a complete handover to government envisaged by the end of 2010.

COORDINATION

School feeding in Lesotho involves coordination between many different bodies, but in practical terms centres on the role of the MOET, which organizes the contracting of caterers at school level, and the Food Management Unit, which ensures the distribution to schools of WFP supplies from its warehouses. Over the years, WFP itself has played a major role, although successive shifts in policy mean that WFP often has to reconsider where it should put the emphasis of its activities in Lesotho. Since 2004 MOET and WFP have had to coordinate in detail, and on a continuing basis, the phasing out of WFP deliveries to primary school feeding and their replacement by the GoL-FPE scheme.

At school level, coordination of school feeding is undertaken by school advisory committees that are mandated to advise school managements on financial issues and to supervise meal programmes. School advisory committees comprise the head teacher, one teacher representative, two parent representatives, the village chief and one church representative. These committees also oversee the efforts of schools to become self-provisioning under the SSRP initiative.

COST-EFFECTIVENESS

Little is known about the true costs of government school feeding (GoL-FPE), which comes under MOET and is supported by donors at central level as part of their general support to the realization of universal primary education in Lesotho. For the WFP 2004–07 project, budgeted costs are available (World Food Programme, 2003). This project covers school meals for 208 300 children in highland schools and 53 000 in lowland schools, as well as take-home rations for 10 000 orphans and herd-boys (phased in over four years). The direct costs of the project were estimated at inception at US$12.2 million, and support costs at US$2.3 million, giving a total budget of US$14.5 million. In other words, if we assume that budgeted total direct costs to WFP of delivered food commodities reasonably reflect their actual value at the point of distribution, US$1.18 budget is required to deliver US$1.00 in direct benefits to recipients.

MARKET EFFECTS

School feeding involves important two-way interactions with food markets, especially the market for maize in a country like Lesotho where maize meal is the main source of dietary energy. On the one hand, provision of school meals protects school children from fluctuations in food prices and availability in the national market, and therefore reduces risk and vulnerability for them and their families. On the other hand, school feeding is not trivial in the overall volume of food it consists of, and therefore how it is sourced may have effects at the margin in weakening or strengthening local food markets. The GoL-FPE scheme procures food locally (indeed, very locally, since school caterers source their supply in local markets) and will therefore tend to strengthen local market functioning. WFP procurement has not in the past had this effect, since it has relied on external supplies; however, stated WFP policy in recent years has been to procure in national markets whenever it can do so without unduly compromising costs and quality or driving up prices.

ASSET BUILDING

School feeding is about contributing to the formation of human capital, although this is a long term intergenerational effect, not the type of asset building that immediately opens up new livelihood opportunities for the current generation of adults. Nevertheless, in the short term school feeding may help to protect assets, since it reduces the burden of food expenditures on the household, and makes it less likely that households with school age children will have to sell assets in order to feed the family in situations of incipient food deficits.

STRENGTHS

School feeding in Lesotho has a number of strengths, which can be listed as follows:

i. It has a long history, and is well established, and its various participants and stakeholders have a lot of experience in its successful implementation.

ii. It meets a need that is widely acknowledged as critical to the future ability of a country like Lesotho to reverse its hitherto weak record in improving the living conditions of its citizens, and all the more so given the food security difficulties faced by the country in the 2000s.

iii. School feeding is one area where there is fairly wide agreement that physical delivery may be preferable to cash transfers, since fluctuating market prices would complicate cash purchase of food by children or by schools (nevertheless, the FPE form of school feeding comes close to being a cash transfer model, via its fixed payment to caterers).

iv. In general, good coordination between the various stakeholders in school feeding in Lesotho seems to have been the norm, with the government and WFP adapting to each other's evolving role in provision.

WEAKNESSES

The programme also has some weaknesses, as revealed in part by fieldwork investigation underlying this case study:

i. The switch from WFP to the GoL-FPE system based on contracted caterers may not be as effortless and successful as it first appears: the private contracting system lends itself to skimping on purchases and quality of ingredients by caterers, especially when local food prices rise, with an associated diminution in the size and nutritional quality of meals received by children – nor is it a simple task to monitor the performance of thousands of caterers.

ii. The attempt to switch school feeding towards home-grown supplies in school farms and gardens (the SSRP scheme) seems to have been unduly optimistic, especially since worldwide experience of this type of endeavour hardly provides an assurance of success: school gardens are always dogged by difficulties of collective decision making, responsibility and motivation, and, in the Lesotho context of persistently deteriorating agricultural performance in the long run, the contextual circumstances were hardly propitious.

iii. The consequence of these factors is that over the past decade there have been gaps in coverage, as well as quite probably a slowly deteriorating food quality; in addition, WFP's role has become uncertain and tenuous where formerly it had a well-understood and routine contribution to make.

POLICY LESSONS

It is unfashionable to champion a prolonged role for WFP in this era where cash transfers are the widely favoured vehicle for conducting social transfers to vulnerable people. Yet WFP-style school feeding in a country with the multiple disadvantages possessed by Lesotho possibly has much to recommend it. In relation to overall development budgets and aid flows, the costs of this type of programme are in fact quite minor. Efforts to get schools to feed themselves from their own farms were poorly conceived in a country where the entire agricultural sector underperforms in the long run.

While there are some strengths in the notion that government can do the same thing through subcontracting food purchases for schools through thousands of small caterers, the implications of widely varying food prices in the broader market for the behaviour of those caterers under fixed payment contracts are yet to be properly understood. Above all else, school feeding requires reliability and stability so that the growing up of the next generation is less blighted by hunger and vulnerability than the one before. It also requires a delivery system that can ensure the size and quality of the meals provided, and protect them to a reasonable degree from actions that jeopardize those objectives.

Case Study 9. Neighbourhood Care Points for orphans and vulnerable children, Swaziland

OVERVIEW

In 2006, Swaziland joined several other African countries in developing National Plans of Action (NPAs) for orphans and vulnerable children (OVC). Included as a central plank in Swaziland's 2006–10 NPA was an approach to the social inclusion of OVC, Neighbourhood Care Points, which had previously been developed as a scheme with intended national coverage (Swaziland, 2006).

A Neighbourhood Care Point (NCP) in simple terms refers to a place or point in a community where neighbours come together to provide care for OVC from the neighbourhood. This can be a house, a church, a community shed, a school or any type of shelter available. Some NCPs begin under a tree, until a roofed structure can be secured. The 'ideal NCP' is a place providing emotional support and care, along with a regular balanced meal, in order to secure improved nutrition, health, hygiene and sanitation for OVC. The wish list for such an NCP includes (Dlamini, 2007):

- basic day-time shelter from rain, wind and cold;
- warm clothing against winter cold;
- basic interaction, and developmental simulation activities for young children;
- availability of first aid treatments and basic health care;
- teaching and story-telling activities to provide life skills and build resilience;
- play, drama, singing and sports opportunities;
- consciousness raising and protection from abuse and HIV infection;
- gardening and keeping of small livestock;
- non-formal and after-school education activities; and
- psychosocial support and counselling for children with special needs.

In Swaziland, NCPs were first established in early 2001 in four communities in Hhohho region with support from UNICEF and World Vision.

They are said to build on the traditional Swazi concept of *bantfwana bend-lunkhulu,* meaning 'children of the big house' (a reference to the traditional socially inclusive responsibilities towards their subjects of local chiefs). The NCP initiative was a substantial component of the Community Action for Child Rights Programme of a UNICEF–Government of Swaziland cooperation agreement running from 2001 to 2005. By the end of 2001 there were NCPs in 18 communities, and by the end of 2002 they were present in 96 communities. In 2003, UNICEF received substantial EU funding to take this initiative further, resulting in 438 new NCPs being established between 2003 and 2006. By the end of 2006, the number of NCPs supported by UNICEF and WFP in partnership with seven NGOs and the Ministry of Regional Development and Youth Affairs had increased to 625.

At the core of the NCP approach are unpaid community volunteers known as 'caregivers', who are essential to the functioning of NCPs. These are usually adult women selected by the neighbourhoods themselves, then ratified by the chief and inner council of the chiefdom, to provide care to the children enrolled at the NCPs. The NCP caregivers receive basic training from organizations that support the NCP project. A management committee comprising community members is usually set up to oversee the affairs of the NCP, monitor NCP activities and assist the caregivers in their duties. Caregivers' responsibilities include the preparation and serving of food, organization and supervision of play and development activities, health promotion activities, training on hygiene, sanitation and basic child self-care, supervision of care for minor ailments (such as diarrhoea or skin infections), education on HIV and AIDS prevention and protection of children from sexual exploitation and abuse. They periodically receive supplies (monthly) to provide meals (one or two meals per day), hygiene (soap and water purification materials), health (first aid kits) and non-formal education services (stationery) to the OVC under their care.

VULNERABILITY

The recognition of an unprecedented social crisis arising from HIV/AIDS began to dawn on politicians and decision makers in Swaziland around the year 2000, and has gathered momentum since. The rising number of children losing one or both parents, caring for sick parents, dropping out of school, living with vulnerable elderly relatives, losing claim to land access owing to their status as minors at the time of parental decease, suffering severe or moderate under-nutrition owing to inability to secure enough food, and being prone to social exclusion or sexual exploitation overwhelmed the capacity of traditional extended family systems to respond adequately. The regional food crisis in 2002 exacerbated this emerging situation, as also did erratic rainfall and food harvest levels in subsequent years.

Swaziland has the highest HIV prevalence rate in the world, the most recent data from UNAIDS suggesting a total of 220000 people living with HIV/AIDS, or 20 per cent of the entire population (UNAIDS, 2007). Owing to the age structure of the population, the prevalence rate is much higher among adults aged 15 years and over, at around 35 per cent. A much-cited statistic on which many HIV/AIDS estimates are based was the finding in 2004 that 42.6 per cent of all pregnant women attending antenatal clinics tested as HIV-positive. These proportions mean that the number of AIDS orphans is projected to rise through to 2013 (World Bank, 2006), leading to an associated rising toll on family welfare caused by caring for the sick, purchasing medicines and meeting funeral costs.

The NPA prepared during 2005 estimated total OVC numbers at 132 000, including 69 000 orphans, 47 000 children in highly vulnerable families, 15 900 disabled children and 300 street children. The total OVC figure represented 25 per cent of all children aged 0–18, and 12 per cent of the total population of 1.1 million.

TARGETING

A national definition of orphans and vulnerable children in Swaziland is codified in the 2006 NPA. According to the NPA an orphan is defined as a child under 18 who has lost one or both parents, and 'a vulnerable child is a child under the age of 18 years who satisfies one or more of the following criteria:

- parents or guardians are incapable of caring for him or her,
- physically challenged,
- staying alone or with poor elderly grandparents,
- lives in a poor sibling-headed household,
- has no fixed place of abode,
- lacks access to health care, education, food, clothing, psychological care, and/or has no shelter to protect from the elements, exposed to sexual or physical abuse including child labour (Swaziland, 2006, p.11).

The principal focus of NCPs has been on children aged 0–10, although older children also participate in NCP activities, both as beneficiaries and as contributors to help with the younger children. The children are selected by the community, in consultation with traditional leadership structures. In most cases, the NCP caregivers in collaboration with other community-based workers such as Rural Health Motivators take the leading role in the selection process.

UNICEF's 2006 evaluation of its OVC projects suggested that selection was not beset by significant problems. This was because selection was done by members of the community with good knowledge of the situation of children in their neighbourhoods. In any event, caregivers were found in general not to enforce a serious policy of excluding children who came to their NCP. They were also mainly found to have made efforts, through house-to-house visits, to ensure that all deserving children were identified and participated in NCP activities.

COVERAGE

The first NCPs in 2001 were created in Hhohho region, with emphasis in the next few years on the three regions of Hhohho, Shiselweni and Lubombo. By 2006 NCP roll-out was occurring in all four regions of the country. Nevertheless, the number of NCPs created and supported has tended to be limited by the level of donor funding, and the 625 NCPs operational at the start of 2007 represented about a quarter of an envisaged total of 2520 neighbourhoods across the country. The 2006–10 NPA foresees NCP coverage rising to 750 by 2010. Since the declared intention is to achieve nationwide coverage, it is possible that 750 is considered sufficient for this purpose, given that a single NCP can serve more than one neighbourhood, and intersections also occur with support provided by schools, churches and other institutions.

COORDINATION

The NCP project is a collaborative effort between UNICEF, the National Emergency Response Council on HIV and AIDS (NERCHA), WFP, the Ministry of Regional Development and Youth Affairs, the Ministry of Health and Social Welfare, the National Disaster Force and NGOs that are addressing OVC issues in Swaziland. It grew out of the evolving strategies and activities of the Community Action for Child Rights Programme (2001–05). All the organizations involved in NCP implementation belong to the Child Protection Network, an umbrella organization open to all agencies with OVC concerns in the country, and encompassing both national and international NGOs. The Child Protection Network, through its quarterly meetings and annual joint planning, seeks to ensure minimum overlap and maximum synergies in the activities of its members. A Child Coordination Unit has been recently established, which once operational is likely to serve as the secretariat of the Child Protection Network.

COST-EFFECTIVENESS

The cost-effectiveness of the NCP project can be assessed in terms of cost-efficiency and the relationship between the stated intentions and actual outcomes of the project. In general, the costs associated with NCPs are for start-up materials, training of caregivers, monitoring, monthly food donations, and occasional provision of non-food supplies. The resource requirement for setting up an average UNICEF supported NCP comprising five caregivers and catering for 75 OVC was roughly US$8500 in 2006. According to the UNICEF data, administration and support costs were only 7 per cent of total NCP establishment costs. It can be inferred that NCPs are a cost-efficient method for delivering care to OVC, since once up and running their subsequent servicing costs are minimal. However, an important factor missing from this picture is the delivery cost and transfer value of food supplied by WFP to NCPs, which seems to be the single most important consideration in their successful operation.

Once started, the UNICEF supported NCPs are left to the communities to run, with occasional visits made for purposes of monitoring and delivering non-food supplies. While WFP's monthly food deliveries are for the children, it has also started a 'food-for-work' distribution programme from which caregivers in some NCPs benefit. This has proved to be an important incentive for the caregivers, who have to juggle NCP responsibilities and their own domestic or work responsibilities, without any pay. However, in some communities the caregivers' food packages have created tension in the community, with other community members agitating to replace existing caregivers in order to benefit from the food-for-work programme.

MARKET EFFECTS

It is not considered that NCPs create significant market effects. The food supplied by WFP to support meal provision for OVC at NCPs is a trivial quantity in relation to the Swaziland food market overall. At the same time, provision of this food does potentially protect the meal component of NCPs from being eroded at times of rising food prices in the domestic market.

ASSET BUILDING

NCPs address the nutrition, health, education, socialization and life skills of vulnerable young children, and therefore address future human capital. They also may have the effect of strengthening collective community responsibility and reciprocity in communities seriously affected by the downstream social effects of HIV/AIDS, although evidence on how far this is actually accomplished is rather mixed.

STRENGTHS

Neighbourhood Care Points display the following considerable strengths:

i.   They seek to build on traditional norms of community solidarity and reciprocity, and may help to strengthen these in the face of adverse trends that otherwise have disintegrating effects.
ii. They are inexpensive to start up relative to the OVC outreach they achieve, and are certainly much more cost-effective than either individually targeted OVC support or the creation of special OVC institutions.
iii. This cost-effectiveness is due to the voluntary work provided by members of the community at the NCPs, typically up to five caregivers in each NCP.
iv. NCPs are incorporated into the 2006–10 National Plan of Action for OVC, which has the stated objective of scaling up to every community by 2010.

WEAKNESSES

UNICEF's 2006 assessment, while in general reaching positive conclusions about NCP experience so far, nevertheless identified a number of weaknesses from interviews with key informants, caregivers and beneficiary OVC:

i.   It is possible that up to one-third of the total NCPs created since their launch in 2001 are non-functioning or barely functioning, the principal reason being failure to secure regular food supplies to provide meals, although other reasons such as intra-community conflict were also noted.
ii. Community support to NCPs is not as robust as the rhetoric of their origins in traditional cultural norms typically suggests: in many

instances caregivers were found to undertake practically all responsibilities, with little assistance and even suspicion and jealousy from other community members.

iii. NCP structures are mostly rudimentary, comprising a shelter of thatch and poles, an earthen floor and no storage facilities; only 17 per cent of sampled NCPs were constructed of brick, 35 per cent had access to a borehole or piped water, and 19 per cent had toilet facilities of any kind.

iv. Provision of meals is the principal and by far the most valued function of NCPs by beneficiaries and their carers, yet their capability to provide this function is highly dependent on WFP support, and efforts to achieve food supplies from OVC fields set aside by communities for cultivation have shown little visible progress to date.

POLICY LESSONS

NCPs seek to address a very real child deprivation problem in Swaziland, and they appear to do so in a cost-effective manner. The potential numbers of children for which they could provide support will grow in the future as the effects of the world's highest recorded rate of HIV infection feed into increased premature death rates of the productive adult population.

The UNICEF assessment of NCP performance up to 2006 concluded that the government commitment to national coverage by 2010 should be followed through, including maintaining a consistent level of start-up support to NCPs, continued training and support to caregivers including remuneration in cash or in kind for the work they perform, upgrading of NCP facilities, and provision of piped water to them. These proposals are in the main addressed in the budgetary provisions of the NPA.

The NPA envisages extending food provision across all currently operating and proposed NCPs, while at the same time reducing the proportion of total food to be met by external supplies (WFP and other agencies) from 100 per cent to 40 per cent between 2006 and 2010. This reflects an intention that a rising proportion of OVC food needs should be met from multiple food production initiatives including NCP gardens, backyard gardens, school farms, CFs and child-headed household farms. Nevertheless, these farming initiatives have proved to be the weakest in terms of outcomes of all the various OVC policy responses devised to date (see Case Study 14). It would seem sensible to be realistic about the future role demanded of WFP in NCP expansion, since the consistent daily provision of meals is undoubtedly the cement that holds together the broadly positive features of NCP experience so far.

Case Study 10. Education Material Fairs, Mozambique

OVERVIEW

Education Material Fairs (EMFs) are a social transfer delivery mechanism designed to motivate school attendance by orphans and vulnerable children (OVC) in families that are unable to meet even the most basic necessities for school attendance owing to financial constraints. EMFs provide a cash transfer in the form of a voucher that can be used to purchase shoes, clothes and educational materials at a fair to which vendors have been invited at a specific date and place. EMFs are thus modelled on Input Trade Fairs (ITFs), which provide farm inputs to vulnerable families in the same way.

EMFs seek (a) to provide choice for children, who are able to exercise their own preferences over what is purchased (the vouchers are physically given to named children, and parents or carers are discouraged from pre-scribing the choices that the children in their care make), (b) to stimulate the local economy by bringing together buyers and sellers at the fair, and (c) to pilot a potentially cost-effective model that could be scaled up for improving enrolment and retention rates in schools of children from the poorest and most vulnerable families.

EMFs in Mozambique have been implemented by Save the Children UK (SC-UK) in the period 2005–06, funded by the Danish International Development Agency (DANIDA). A pilot fair was held in 2005, in which 934 school age OVC were given vouchers with a cash value of Mtn130 (US$6.5). In 2006, five separate fairs were held in which a total of 3462 school aged children were provided with vouchers with a cash value of Mtn150 (US$6.0).

SC-UK operates mainly in Zambezia Province in Mozambique, and this is where the EMFs in 2005 and 2006 were held, in Morrumbala District (four fairs) and Mopeia District (two fairs). In the preparation for this as well as other activities in Zambezia Province, SC-UK had encouraged communities to form OVC committees and had succeeded in establishing 36 such committees in six districts. The OVC committees in communities chosen for EMFs were informed and trained regarding the project rationale and beneficiary selection criteria, and they also assisted in the organization of the fairs in conjunction with the headmasters of the nearby schools. Fairs were held adjacent to schools for ease of involvement of school staff as well as community volunteers in their organization.

Prior to the day of the fair, vendors were invited to attend and were informed about the range of items the vouchers would cover. This included shoes, clothing and a typical range of educational materials (pencils, pens, exercise books, etc.). The selected children were required to present themselves to project staff the day before the fair and then on the day of the fair were provided with a voucher valid only for that day.

VULNERABILITY

The EMFs target orphans and vulnerable children of school age who only intermittently attend school or who have dropped out altogether. Families of OVCs are vulnerable for many reasons, including (a) recurrent droughts that cause agricultural production failures, (b) floods that destroy household and productive assets, and (c) the rising rate of HIV and AIDS in Mozambique creating greater numbers of AIDS orphans as well as households lacking sufficient able-bodied adult labour to generate a sufficient livelihood for the family. The HIV prevalence rate in adults aged 15–49 is estimated to be 16.1 per cent, and there are 510 000 AIDS orphans in Mozambique (UNAIDS, 2006a).

EMFs address particular outcomes of these causes of vulnerability rather than the causes themselves. They seek to break the cycle of impoverishment and destitution by improving the life chances of some of the worst affected children through attendance at school.

TARGETING

The primary target group of EMFs is school age children identified by local communities as vulnerable or as orphans, and who have been enrolled for at least one year at school at any time in the past. The secondary target group is the parents or guardians of the OVC who have responsibility for ensuring or encouraging the education of the targeted children. The main eligibility criteria relate to vulnerability:

- as recognized by the community with regard to children (orphans, children living with elderly or chronically sick persons, and children themselves infected by HIV) and families (female-, elderly- and child-headed households);

- living in communities with reasonable access to at least one primary school;
- lacking any other form of direct material support to education (for example, provided by other NGOs).

The OVC committees were responsible for compiling the initial list of vulnerable households containing children who meet these criteria. This list was then debated between the OVC committee and project enumerators. The latter were selected by SC-UK at the local level and comprised students, workers and other people with some level of education and the ability and willingness to assist in the process of identifying beneficiaries. The outcomes of the joint committee–enumerator selection process were then discussed with EMF project staff and local level education officials.

Despite being small scale intensively managed schemes, EMFs were not entirely free of the kind of slippages in beneficiary selection that are widely associated with use of proxy vulnerability criteria. In one recorded instance, the OVC committee produced a beneficiary list that included 85 children who did not exist, subsequently attributing the action (when discovered) to a misunderstanding that they had to reach a target number.

COVERAGE

The EMFs were pilot projects conducted in six communities of two districts in a single province (Zambezia). The first fair was held in 2005 in the community of Mepinha-Chivungure in Morrumbala District. In 2006, fairs were held at Megaza, Pinda and again at Mepinha-Chivungure in Morrumbala District; and at Chimuara and Mopeia-Sede in Mopeia-District (see Table C10.1).

Table C10.1   Basic data on EMFs held in Zambezia Province, Mozambique, 2006

Community	Beneficiary OVC	Girls (%)	Vendors
Megaza	979	40.9	27
Pinda	500	44.0	33
Chimuara	428	50.0	11
Mepinha-Chivungure	763	50.2	60
Mopeia-Sede	762	47.6	23
Total	3432	46.0	154

Source: Mole & Giva (2007)

Clearly, coverage of EMFs has been minuscule in terms of the overall scale of vulnerable OVC in Mozambique. The total number of school age children reached in the six fairs held in both 2005 and 2006 was 4396. This is, for example, a mere 0.8 per cent of the estimated number of AIDS orphans in the country as a whole. The success or failure of EMFs cannot therefore be judged by reference to relative national coverage, but rather in terms of whether they represent a model that could or should be multiplied up as a policy device to encourage attendance and retention in school of OVC more widely in Mozambique.

COORDINATION

SC-UK coordinates its EMF work with district level representatives of the Ministries of Education and Women and Social Affairs (MMAS). The scheme is a decentralized provincial and district level social transfer mechanism. EMFs require early preparation one to two months in advance of the academic year, so that fairs can be held before the next school year starts. Therefore consultations with education and social welfare officials take place at the beginning of that preparation period, followed by community and beneficiary selection as already described under 'Targeting' above. There is no evidence of strong official or SC-UK influence on the list of beneficiaries that emerges from OVC committees in consultation with enumerators, although this list is subject to final verification by SC-UK and local education officials.

COST-EFFECTIVENESS

The total cost of the five EMFs held in 2006 was US$26 124, giving a cost per beneficiary of US$7.5. The cash value of the voucher transferred to beneficiaries was US$6.2. Therefore the average implementation cost per voucher was US$1.3, and a total budget of US$1.2 was required to deliver a US$1.00 level of benefit. In comparative terms of social transfer schemes this was a cost-efficient intervention.

In addition to the efficiency of delivering a transfer, cost-effectiveness is concerned with the success of a social transfer in terms of achieving its goals, in this instance getting vulnerable children to enrol in school and to remain in school thereafter. SC-UK has put in place a monitoring capability at selected sites, one of which is Mepinha community and school, which was the location of the 2005 pilot EMF. Data show that the Mepinha school enrolment rate rose by 36 per cent from 911 students in 2004 to 1240

*Table C10.2   Purchase preferences of children in the EMFs held in
                 2006 (mean numbers of items purchased per child)*

Exercise books	8.55
Pens	2.50
Pencils	1.10
Flip-flops	0.95
Soap/detergents	0.90
Shirts	0.50

Source: Mole & Giva (2007)

in 2005. Community members attribute most of this rise to the EMF. For the EMFs held in 2006, 46 per cent of the 3432 students assisted were girls. The results of longer term monitoring are still awaited, but it is worth emphasizing that downstream monitoring is rare in social transfer schemes of this kind, and SC-UK is to be commended for following up in this way.

SC-UK also monitored the use made of the vouchers by beneficiary children in the 2006 EMFs, as shown in Table C10.2. While educational materials ranked high on children's priorities, so too did cleanliness and clothing. In particular, a pair of flip-flops was on almost all children's preference list, and half the children purchased shirts as well. This confirms well-substantiated behaviour that children feel the need to conform to minimum social norms in order to have the self-confidence to attend school and integrate socially with other pupils.

MARKET EFFECTS

A stated objective of EMFs is to stimulate the local economy by holding the fairs. It is true that, in relative terms, an EMF channels a considerable sum of money into the project sites for expenditure on the day of the fair, and this is an attractive business opportunity for sellers of clothes and educational materials. According to a study undertaken for SC-UK, total takings at the five fairs held in 2006 were Mtn510 505 (US$21 271). On average, 154 vendors participated in each fair, and each vendor turned over Mtn3426 (US$143) in sales. The data are provided in Table C10.3.

Clearly EMFs on the scale conducted by SC-UK in 2006 have no significant impact on the broader market availability or price levels of educational materials. The fair itself is a one-off event, and for this reason, too,

Table C10.3   Voucher values spent, EMF fairs, 2006

Community	Voucher Value Delivered (Mtn)	Mean Vendor Receipts (Mtn)
Megaza	144 959	5 369
Pinda	74 570	2 260
Chimuara	64 950	7 217
Mepinha-Chivungure	113 259	1 857
Mopeia-Sede	112 767	4 903
Total	510 505	3 426

Source: Mole & Giva (2007)

stimulation of the local economy is brief and unlikely to result in sustained changes in cash-based economic activity.

ASSET BUILDING

EMFs are an intervention supporting households with low or depleted assets. Beneficiary children are expected to remain in school and progress at least towards completion of primary education, in this way building up the human capital of the next generation. In this the EMFs can be seen as complementing broader national efforts by government and donors to increase the education level of Mozambique's citizens in the future, as also envisaged in the Millennium Development Goal (MDG) goal for education which the Government of Mozambique is trying to meet.

STRENGTHS

The EMF social transfer approach has a variety of strengths that can be identified as follows:

i.   It is a true social transfer, not an emergency response, and is designed to meet a specific social objective, which is the generally poor participation of OVC in the education system.
ii. It provides the children themselves with a voucher, and permits them to make their own decisions about what to purchase up to the cash value, thus empowering them and increasing their self-esteem.

iii. It involves communities in selecting social transfer beneficiaries, as well as in helping to organize the fairs in collaboration with the staff of schools, therefore reinforcing beneficial social interaction both ways between the schools and the community.

iv. SC-UK is making an effort to monitor subsequent outcomes of the fairs in terms of school enrolment and attendance, which is unusual for experimental or limited duration social transfer schemes.

WEAKNESSES

The EMFs in Mozambique display certain obvious weaknesses from the broader perspective of reaching the vulnerable on a national scale, supporting them in a sustainable way, and ensuring the educational participation of orphans and vulnerable children:

i. These are tiny projects, part of diverse NGO efforts to address the many different facets of chronic poverty and vulnerability in a country like Mozambique, but with scarcely any evidence regarding cumulative or sustainable impacts.

ii. The recognized beneficial impacts are personal (to the children concerned) and may or may not produce longer term results for improving the future well-being of those children, their families or the communities in which they live.

iii. The one-off (and one-day) character of the EMFs means that the hoped for stimulation of local economic activity from holding them is unlikely to eventuate.

POLICY LESSONS

The EMFs demonstrate that careful and considered execution can result in local level success, albeit on such a small scale. In this instance, the local knowledge of SC-UK, coupled with the dedication of its staff, meant that timing, coordination, community selection of beneficiaries and implementation worked well within the parameters set. It is possible that downstream monitoring will demonstrate that this is an effective way of motivating vulnerable children to return to school, and keeping them there once they are enrolled. However, broader policy questions are then raised about replicability within the framework of national education policy and the role of the Ministry of Education. On the one hand, larger scale roll-out (to reach more vulnerable children) and repetition (to ensure they stay in school, and to achieve the market stimulation goal of EMFs) would require substantial and rising donor commitments. On the other hand, this would conflict with donor preferences towards supporting education through general budget support to the government, and also with the Ministry of Education's own mandate to supply adequate educational materials to schools and to ensure the widest possible participation of all children in the education system.

Case Study 11.   Input Subsidy Programme, Malawi

OVERVIEW

The Input Subsidy Programme (ISP) in Malawi is a fertilizer and maize seed subsidy programme covering the entire country. It has operated since 2005/06 and 2006/07, and is a successor to earlier input subsidy schemes such as the Targeted Input Programme (2000–04) and Starter Pack (1998–2000). ISP is funded by the Government of Malawi and implemented by the Ministry of Agriculture, as well as by the public fertilizer distribution agencies Agricultural Development and Marketing Corporation (ADMARC) and the Smallholder Farmers Fertilizer Revolving Fund Malawi (SFFRFM).

ISP is a coupon-based subsidy scheme. Eligible small maize farmers receive two coupons, one for 50 kilograms basal dressing (NPK 23–21–0) and one for 50 kilograms urea, entitling the holder to purchase the fertilizer at MK950 (US$6.8) per bag. Coupons are also issued to tobacco farmers for compound D and CAN ('tobacco fertilizers'). In 2005/06 the subsidized purchase price of tobacco fertilizers was higher than for maize, at MK1450 (US$10.4) per bag, while in 2006/07 the single price of MK950 per bag was used across all fertilizers. In addition, in 2006/07 maize seed coupons were issued permitting purchase at MK400 per 3-kilogram bag. The overall cost of the scheme, net of sales revenue, was US$51.4 million in 2005/06 and US$73.9 million in 2006/07, representing almost half of the Ministry of Agriculture's budget in 2006/07. Donors contributed around 13 per cent of net costs in 2006/07, mainly covering seed supply, transport and logistics (Dorward *et al.*, 2008).

Organization of the ISP involves three main stages: coupon allocation and distribution, fertilizer procurement and distribution, and coupon redemption by recipient farmers. These stages clearly interact (for example, fertilizer available must match coupon allocation) and operate at different scales (from centre down to the village level). The timing of the stages is critical if farmers are to take delivery of the fertilizer by the onset of the rains in late October or early November.

Coupons are allocated to each district according to a distribution matrix constructed by the Ministry of Agriculture. This matrix involved three main sequential decisions: coupons for maize fertilizer and seed are allocated in proportion to the maize area in each district; these proportions are then adjusted to reflect variations in expected demand in each district (for 2006/07 this was based on 2005/06 uptakes); then district level coupons are divided between extension planning areas (EPAs) in proportion to each EPA's maize area.

Once in the district, coupon distribution is the responsibility of the District Commissioner acting through successively lower level committees, from the District Coordinating Committee to the Area Development Committee and Village Development Committee (VDC). Each of these committees has a wide membership drawn from non-elected officials as well as elected representatives; for example, the VDC comprises the group village headman, village headmen, the extension officer, the village police committee chair, the local MP, and two male and two female small farmer representatives.

ADMARC and SFFRFM are mainly responsible for fertilizer distribution, substantially reducing the market share of private traders who formerly delivered full-price fertilizer to better off farmers. Initial delivery takes place into three SFFRFM depots located in Blantyre, Lilongwe and Mzuzu. From these depots, outward distribution occurs to storage and sales facilities at district and EPA levels. Delays in procurement and outward distribution were widely reported in 2005/06 and 2006/07, with some farmers not being able to exchange their coupons until January when crops are already in mid-growth.

The final stage of ISP organization is redemption of coupons by farmers. In 2006/07, each coupon comprised a booklet in triplicate bearing a unique serial number including a district identifier, and different colour coupons for different inputs. Redemption required matching up the correct colour coupon against the type of fertilizer purchased, and copies of the coupon and sales invoice being held after the transaction by both the seller and the buyer.

VULNERABILITY

The aim of fertilizer and seed subsidies is to raise small farm agricultural production by the timely use of improved farm inputs and associated cultivation practices. In this way, vulnerability arising from seasonal subsistence food gaps at household level is reduced, overall grain and tobacco production rises, and cash income rises for those farmers who are able to produce a marketed surplus. By definition, a social transfer that requires a minimum payment by its recipient does not reach the most vulnerable groups in society, who would be unable to pay even the subsidized price. However, an indirectly beneficial effect may occur owing to lower market prices following higher harvests, benefiting food deficit households while moderating the income gains of surplus farmers. Moreover, higher cash in circulation in rural areas is expected to have multiplier effects in the local economy.

TARGETING

In both 2005/06 and 2006/07 there was a lack of clarity in the criteria for determining eligibility for coupons. On the one hand, a widespread interpretation was that all farmers were eligible, and indeed in some places village heads registered all their households to receive coupons. On the other hand, the ISP was not formulated by government as a safety net, but rather as a boost to agricultural productivity for those with land, labour and the ability to purchase inputs at the subsidized price. In practice, it seems that local leaders adopted a variety of different beneficiary selection methods, noted in different places as follows:

- all eligible, including non-farmers resident in towns with family in the village;
- ownership of a piece of land;
- demonstrated ability to pay the subsidized price;
- participation in community development projects;
- participation in cash-for-work schemes, with the cash then allocated to input purchase;
- adherence to a new maize cultivation method known locally as sasakawa (this is a recommended maize cultivation process that involves planting single seeds on a grid pattern, with fertilizer targeted precisely to each 'planting station');
- first-come, first-served;
- none of the above: non-transparent allocations in which leaders, police, chiefs, friends and relatives received the bulk of coupon allocations.

It is possible that this rather fluid experience did not matter too much at national scale, where overall fertilizer use rose substantially, with resulting positive impacts on output and national food security. However, at local levels considerable social stress arose from uncertainties about eligibility, compounded in many instances by delivered coupon numbers being lower than the recipient lists already drawn up by VDCs. In such instances, rationing occurred, with consequent tensions between included and excluded farmers.

COVERAGE

It is estimated that 131 000 and 174 688 tons of subsidized fertilizer were sold to farmers in 2005/06 and 2006/07 respectively. This implies the issue of 2.6 million and 3.5 million coupons in each year, possibly reaching 1.3 million and 1.75 million farmers. This is on the working assumption that each beneficiary farmer received and used two coupons. In fact, coupon and beneficiary numbers are more difficult to derive than this owing to extra coupon printing in both years, unutilized coupons, many farmers only getting one coupon, and unintended exclusions due to poor targeting practices (see Box C11.1). Since there are an estimated 3.1 million maize farm households in Malawi, coverage in those years was around 45 to 55 per cent.

COORDINATION

Given its size and logistical complexity, the ISP seems to have been coordinated fairly well in both years, with problems tending to arise owing to local variations in implementation rather than to national level failures in coupon and fertilizer procurement and distribution to districts, although lateness has been an issue. The Logistical Unit of the Ministry of Agriculture is chiefly responsible for coordination at this national scale, and arrangements are made with ADMARC, SFFRFM, private traders, and transporters to ensure that delivery occurs according to agreed allocations.

COST-EFFECTIVENESS

The calculations given in this paragraph are based on data contained in an evaluation of the 2006/07 ISP conducted by a team led by Imperial College (Dorward *et al.*, 2008). Excluding the seeds component, total programme cost for distribution of 174 688 tons of fertilizer by the parastatals and participating private traders amounted to MK12.0 billion (MK3434 per 50-kilogram bag or US$490 per ton), although it is possible that the parastatals' handling costs were understated. The coupon price of MK950 paid by farmers implies a subsidy of MK2484 per bag (US$355 per ton), or 72 per cent of the total delivery cost. Of total cost, procurement cost amounted

BOX C11.1:   EXPERIENCES OF THE 2006/07 INPUT SUBSIDY IN FOUR DISTRICTS

Research for this case study examined rural people's experiences of the 2006/07 fertilizer subsidy, involving interviews with 192 farm households, 17 focus group discussions and 16 key informants in the four districts of Chiradzulu and Machinga in the south, Kasungu in central, and Mzimba in the north of Malawi.

Household and community experiences of ISP implementation varied widely between districts:

● Some chiefs invented non-existent households to increase the number of coupons for their villages.

● Coupon delivery was often less than registered households, resulting in coupon rationing and households receiving just one coupon or sharing one coupon.

● Relatives and friends of chiefs and policemen were given preferential treatment during distribution of coupons, as well as in the subsequent procurement of the inputs.

● Incidents occurred where police officers and ADMARC/SFFRFM staff demanded cash payments (MK200–500) to deliver inputs against coupons.

● In some communities only one type of coupon appeared, reputedly owing to theft of the other coupon further up the system.

● Some participants received invalid single parts of the multi-part coupon, which could not be utilized.

● In some places coupon distribution occurred surreptitiously (for example, at night), and recipients were sold the coupons at MK1000–1500 instead of the stipulated MK950.

● A considerable secondary market in coupons existed in which the coupons were being sold at MK2000–2600.

● In the quantitative survey, 78 per cent of sampled households received coupons; half of those received just one coupon (with wide variation across districts in this proportion); 62 per cent reported buying just one bag of fertilizer, while 32 per cent bought two bags and 5 per cent bought three or more bags.

> Overall, fraud, theft, nepotism, diversion of coupons, secondary markets, fake fees for delivery, etc. were reported, with wide variation in experiences within and between districts. Nevertheless, the subsequent maize crop was outstanding, leading to observations such as:
>
> *'. . . since this programme started, we can just say there is no more hunger here. . . we have plenty of food such that some people are throwing away maize meal. . .'* (female focus group participant, Machinga)
>
> *'. . . this year we don't even know where we will sell all this maize, and markets will be a problem if ADMARC will not open its depots as has been the case in the last couple of years . . .'* (woman in her 30s, Chiradzulu)
>
> *'. . . households that received the coupons will harvest six to ten more bags than those that did not apply any fertilizers at all . . .'* (45-year-old man, Chiradzulu)
>
> *Source:* Kadzandira (2007)

to an estimated MK10.8 billion (US$442 per ton), suggesting that operations were cost-efficient, with US$1.11 total cost for each US$1 spent on procurement. According to Dorward *et al.* (2008, p.27), private sector costs per ton of fertilizer sold were also about US$490 and, if we take this as an indication of the average market value of fertilizer at point of sale, this suggests that the ISP spent just US$1 to transfer each US$1 worth of fertilizer (or subsidy) to beneficiaries and would tend to confirm its cost-efficiency.

The effectiveness of a social transfer is of course about not just its cost-efficiency, but also the quality, impact and sustainability of transfer outcomes for beneficiaries. In the case of ISP, maize output rose from a five-year mean level of 1.55 million tons (2001–05) to 2.72 million tons in 2005/06 and a reported 3.4 million tons in 2006/07. Of course not all of this substantial increase can be attributed to ISP. The climate in both 2005/06 and 2006/07 provided excellent growing conditions for maize in Malawi, and especially so in the latter year. Nevertheless, econometric analysis suggests that the subsidy may have contributed 300000–400000 tons to the rise in output in 2005/06 and 500000–900000 tons in 2006/07. While the programme appears to have yielded significant household food security dividends through raising wage rates and lowering food prices, its cost-effectiveness will ultimately depend on several factors, some difficult to predict. Depending on assumptions about how much the subsidy displaced commercial fertilizer sales (discussed below) and contributed to increased output, and future national and regional maize prices, a benefit–cost ratio has been estimated in the range 0.76–1.36 for 2006/07, and 0.65–1.59 over the following five years (Dorward *et al.*, 2008, Annex B).

MARKET EFFECTS

A social transfer on the scale of the Malawi ISP has very considerable effects in input and output markets. On the input side, subsidized fertilizer sales increase overall fertilizer use, but net additional use is less than total subsidized sales, because better off farmers who would otherwise have purchased fertilizers at market prices switch to subsidized supplies.

According to available figures, fertilizer use in Malawi rose from 228 000 tons in 2004/05 to 292 000 tons in 2005/06 and 296 300 tons in 2006/07. In 2005/06 131 000 tons were subsidized, and it is estimated that 80 per cent of this represented incremental use created by the subsidy, while 20 per cent represented displacement of commercial sales. Likewise in 2006/07, of 178 000 tons subsidized, 60–70 per cent is thought to represent incremental use, as against 30–40 per cent displacement (Dorward *et al.*, 2008).

ISP also has impacts on maize prices. The national average retail price for maize, which had varied between MK20 and MK50 per kilogram in the hungry season of 2005/06, fell steeply after the successful 2006 harvest and then rose only moderately in the 2006/07 hungry season, before falling again in late 2006 and early 2007 as farmers and traders sold off stocks that they had been keeping from the 2005/06 harvest (Figure C11.1). This decline continued through the harvest period in 2007 to reach a low for recent history of MK14 per kilogram in June 2007. Low maize prices are, of course, good for food deficit vulnerable groups in Malawi, but below a certain point in real terms they are likely to defeat the purpose of the ISP, which is to stimulate agriculture to act as the engine of sustained long run growth in the country.

A final market effect of the ISP has been noted in the rural labour market. This is a decline in the supply of labour to *ganyu* (casual work on bigger farms) during the hungry season, causing upward pressure on *ganyu* rates of remuneration, and a rising preference by employees for cash wages rather than other forms of remuneration.

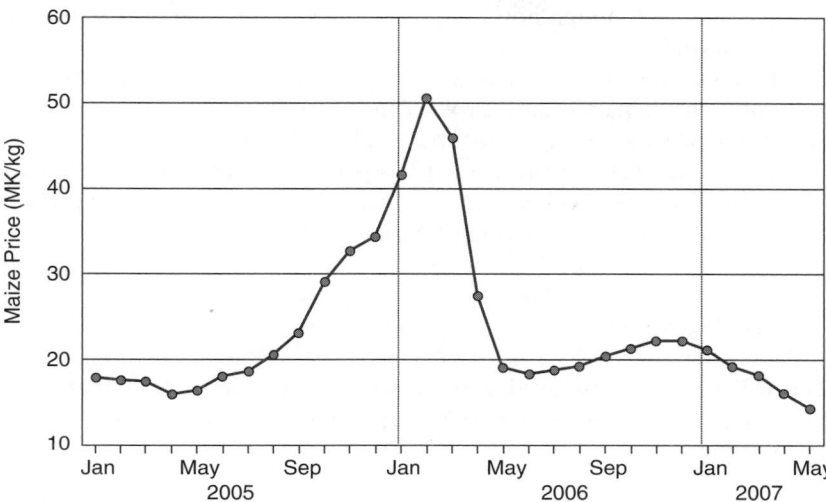

Figure C11.1   Trend in maize prices in Malawi, 2005–07, MK per kilogram

ASSET BUILDING

The ISP has no direct asset-building purpose, but, to the extent that it encourages savings and new investment in Malawian agriculture, this could be considered an indirect asset-building effect. In one important way, ISP has had a damaging effect on assets, and that is on the distribution infrastructure of private input suppliers who were cut out of the fertilizer market by the advent of subsidized sales.

STRENGTHS

The ISP has surprised many observers, including sceptical members of the aid community, by strengths that have been revealed in its implementation:

i.   The Malawi government was decisive about embarking on the programme despite resistance from donors, and has funded it from central revenues.
ii. The big logistical challenges – procurement, coupon distribution, fertilizer distribution, etc. – have generally been effectively handled, with reasonably clear rules for district allocations of coupons, and

successful (although not always timely) country-wide distribution of the fertilizer.

iii. Lessons were taken on board between the first and second years, improving in particular the role of the private sector in the second year.

iv. Impressive agricultural outturns in 2005/06 and 2006/07 may not be solely due to the subsidy, but it has played its due part and created a positive association between input use, improved cultivation practices and output gains across the whole of rural Malawi.

WEAKNESSES

The ISP has also displayed weaknesses, and it is important that these are not lost sight of owing to the apparent aggregate success of the programme:

i. At sub-district level and down to community level, the handling of coupon allocations has been highly variable, with, in the worst instances, fraudulent loss of coupons to officials, politicians, policemen, chiefs, headmen and so on.

ii. Fraudulent practices have included splitting coupon booklets, giving villagers invalid single copies of coupons, using blocks of coupons to acquire fertilizer then sold on to farmers above the subsidized price, and many others.

iii. These instances resulted in widely varying access by ordinary farmers to coupons, and to physical fertilizer, in different parts of the country, across and within districts.

iv. Ambiguity in targeting criteria meant widely varying practice across the country regarding who was prioritized to receive coupons by local committees (VDCs) and village leaders.

v. The exclusion of private traders from dealing in subsidized fertilizer had a serious effect on private input trading networks, gradually nurtured from non-existent beginnings from the late 1980s onwards.

vi. This also means that parastatals like ADMARC that had become near moribund at the beginning of the 2000s have been able to reassert their importance in the institutional framework of Malawian agriculture, a shift that has ambiguous connotations for the working of input and output markets in the future.

POLICY LESSONS

The Malawi ISP is more an agricultural policy instrument than a strict social transfer (even though it has a transfer element in the form of the subsidy), and it marks something of a renaissance in the notion that large scale public intervention in agricultural markets can deliver more rapid agricultural growth and poverty reduction in rural areas than market-led alternatives. This may be so as long as most of the subsidy does reach ordinary small farmers, leakages into secondary markets are minimized, and the government can sustain the subsidy from general revenue.

Case Study 12.   Food Security Pack, Zambia

OVERVIEW

The Food Security Pack (FSP) was initiated in the 2000/01 agricultural season as a Government of the Republic of Zambia (GRZ) funded programme covering all the country's 72 agricultural districts. A national food security NGO established in 1992, the Programme Against Malnutrition (PAM) is the lead implementing agency for FSP. PAM distributes farm input packs to districts and beneficiaries utilizing a network of district-based NGOs. FSP targets 'vulnerable but viable' farm households, defined according to a set of multiple criteria. FSP initially set out with ten objectives and four modalities for achieving those objectives. However, only the key ones of these have ever been met, and these may be summarized as (i) to provide a basic level of farm inputs to households that have lost the ability to source such inputs themselves, (ii) to encourage crop diversification in farmers' fields, and (iii) to promote conservation farming practices in Zambian smallholder farming (Tembo, 2007).

Originally planned to last three years, FSP is still running after seven years, albeit at a greatly reduced scale. The original concept was to attain a beneficiary level of 200 000 households each year, most of these 'graduating' out of the scheme after two years. However, having reached 145 000 by 2003/04, actual beneficiary numbers fell precipitously, averaging only 26 000 from 2004/05 to 2006/07. With beneficiaries receiving packs for one to three successive years, the net number of unique beneficiaries reached by the programme over its seven-year duration so far has been around 220 000 farm households.

The input pack received by beneficiaries is supposed to constitute 0.75 hectare of inputs, comprising 0.25 hectare cereal seed, 0.25 hectare pulses seed and 0.25 hectare cassava/sweet potato tubers, as well as the correct fertilizer type and amount for the cereal, and lime for areas with acidic soils. A review of studies about PAM suggests that this pack has never been delivered in its entirety, owing either to procurement difficulties for particular components or to insufficient funding resulting in a trade-off between number of beneficiaries and size of pack. For example, in the 2005/06 season most beneficiaries received only maize seed and fertilizer.

FSP involves procurement of the inputs (seeds, fertilizers, roots and tubers) required to make up a sufficient number of packs, conveyance of these packs to districts, and their distribution to areas and communities. PAM itself is responsible for the first stages of this sequence, and has partnership agreements with district-based NGOs for local delivery. The delivery and distribution process at district level is overseen by the District Food Security Committee, while selection of beneficiaries is undertaken by AFSCs or CWACs. With the low overall level of deliveries in recent years, area and community distribution is restricted to just a few adjacent sites in each district, with these being rotated each year to achieve as much coverage as possible for a limited resource.

VULNERABILITY

FSP arose out of a specific set of circumstances evolving throughout the 1990s in which the small farm sector failed to recover from successive shocks, and fertilizer and certified seed use declined, as also therefore did crop yields. This resulted of course in heightened vulnerability to food deficits, handled mainly in the 1990s by food aid deliveries in which PAM was significantly involved. FSP sought to reverse this process by providing a base level of inputs, encouraging diversification of crop outputs, and promoting conservation farming practices that are believed by agronomists to hold promise for agricultural regeneration in Zambia.

The chief method advocated by FSP has been 'conservation farming basins', known colloquially in Zambia as 'potholing'. In this, farmers prepare fields by digging out shallow depressions in a grid formation. Seeds are sown only at the bottom of each basin, and this is where fertilizer is also directed. The basins help to conserve moisture, especially if also manured or mulched. The use of conservation farming basins has spread widely in Zambia, partly owing to FSP, as well as broader promotion by the Ministry of Agriculture and Cooperatives (MACO) and the agricultural extension services. However, in areas receiving reasonably reliable rainfall farmers have not always persisted with the method, owing to the extra labour it requires in field preparation compared to customary methods.

TARGETING

From the outset, the target beneficiaries of the FSP have been so-called 'vulnerable but viable' small farm households, meaning that they satisfy a range of criteria with regard to their vulnerability, but at the same time have sufficient able-bodied labour to take advantage of the inputs package delivered. In recent years, the criteria for beneficiary selection have had two tiers: a primary level and a secondary level, with fulfilment of all primary level criteria as prerequisites for qualification under the secondary tier criteria. The primary criteria are:

- access to land, but cultivating less than one hectare;
- having adequate labour;
- not in gainful employment.

The secondary criteria are:

- female-headed households, not in gainful employment (widows, single mothers, etc.);
- households keeping orphans and abandoned children, not in gainful employment;
- child-headed households;
- terminally ill-headed households;
- disabled households;
- unemployed youth;
- the elderly, but with access to labour.

Beneficiary selection in the FSP is undertaken by CWACs or, in their absence, AFSCs. The function of CWACs in Zambia is outlined in Case Study 5 on Social Cash Transfers. AFSCs in rural Zambia are local stakeholder committees responsible for eight villages, and they discuss and modify beneficiary lists initially drawn up by village headmen. This method is prone to inclusion and exclusion errors owing to elite capture by kin and cronies of headmen.

COVERAGE

The FSP has an official mandate to cover all 72 of Zambia's rural districts, and PAM has had to comply with this mandate irrespective of the number of beneficiaries that could actually be funded once budgetary transfers have been made. The original beneficiary target of 200 000 (that is, around 2800

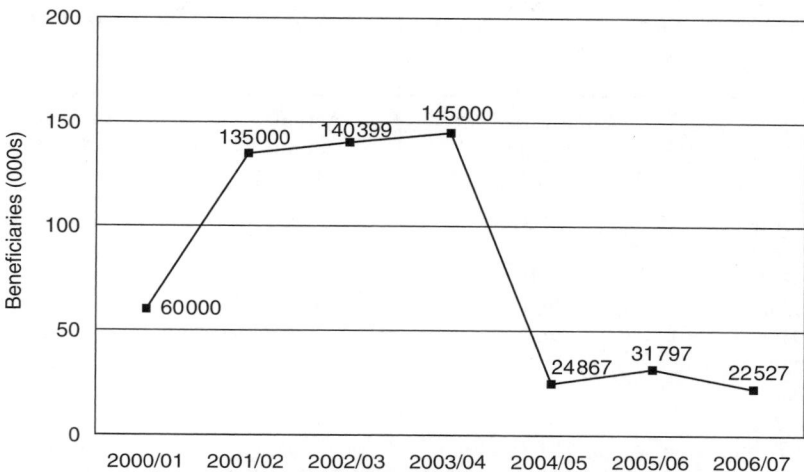

Figure C12.1   Trend in FSP beneficiary numbers, 2000–07

per district) would have covered roughly 20 per cent of the estimated one million Zambian farm households that could be eligible for the scheme each year, given its targeting criteria. With two- to three-year repeats to the same beneficiaries, it is probable that the net total of unique recipients reached has been around 220 000 households, or 22 per cent of eligible households, for the whole period to 2006/07.

The trend in total beneficiary numbers has been somewhat erratic, as demonstrated in Figure C12.1. This has reflected similar gyrations in actual funding to PAM, which has received only 30 per cent of the amounts written into GRZ annual budgets for the FSP overall, with the full budgetary allocation made available only in the first year and only 6 per cent of allocation received in 2006/07 (Table C12.1).

Unpredictable and often late funding creates serious logistical problems for an input delivery programme where timing of delivery to beneficiaries is critical. Moreover, low total beneficiary numbers stretch the credibility of all-district coverage. For example, the 2006/07 beneficiary level of 22 527 households equates to around 230 input packs per district. PAM deals with the unit delivery cost problem posed by this low level of packs by localizing its operations within districts. In effect, within-district geographical rationing has become an unplanned feature of the programme.

The erratic funding has also affected pack composition, compromising a central FSP goal of fostering crop diversification in farmers' fields. Cassava and sweet potato planting materials disappeared from the pack from the

Table C12.1 Budgeted and actual resource allocations to PAM, 2000/01 to 2006/07

Budget Year	Budgeted Amount (ZMK bn)	Actual Amount (ZMK bn)	Funding Gap %
2000/01	32.0	32.0	0.0
2001/02	32.0	3.9	87.8
2002/03	58.0	26.0	55.2
2003/04	89.0	43.0	51.7
2004/05	32.0	9.0	71.9
2005/06	112.0	21.1	81.2
2006/07	85.6	16.2	81.1
2007/08	70.3	4.3	94.0
All Years	510.9	155.5	69.6

Source: Tembo (2007) on the basis of data provided by PAM

2003 planting season onwards. The legume (pulses) component has been at lower-than-stipulated levels, or entirely absent, in all years. An effort was made in one year (2005/06) to increase the maize seed and fertilizer component, but these were then the sole inputs provided in most districts. PAM has had to trade off total packs supplied against pack composition, against a background of never receiving sufficient funding to comply with original targets. While 'pack-splitting' is prohibited under PAM's delivery rules, evidence from field visits by researchers indicates this practice is, in fact, commonplace.

COORDINATION

FSP comes under the Ministry of Community Development and Social Services (MCDSS), but is jointly coordinated with MACO and the Ministry of Finance and National Planning (MoFNP). A National Steering Committee made up of representatives of these three and other key stakeholders oversees the programme. This is chaired by MCDSS, has its secretariat in MACO, and is advised by a parallel National Technical Committee. The FSP receives funding under a MoFNP budget line.

It is probable that the Fertilizer Support Programme (unfortunately with the same acronym), started in 2002, has conflicted with the FSP for central government resource allocations to agriculture. The Fertilizer Support Programme began with fertilizer sales at 50 per cent of cost to farmers, reduced to 40 per cent following the 2006 elections. To take advantage of this farmers must be able to pay the subsidized price, and so are probably better off than FSP beneficiaries (Jayne *et al.*, 2006). This could be construed as a sensible division of responsibility between complementary schemes, with FSP enabling poor, vulnerable farmers to 'graduate' to the fertilizer subsidy. However, the subsequent stability and consolidation of the fertilizer subsidy as compared to the erratic enfeebling of the FSP suggest that no such wise oversight of the two programmes has occurred either in theory or in practice.

COST-EFFECTIVENESS

Recent evidence on the cost-efficiency of FSP is unfortunately lacking; nevertheless historical data up to 2003/04 suggest rising efficiency during its first four years, although from a rather inefficient start-up owing to high overhead costs relative to deliveries achieved in the first year. Even in 2003/04, when deliveries peaked, the overall cost of delivering US$1.00 worth of inputs at procurement value was as high as US$1.78. For the same year, an analysis conducted for DFID by White and McCord (2006) put the total cost to transfer US$1.00 worth of inputs valued at current market prices at US$1.67. Cost-efficiency is likely to have declined considerably since 2003/04, with lower beneficiary numbers in all years, while PAM overhead costs will not have been able to adjust proportionately.

Cost-effectiveness is not just about cost-efficiency, but also about impacts and outcomes made possible by the social transfer. Here there is no reliable evidence concerning the impacts of FSP on farm yields and household incomes, in either the short or the medium term. PAM monitoring systems have largely been limited to pack delivery and financial accountability, rather than on-farm impacts. Official reports indicating that 8–12 per cent of recipients subsequently 'graduated' from FSP by joining the Fertilizer Support Programme are difficult to interpret as evidence of FSP impacts, but this proportion is anyway significantly below expectations at the design stage.

MARKET EFFECTS

The FSP has influences in both input and output markets; however, the strength of such influences is dependent on the scale of the scheme relative to the overall size of the markets within which it functions. On the input side, the receipt of a package of farm inputs at near zero cost implies a 100 per cent subsidy on those inputs, and would be expected to provoke high demand for them at low prices. This is likely to have created considerable pressure for diversion of packs into secondary markets, and splitting of packs in order to sell part of them to other farmers or traders. Since 2002, the input market effects of the FSP will have been overshadowed by the larger effects of the Fertilizer Support Programme.

On the output side, a fully functioning FSP might have been expected to have a measurable impact on the supply of crops, especially maize, pulses and root crops. However, as already described, the FSP has never functioned at its original intended scale, and its recent coverage will have made scarcely any discernible difference in output markets, owing to the much bigger impact of other factors (including rainfall and the Fertilizer Support Programme).

ASSET BUILDING

The FSP is principally about input supply rather than asset building; however, an original FSP intention was to create community level cereal and seed banks, by requiring beneficiaries to pay a small proportion of their output into a common pool called 'recoveries'. Part of the thinking here seems to have been to institute a 'part repayment' of the 'loan' provided to beneficiaries through their receipt of packs, thus creating the capability in successive annual cycles to expand the programme from internal resources instead of relying only on new procurement. Partly also, the idea was to avoid recipient farmers treating their packs just as a free hand-out. According to PAM publicity, FSP is 'not a free handout . . . it is a low loan repayment support that is designed . . . to inculcate in beneficiaries the spirit of honouring loans'. The 'recovery' is set at 60 kilograms maize grain, to be set aside after harvest, for beneficiaries who receive 50 kilograms each of basal and top dressing fertilizer plus 5 kilograms maize seed.

In practice, the seed bank component never really took off; however, 'recoveries' of output according to the stipulated share of crop harvests widely occurred. In some instances, these recoveries were then sold by communities in order to purchase extra FSP packs for additional members of their communities. In other instances, recoveries were sold for other purposes such as livestock purchase and distribution of breeding stock amongst community members. Thus in a minor and rather fragmented way, the FSP in some of its bigger years probably did create some capital at individual and community level in rural Zambia.

STRENGTHS

The Food Security Pack has a number of notable strengths, although some of these are more notable in concept than in practice over the past seven years:

   i.   In concept, it is a scaled up programme with national coverage, and a mechanism for ensuring all potential beneficiaries might eventually be reached.
  ii.   It builds crop diversification in farmers' fields into the input pack delivered, encouraging a shift away from undue reliance on maize towards a balanced mix of grains, pulses and root crops.
 iii.   It builds in innovative farming practices that are widely recommended for improving the stability and level of crop yields in Zambia.

WEAKNESSES

Alas, almost from its inception FSP has also exhibited serious weaknesses, many of which are evident from the discussion so far:

   i.   The programme was initially far too ambitious in almost all respects: its coverage (all districts), its pack size and composition (grain, pulses, roots and fertilizer), and its goals (ten goals covering such disparate aims as new cultivation methods, livelihood diversification and entrepreneurship).
  ii.   In this respect it is perhaps illustrative of the policy principle that something simple accomplished well is likely to have a much greater beneficial impact than something complicated done badly.
 iii.   Delayed, erratic and unpredictable funding have been a major flaw, and government thinking behind retaining a programme that operates under such a high degree of instability is difficult to decipher.
  iv.   Many individual goals were never realized, and even those that were central to scheme success have only ever been partially met, owing to massive fluctuations in effective coverage.
   v.   Failure to monitor outcomes of pack delivery with a sample of recipient farmers means that there is no knowledge base from which to build in the future on proven strengths of the scheme.

POLICY LESSONS

The Food Security Pack contains many rather obvious policy lessons for social transfer policies. A first is that scaling up should not take place unless and until stable resources have been committed to a programme for a predictable run of years. This is not the only example amongst these case studies, but it is unfortunately one of the most high profile ones, of impact and outcome failures due to short term, unstable and unpredictable funding. A second lesson concerns the intricate ambitions of a scheme with too many, poorly integrated, targets and objectives. At a national scale, just a single well-defined transfer objective is likely to confront formidable logistical difficulties in order to achieve effective country-wide coverage. However, a scheme with ten objectives, many of them individually rather complicated in their specification (such as setting up seed banks in villages), never really had the remotest chance of success. A third lesson concerns lesson learning from mistakes. Since FSP did not monitor outcomes, despite delivering to many of the same beneficiaries in three successive seasons, no evidence base exists from which to distinguish the components of the scheme that worked from those that did not, nor the reasons for those differing impacts and outcomes.

Case Study 13.   Input Trade Fairs, Mozambique

OVERVIEW

Input Trade Fairs (ITFs) are a mechanism for providing poor and vulnerable farm families with access to farm inputs, especially certified seed, in the wake of a disaster such as drought or floods that has destroyed their ability to restart agricultural production in the next season. In Mozambique, ITFs are considered a response to emergencies rather than a vehicle for ameliorating chronic vulnerability; nevertheless they provide a model that could apply equally to either objective. The basic format is to provide beneficiaries with a voucher of a given cash value that can be used to buy farm inputs at an input fair to which traders have been invited at a specific date and place. The fair typically lasts just one day, but provides a marketplace that can be attended by any number of buyers and sellers of inputs, farm produce and consumer goods in addition to those traders registered to receive vouchers from beneficiaries.

ITFs in Mozambique are organized by the Ministry of Agriculture (MINAG) and Provincial and District Directorates of Agriculture in partnership with FAO. Pilot ITFs were tried out in 2001, in the wake of severe floods in the 2000–01 agricultural season, and they have subsequently been organized every year since 2003. Between 2003 and 2007, a total of 323 fairs were organized covering 266 030 beneficiaries mainly in the seven provinces of Maputo, Gaza, Inhambane, Tete, Manica, Sofala and Cabo Delgado. The total budgetary cost of ITFs in Mozambique in this period was of the order of US$3.3 million. The value of the voucher transferred to beneficiaries was Mtn180 (US$7) in 2003–05, rising to Mtn190 (US$8) and then Mtn300 (US$12) in 2006, and Mtn400 (US$15) in 2007. In order to provoke a sense of personal 'ownership' of vouchers, beneficiaries are expected to pay a nominal amount for them (Mtn20).

The choice of locations to hold ITFs is made at province and district levels, in consultations between FAO and local level MINAG officials, and taking into account the results of national vulnerability assessments. Once this decision has been made, seed suppliers and other input traders are invited to submit applications to be registered for participation at the fair. This process is required, since only registered vendors are able to exchange the vouchers that they receive at the point of sale for cash, after the fair is completed. There is no restriction, however, on the numbers and types of non-registered traders that can turn up at a fair.

On the day of the fair, beneficiaries are provided with a voucher booklet containing coupons of different cash denominations, summing to the overall value that has been specified (Mtn400 in 2007). They can spend these vouchers on any items offered for sale by the registered vendors, including seeds, fertilizer, pesticides, pumps, implements and so on. It is not uncommon for beneficiaries to club together in order to purchase amounts or items in excess of the purchasing power of each individual, or in order to resolve difficulties with the indivisibility of the coupons that are available in the voucher.

VULNERABILITY

The ITFs in Mozambique respond to specific risks and are targeted geographically at locations that are identified in vulnerability assessments as most prone to food insecurity and agricultural production failure caused by the two hazards of drought and floods. As in other southern African countries, specific trigger causes such as drought and floods occur against a backdrop of longer term and persistent factors contributing to high and widespread vulnerability to livelihood collapse, especially in rural areas. While poverty is thought to have declined in recent years from its extraordinarily high levels of the early 1990s, the most recent poverty assessment conducted in 2003 nevertheless shows poverty overall at 54.1 per cent and rural poverty at 55.3 per cent. The HIV prevalence rate in Mozambique is estimated at 16.2 per cent of the adult population, with the attendant effects of loss of able-bodied labour and depletion of household assets in order to pay for medical and funeral costs.

TARGETING

The target group for ITFs in Mozambique comprises poor farm families who have lost their capability to restart agricultural production following drought or floods; priority is given to female-headed households, widows, the elderly and child-headed households. Eligibility criteria for receipt of vouchers are:

  i. poor families strongly affected by floods or drought resulting in loss of crop output, housing or family members;
  ii. insufficient food reserves to secure future consumption due to crop loss;

iii. fewer resources compared to other households in the community;
iv. nevertheless, still possessing a minimum capacity to produce.

These criteria have been applied differently at different ITF sites because of differing interpretations, community conditions or local social institutions. Alternative and complementary criteria have been stated as: (a) being an active farmer, (b) having lost seeds in the previous crop season, (c) having low purchasing power compared to other local farmers, and (d) being a female-headed household. Consultation occurs with community leaders concerning who should be included in the beneficiary list, with this list then being verified by the District Directorate of Agriculture.

While disaster-affected poor farm families are the principal focus of ITFs, a secondary, indirect, target group are considered to be the small traders who can participate in the fairs, many of whom are women who come to the fairs to market different crops.

COVERAGE

ITFs in Mozambique have covered selected districts and sites in all of the country's ten provinces, although with considerable variation between them in terms of frequency. Maputo, Gaza, Inhambane and Tete provinces have been allocated fairs in most years, while Niassa and Nampula provinces have participated in only a few seasons. In general, efforts are focused on locations that have been hit by known adverse natural events (floods, rainfall failure), and where vulnerability assessments indicate the presence of high numbers of families that have lost their capability to recover.

Since 2002–03, ITFs have reached 266 030 families, broken down seasonally and across years as shown in Table C13.1. This table also provides information on the number of ITFs held and the value of the vouchers transferred in each season. While total number reached seems impressive, it is put in perspective by noting that there are approximately 3.3 million rural families in Mozambique, so ITF cumulative coverage has been about 8 per cent, consisting of a once-only transfer per beneficiary. Of course, not all rural families are poor or prone to devastating natural hazards, but nevertheless the coverage of those who do fall into these categories is likely to have been modest overall.

COORDINATION

It is widely considered that ITFs in Mozambique have involved good coordination between the various parties and stakeholders involved in their

Table C13.1   ITF coverage, 2002–07

Season	ITFs Held	Districts	Recipients	Transfer Value US$
2002–03	26	14	12 750	89 250
2003–04	100	116	49 720	348 040
2004–05	54	n/a	26 060	182 420
2005–06	85	52	79 000	584 000
2006–07	58	58	98 500	1 353 000
TOTAL	323	240	266 030	2 556 710

Source: Mole & Vasco (2007); FAO Mozambique (2007a)

planning and implementation. ITFs are an established part of MINAG's strategic planning for crop losses caused by natural disasters, and in some years the Ministry has funded additional ITFs and beneficiaries in excess of those funded by donors through FAO.

COST-EFFECTIVENESS

Data contained in documents provided by the FAO office in Maputo yield cost-efficiency indicators for two recent ITF projects as shown in Table C13.2. These suggest that it has taken between US$1.25 and US$1.29 to deliver US$1.00 of transfer value to beneficiaries in recent times. These data should be interpreted cautiously. FAO budgets and costs represent only part of the logistical support required to organize an ITF at a selected site, with MINAG being responsible for a considerable proportion of the expenses involved. There is also a degree of inconsistency in figures produced by FAO on the budgets and value of ITF transfers in different reports written at different times.

   Since monitoring of outcomes of ITFs was negligible until 2007, data on broader indicators of cost-effectiveness, for example the additional farm output they have made possible, are unavailable. However, it is understood that efforts have been made to redress this deficit since then.

MARKET EFFECTS

ITFs both respond to perceived failures in input markets in Mozambique and have the objective of stimulating rural markets in inputs, outputs and consumer goods through holding the fairs. ITFs respond to the failure of

Table C13.2　Data on budgets and transfers, ITF projects, 2006–07

Indicators	2006–07	2006–07
Funding agency	EU	CERF
Planting period	Oct.–Jan.	Feb.–Apr.
No. of beneficiaries	30 000	57 000
Budgetary cost US$	450 000	1 102 609
Cost per beneficiary US$	15.00	19.34
Transfer value US$	360 000	855 000
Value per beneficiary US$	12.00	15.00
Ratio total cost: transfer value	1.25	1.29

Source:　FAO Mozambique (2007b, 2007c)

certified seeds to reach poor and remote rural areas, owing to low purchasing power and high transport costs. This seed market failure means
that seeds for purchase are typically unavailable in drought and flood-prone
areas after disaster has occurred. By guaranteeing a market of a predictable
size at a stated date and location, and by widely informing seed distributors
and other input vendors of each event, ITFs create the conditions for such
input market failures to be overcome in the short term. However, ITFs also
hope to stimulate rural markets in the longer term by demonstrating
to traders that there is enough rural demand to justify holding markets
regularly in rural areas.

Monitoring of the use to which coupons are put in a range of ITFs
reveals that in practice farmers are often more interested in implements
than in seeds or fertilizers, with hoes and machetes being priority items for
purchase. This preference for implements over seeds is more pronounced in
remote areas with poorly functioning markets. An explanation for this
could be that farmers in such locations are more accustomed to exchang-
ing seeds between themselves. For seeds, the preference is strongly in favour
of maize (around 90 per cent of cereal seed sales in ITFs).

ASSET BUILDING

ITFs can be considered as contributing to rural asset building at a number of
different levels. As just discussed, many poor farmers use their coupons to
purchase agricultural implements rather than seeds or fertilizer at the ITFs,
thus directly increasing their ownership of productive farm assets. It is possible also that ITFs can be seen as invigorating social networks through the

intense social interaction that occurs at the fairs (social capital). At a different level ITFs are thought to contribute to capacity building in agricultural administration and services at district and provincial levels in Mozambique.

STRENGTHS

The ITF schemes in Mozambique have displayed particular strengths that are worth highlighting:

i.   The transfer of coupons rather than a physical input package gives beneficiaries choice about which inputs to purchase, according to their own priorities.
ii. Input sales at ITFs in Mozambique appear to exceed the value of the vouchers distributed to beneficiaries, suggesting that the ITFs have a stimulating effect on trade and inputs beyond that attributed to the voucher transfers themselves.
iii. As emphasized in much of their internal documentation, the ITFs themselves are social gatherings that are attended not just by beneficiaries, and they enable other worthwhile social goals to be pursued at the same time, such as dissemination of information on HIV and AIDS in local communities.
iv. The coordination achieved between FAO, the Ministry of Agriculture, provincial and district public agricultural institutions, and community leaders can be considered as a positive strength of the ITFs.
v.   So too are the adoption and formal inclusion of ITFs within the MINAG strategic approach to supporting vulnerable farm families in the event of disasters such as droughts and floods.

WEAKNESSES

ITFs in Mozambique also, however, reveal some downsides to this approach to social transfers. Some of these weaknesses are unique to the ITF approach, while others are common across many different types of social transfers that try to isolate beneficiaries using complex proxy indicators for vulnerability:

i.   Where farm inputs are the social transfer focus, timing is critical: any slippage in organization or delivery means that inputs reach farmers too late to make a valuable contribution to the next season's crop, and this has occurred with some of the ITFs in Mozambique.

ii. Lack of continuity or repetition in locations and venues: certainly so far, ITF policy in Mozambique has been never to repeat a fair in the same place. While there seem to be good enough reasons for this, such as selecting the most vulnerable places (which differ from season to season) and ensuring as wide as possible participation in at least one ITF by potential beneficiaries, the downside is that no cumulative momentum is provided for rural market development, and the sustainability of market effects is therefore compromised.

iii. While not fully empirically substantiated, interviews in ITF communities suggest that inclusion and exclusion errors have been prevalent in ITFs, as they are indeed in most schemes that rely on the fulfilment of complex qualitative criteria for the selection of beneficiaries.

iv. It is probable that ITFs are a fairly costly way of delivering a certain type and level of transfer to vulnerable rural beneficiaries, owing to the high gearing up costs around a series of one-off large events, the logistical costs of holding such events in remote rural areas, and the time and effort required to inform and persuade seed distributors and traders to turn up for the fairs.

v. Little if any downstream monitoring had occurred at ITF sites up to 2007, so no reliable information was available concerning the true incremental impact on the farm outputs of beneficiaries from their participation in the fairs, although this problem was being addressed by FAO with the introduction of a new monitoring and evaluation instrument for ITFs in Mozambique and Swaziland.

POLICY LESSONS

ITFs set out to provide a bridge between effective emergency response towards people in crisis (in this instance poor farmers who have lost their ability to plant for the next season) and the promotion of livelihoods (by creating access to inputs that can ensure future success in agricultural production). A subsidiary objective is to stimulate rural markets, therefore creating the conditions for more cash transactions and greater economic dynamism in rural areas. There are tensions between these different objectives, manifested in particular by insufficient continuity to make much difference to livelihood or market promotion in the medium and long term, while the short run impact on next season's crop for beneficiary farm households is unmeasured and therefore unknown.

A questioning stance on ITFs does not mean that they are unsuccessful at what they achieve on the day of the fair, which is to support vulnerable farmers to rebuild agricultural production, give beneficiaries choice over the input items they think are most important for them to do this, create a large social event with widespread participation by surrounding communities, and stimulate rural trade and exchange on the day. However, the extreme brevity of the transfer process (one day), its once-only support to any individual recipient (one coupon) and its 'nomadic' character (ITFs pop up in different places in successive seasons) all add up to a social transfer that is somewhat fragmented and in all probability lacks cumulative or sustained impact. It is also possible that this is a relatively high cost way of dealing with persistent vulnerability and the humanitarian crises to which it gives rise.

Case Study 14. Chiefs' Fields for orphans and vulnerable children, Swaziland

OVERVIEW

The CFs originated in 2004 as an initiative of the Swaziland National Emergency Response Council on HIV and AIDS (NERCHA). The initiative is called *indlunkhulu* in Swazi, meaning 'the big house' (a reference to the traditional socially inclusive responsibilities of local chiefs towards their subjects). The initiative sought to revive an ancient tradition by which local chiefs set aside fields to provide for destitute members of their communities, or those unable because of illness, accident or old age to cultivate fields for themselves. In the context of orphans and vulnerable children (OVC), the intention was to find a long term solution to their food security, since there had hitherto been a heavy reliance on feeding programmes involving external agencies like WFP to provide this.

The CFs initiative is overseen by NERCHA. At the local level decisions are made by an *indlunkhulu* committee, established in each participating community, and comprising representatives of community institutions, chiefdom officials and local civil servants. NERCHA partnered with the Ministry of Agriculture and Cooperatives (MOAC) to act as the implementing agency providing tractor services, and procuring seeds and fertilizers from private sector suppliers and delivering these to project sites. The *indlunkhulu* committee allocates the inputs between beneficiaries. MOAC also trains beneficiaries in grain store construction to minimize post-harvest losses to rodents and pests.

Chiefs' Fields consist of a single 3-hectare community farm, made available in each of Swaziland's 360 chiefdoms. In addition, a subsidiary project funded by the Japanese aid agency JICA allocates 0.5-hectare plots in 320 chiefdoms to be farmed individually by child-headed households. JICA committed external resources amounting to E24 million (US$3.4 million) to this child-headed household project for three years from 2004 to 2007. The JICA sub-project conforms with CFs in the roles played by NERCHA, MOAC and the *indlunkhulu* committees.

However, in one important respect the JICA sub-project has a different agenda to the main CFs initiative. This is to protect the land rights of child-headed households, ensuring them a long term future stake in farming as an occupation, an option that might otherwise be denied them owing to their status as minors at the time of the death of their parents. Under a Swazi custom known as *kukhonta*, unutilized land can be reallocated by the chief or claimed by new settlers arriving in a community, and it was found that many AIDS orphans and other vulnerable children were losing their hereditary claim to their families' own land owing to this custom. The child-headed household scheme seeks to reinstate the sense of land entitlement for such OVC, and to provide them with the skills and experience to enable them to pursue farming as a career. In this way, also, the rural social structure based on family farming is intended to be protected to some degree from disintegration caused by the demographic effects of AIDS-related mortality.

VULNERABILITY

The underlying dimensions of childhood vulnerability arising from AIDS mortality in Swaziland are set out in Case Study 9 on Neighbourhood Care Points (NCPs). To repeat the key data from there, the 2006 National Plan of Action (NPA) report estimated the total number of OVC in the country at 132 000, representing 25 per cent of all children aged 0–18, and 12 per cent of the total population of 1.1 million (Swaziland, 2006).

The vulnerability addressed by CFs is lack of access by OVC to reliable sources of food. In the early 2000s, there was heavy reliance on WFP to supply ingredients for OVC feeding at NCPs and schools. Some policy documents argued that this reliance was justifiable, and that the role of WFP should if anything be extended in order to ensure nationwide access of OVC to regular and nutritious meals, whether in the community or in school. However, the CFs initiative takes the viewpoint that Swaziland needed to develop a long term and sustainable food supply response of its own to overcome OVC food insecurity, in the process reinvigorating customary collective responsibility towards those in need in local communities and providing OVC with farming skills that would serve them in the future.

TARGETING

The criteria defining OVC in Swaziland are set out in Case Study 9. Compiling a list of individuals and families to benefit from CFs according to these criteria is the task of the *indlunkhulu* committee in each chiefdom. Evidence from key informants at field sites suggested that the criteria leave fairly wide scope for local differences of interpretation, especially with regard to the vulnerability aspect of the OVC definition. While the vulnerable situation of the elderly looking after young children is understood, other causes of OVC vulnerability such as disability may be overlooked by the *indlunkhulu* committee. This may be because disabled children are considered unable to participate in farming; however, this also means that their food needs may be inadequately acknowledged, especially if CFs production is meant eventually to replace community or school feeding arrangements.

The concept of a child-headed household is a sub-set of the overall OVC definition; however, it is a difficult one to pin down precisely. It rarely means that a child is literally running a multi-person household, although this can occur with older OVC in their mid- to late teens. More commonly, it means that the child even though a minor is regarded by the community as the successor 'head' to the household head who has died, even though that child and his or her siblings are most likely living with one or more grandparents, aunts, uncles, cousins or more remote adult relatives. The term 'child-headed household' therefore recognizes a future condition that would have occurred if the child's parents had lived a normal lifespan and the child in due course would have become the household head. Child-headed households can be quite large, perhaps five to seven people, and comprise the orphaned or abandoned siblings of the 'household head' as well as the adult relatives who have some sort of caring or guardian relationship to them.

COVERAGE

In 2004, the government issued an instruction that each of the country's 360 chiefs should set aside land for *indlunkhulu* fields, and should oversee the planting, cultivation and harvesting of food crops for OVC. By the beginning of 2007, some 339 chiefdoms had complied with this instruction, through provision of 3-hectare collective fields as well as the 0.5-hectare individual plots for the JICA-funded child-headed households scheme, which covered 320 chiefdoms.

Coverage in this context must consider the food security contribution of these initiatives as well as their land allocations. In early 2007, there were 81 253 OVC registered as participants in CFs, implying 274 OVC per participating chiefdom supposedly sharing the output of a 3-hectare plot. This suggests that the collective fields could only minimally cover the annual food needs of their OVC participants.

The JICA-funded scheme involves 26 individual 0.5-hectare plots being made available per chiefdom, implying coverage of 8320 households overall. On the assumption that there are perhaps three OVC per child-headed household, this would mean that around 25 000 OVC could eventually be reached overall by the scheme, that is, about 20 per cent of all OVC. However, this is admittedly a very crude estimate. Also relevant is that vulnerable adults in the same households could benefit from the scheme, if the farms are successful at producing their intended outputs.

In 2005, the area planted under the different crops for OVC child-headed households was 219.5 hectares of maize and 5.7 hectares of legumes (beans or cowpeas) across all four regions. While available information for 2006 suggested a possible small increase in this, these areas are substantially below the 4160 hectares of cultivation envisaged in overall scheme design.

COORDINATION

The CFs initiative appears not to be coordinated by the 2006 NPA, since it is neither mentioned nor budgeted for in the plan document. Rather NERCHA has an overseeing role and MOAC is the main implementing agency. However, successful implementation also requires MOAC to line up with decisions made by chiefs (on land allocations), *indlunkhulu* committees (on beneficiaries), and community members for logistical support and labour inputs. Moreover, there is a meso-level, comprising the regional administrations, which are supposed to have intermediary roles in overseeing implementation. This adds up to a multi-layered array of stakeholders, and unsurprisingly results in varying success in scheme management in different localities.

With respect to the JICA-funded individual farms, key informant interviews suggest serious lack of coordination between this scheme and other OVC initiatives such as NCPs, backyard gardens, school farms and so on. This has detrimental effects on the prospects for scheme success. The key problem is the disconnection between delivering inputs and preparing beneficiaries for farming. Inputs are delivered (often late), but the 'child heads' and their families are unprepared for the tasks and teamwork involved, and may even include small children under 10 who have no idea how to start such an endeavour.

This problem is exacerbated by beneficiary selection practices that do not ascertain whether would-be beneficiaries have any interest in farming or access to the requisite able-bodied labour or skills to go about cultivation activities. A farm may be allocated, for example, to a household containing four OVC under 8 years old and two elderly and infirm grandparents, none of whom are able to engage in farming tasks with any degree of competence.

A side-effect of this failure to match the technology profile of the scheme (the farm inputs) to the social and demographic profile of the beneficiaries is that the inputs delivered go astray. They are understandably commandeered by other farmers if left unattended or unutilized for any period of time after delivery. This may mean plots remain idle, or are only partially planted with the few seeds that remain available after others have helped themselves. The resulting crop outputs are negligible relative to the intended outcomes of the scheme.

COST-EFFECTIVENESS

No evidence is available on the cost-effectiveness of CFs. Fragmentary evidence indicates that their yields have been disappointingly low, owing to rainfall failures, insufficient inputs, late delivery of inputs and low levels of community participation (Hlanze, 2007). Moreover, even if their yields attained local norms, their 3-hectare size means that their output levels could at best make a minor contribution to the annual food needs of participating OVC.

In the case of the JICA-funded individual farms, the overall budget per beneficiary household was E2900 (US$409). On the face of it, this seems unusually high for providing free farm inputs in very small amounts to act as a catalyst for the household's successful engagement in food production. Intended outputs consist of 20 times 70 kilograms of maize per farm, with an estimated output value of E2000, and three times 50 kilograms of pulses (for example, beans or cowpeas), with a projected value of E1200. Thus E2900 is put in for a proposed output worth E3200, implying a slim margin of E300 to represent the gains from engaging in productive activity over an agricultural season. These figures suggest that the food security of child-headed OVC households might be more effectively achieved by providing E2900 as a cash transfer. Project documents state that, if intended outputs were reached, they would feed a family of seven with staple food for a year. However, no evidence exists about actual outputs obtained from these plots, nor apparently are data collected that would permit this evidence to be compiled.

MARKET EFFECTS

The market effects of these initiatives are almost certainly trivial in terms of national aggregate levels of farm inputs and outputs. Providing free farm inputs to some farms, while most farmers must meet the full cost of such inputs, almost certainly results in leakages from the free input segment as a secondary market for the free supplies arises (or they are directly re-assigned).

ASSET BUILDING

The CFs initiative involves re-allocating existing assets (land), potentially building up the human capital of OVC (by providing them with agricultural skills), and protecting the household assets of vulnerable families (by reducing the necessity for such assets to be sold in order to buy food). In the case of the individual 0.5-hectare plots in the JICA-funded scheme, an explicit objective was to protect the land entitlement of child-headed households that otherwise would have been lost owing to their status as minors at the time of their parents' death, or their abandonment by one or both parents. In this sense the scheme seeks to support the continuity of rural social relations.

STRENGTHS

The CFs initiatives for ensuring the long term food security of orphans and vulnerable children in Swaziland appear to have some important strengths:

i.   The notion of CFs appeals to an ancient tradition whereby the chiefs used to provide land, and instructed their subjects to cultivate such land, for the benefit of the destitute and needy in their communities.

ii. While this old tradition had all but disappeared by the early 2000s, its reinvention in the form of collective (3-hectare) and individual (0.5-hectare) CFs is regarded in Swaziland as a positive project that could help to arrest other manifestations of the decline in community solidarity over time.

iii. The initiative seems to be supported strongly by the Swazi royal family, and to be reasonably well coordinated in principle between the various parties that are involved in its implementation, namely NERCHA, MOAC, the regional administrations and the chiefs.

iv. For the JICA-funded individual OVC farms, the erosion in social cohesion caused by the loss of customary land entitlement of children who become orphans through the premature death of their parents is properly acknowledged, and redress is sought.

WEAKNESSES

However, as a platform for ensuring the food security of expected rising OVC numbers in Swaziland, the CFs initiatives display certain fundamental flaws:

i. CFs are unable to guarantee security of food supply to OVC since they are just as prone as any other farms in Swaziland to the vagaries of climate, and will experience harvest failure at the same time as other farms.
ii. This problem of reliability is exacerbated by the experience to date of lower yields on the collective fields than on privately tilled farms, indicating in all probability that the collective fields are relatively neglected by community members in comparison to achieving the best they can on their own fields.
iii. With respect to the individual 0.5-hectare plots, a fundamental gap exists between the selection of beneficiaries (including their aptitude and preparedness for agricultural production) and the delivery of the free farm inputs (often rather late in the agricultural calendar).
iv. This gap means that inputs have often been delivered to beneficiaries at best unprepared for, and at worst totally disinterested in, taking up farming as an immediate occupation.
v. In part there is a demographic factor at work here, in that in the mid-2000s AIDS orphans have conformed to a demographic pyramid with small numbers of older children (perhaps capable of and interested in farming) at the top, and ever larger numbers of younger children (ever less capable of taking up agriculture) at the bottom.
vi. The CFs initiative lacks output and outcome monitoring and evaluation capability, with the consequence that beyond the delivery of inputs almost nothing is known at aggregate level about their relative success or failure at achieving intended results.

POLICY LESSONS

The National Plan of Action for OVC 2006–10 does not include the CFs initiative in its overall portfolio of policy responses. What the NPA does have is a portfolio of agriculture-related activities (NCP gardens, backyard gardens, school gardens) that come under its food budget, and that seem likely to conflict with both collective and individual CFs in terms of spreading community commitment too thinly across multiple separate initiatives.

CFs face a number of policy challenges. One is to ensure that the free inputs that are the basis of their productive potential are delivered in the correct quantities and on time for the beginning of the agricultural season. This is the responsibility of MOAC, and it is a difficult and costly task because neither the collective nor the individual CFs are big, and they are scattered across the landscape. However, the really major challenge of CFs is to secure genuine participation by community members and beneficiaries.

Attempts to reinvent discarded traditions often founder, not because the old tradition was faulty in its own context, but because objective circumstances have changed radically in the intervening period. CFs seem to be predicated on false expectations about the ability of people whose livelihoods are under stress to respond to additional burdens. It will not be surprising, therefore, if they turn out to make considerably less contribution to the food security of OVC in Swaziland than their champions currently envisage.

The JICA-funded individual farm scheme has the additional substantive policy objective of protecting the land entitlement of AIDS and other orphans. However, the conflation of this objective with the food security and community farming aspects of CFs invites the question whether the same aim could have been met through a different policy vehicle. In effect, if the food security aims of CFs fail, so too will the restitution of land entitlements to OVC, thus also failing to reverse or ameliorate their social exclusion in rural Swaziland.

Case Study 15.   Small Livestock Transfers, Zimbabwe

OVERVIEW

The Catholic Relief Services (CRS) Small Livestock Transfers project in Zimbabwe transfers livestock such as goats and chickens to vulnerable families in selected rural districts. The project is managed by CRS Zimbabwe through a partnership with the Organisation of Rural Associations for Progress (ORAP), a local NGO founded in 1981 that has built up a substantial track record of problem solving in local communities using participatory and inclusive approaches. ORAP in turn works through community-based organizations at the local level. The project comes under the umbrella of DFID Zimbabwe's Protracted Relief Programme (PRP). The purpose of PRP is to stabilize food security and protect the livelihoods of vulnerable households in Zimbabwe, particularly those affected by HIV/AIDS. PRP is implemented by 12 NGOs (of which CRS is one) and their local partners.

The first phase of PRP ran from 2004 to 2007, with an extension to 2008. A new phase was in the pipeline for 2008 onwards. In its first phase, the PRP reached about 1.5 million beneficiaries per year within an overall budget of £36 million sterling (US$72 million). It is a mainly rural-based relief and livelihoods improvement effort intended to support agricultural production through advice and inputs, as well as to provide clean water and to support destitute people and those living with HIV/AIDS. The Small Livestock Transfers project is just one among a range of agricultural support projects funded by the PRP, including several farm input delivery schemes.

The part of the CRS Small Livestock Transfers project reviewed here covers livestock transfers to two districts in Matabeleland called Hwange and Bubi Districts. The project began in October 2004, and these two districts were among the earliest to benefit from the transfers, from an intended eventual coverage of 22 districts. By the end of 2006, beneficiaries in the two districts had received 1634 goats, 10 pigs, 41 sheep, 3103 chickens, 5225 guinea fowl and 16 ducks (Dzingirai, 2007, p.12).

The CRS Small Livestock Transfers project utilizes a number of different mechanisms for transferring stock to vulnerable families and multiplying up the benefits of the scheme. It attempts to source livestock locally, or in closely adjacent districts, in order to minimize adaptation risks to local environments. In some cases livestock are transferred directly to beneficiaries, while in others beneficiaries are provided with a livestock purchase voucher that can be spent at a livestock fair organized by ORAP. These fairs are similar in intention and organization to the education and input fairs described in Case Studies 10 and 13. The transfer process does not, however, stop at the first round acquisition of livestock by beneficiaries. The first recipients are required to 'pass on' a proportion of the successful multiplication up of animals or birds to other beneficiaries on the list, thus ensuring that the final number of beneficiaries is some multiple of the number of original recipients.

VULNERABILITY

The broad features of rising vulnerability to hunger in Zimbabwe are outlined in Case Study 6. The Small Livestock Transfers project recognizes the critical role that livestock plays in ensuring livelihood security for poor rural people, especially in semi-arid areas and places with large annual fluctuations in rainfall. Livestock are a direct source of consumption, a store of wealth (a 'walking bank'), and an asset that can be sold quickly at times of dire necessity. The districts targeted by the project are places where serious livestock depletion had occurred, owing to natural disasters and animal diseases.

TARGETING

In Hwange and Bubi Districts, the Small Livestock Transfers project aimed to target the most vulnerable families, defined especially by widowhood from AIDS deaths and destitute families caring for small children or orphans. As specified by ORAP in 2004, its interest was in *umunthu uyadubeka*, meaning any person struggling to survive. Typically these are people 'without means of support', or those without cattle or goats.

Traditional leaders, especially village heads, participated in the compilation of beneficiary lists, with ORAP playing a verification role. It seems that targeting may have been reasonably accurate, since, as of late 2006, 65 per cent of beneficiaries were widows or families caring for orphans. Apart from women and vulnerable children, the project sought to include others struggling to survive, including the sick, caregivers to the chronically sick, the elderly, those with no remittances, and those with large families and high dependency ratios.

As occurs in many such projects, 'elite capture' was an ever present pressure in the beneficiary selection procedure. ORAP reported several cases where beneficiaries were de-registered when it was discovered that they were from the wealthiest families in the community. This included several cases where village headmen inserted their names into beneficiary lists. This problem applied also to prioritization within the list, once the list had been compiled to the satisfaction of ORAP. Thus relatives or friends of more powerful individuals in villages tended to rise to the top of the list in terms of being the first to receive livestock transfers (or vouchers to spend at livestock fairs), while 'pass-on' rules were sometimes found to have been flouted such that livestock that were passed on went to these better off individuals.

Also present in the Small Livestock Transfers project was a social envy dimension, observed also in other social transfer case studies. This arises from the perception often articulated by villagers themselves that 'we are all poor here', and therefore community members find it difficult to accept that some need assistance more than others. In some beneficiary villages, conflict emerged between the included and the excluded from the project, and, at one livestock fair in Hwange District, fights apparently broke out between these groups (Dzingirai, 2007, p.12).

COVERAGE

It is difficult to gauge the coverage of the CRS Small Livestock Transfers project from information obtained from just two beneficiary districts. According to data contained in Dzingirai (2007, pp. 8–9), in 2004 and 2005 combined there were 1187 beneficiaries in Bubi District and 1310 in Hwange District. These beneficiaries were spread across 17 wards in the two districts, implying around 150 recipients on average in each ward, and a good geographical spread in the outreach of the project. Each recipient typically received two to three stock, consisting perhaps of a goat and two chickens, or a goat and two guinea fowl.

The success of the scheme rests heavily on the continued good health of the livestock delivered, and also on successful breeding from the initial transfer in order to multiply up animal or bird numbers. Evidence from field sites suggests mixed success in this regard. Unfortunately no data are available on pass-on rates at project sites, suggesting perhaps a monitoring weakness at that level. On the other hand, individual examples were found of successful multiplication up of chickens and goats, resulting in cumulative strengthening of livelihoods from the initial transfer.

While some respondents reported wholly positive experiences from being included in the scheme, others had different stories to tell. Most of these in one way or another concerned the adverse impacts of animal diseases, especially Newcastle disease in chickens and various tick-borne diseases in goats and sheep. Some respondents had simply lost their initial stake quite quickly to disease. Others reported having to sell other assets in order to pay for vaccines for their newly acquired stock, resulting in little net gain in their overall livelihood position. Still others reported the loss of help that they used to receive from better off relatives in the community, owing to being included in the scheme.

COORDINATION

As far as can be ascertained from available documentation, coordination of this project worked well in terms of the partnerships between the DFID PRP, CRS and ORAP. Monthly reports published on the PRP website show that CRS has an excellent reporting record to the PRP, as well as in balancing its books on the projects for which it is funded. Less is known about the success of the collaboration between CRS and ORAP. However, both organizations have substantial experience in the areas in which they work, and both have multiple project portfolios under their management.

In Zimbabwe, there is inevitably considerable ambiguity in the relationship between projects like the Small Livestock Transfers scheme and the Government of Zimbabwe at different levels, down to the district. While the umbrella PRP programme undertakes quite a few initiatives in collaboration with government agencies, the bulk of its projects are handled by international and local NGOs outside government. This can, of course, result in government agencies at local level perceiving that they have been bypassed by projects, resulting in an unwillingness to lend support that they could provide. In the case of the Small Livestock Transfers scheme, several key informants stated that this was so in the relationship of the project to the district veterinary services, which did not make themselves available to help with vaccination or disease control.

COST-EFFECTIVENESS

The October 2006 output to purpose review of the PRP (Jones *et al.*, 2006) noted that, with multiple NGO implementing partners each involved in several PRP activities, budget and cost information disaggregated by activity was often lacking. This applies in the case of CRS, which has been involved in several different activities alongside – and to some extent integrated with – its small livestock scheme, and to PRP livestock activities in general, which have been implemented by several of the NGOs. The review also noted the paucity of data collected during implementation that might be used to assess impacts of individual activities.

However, a subsequent PRP cost–benefit study (Woolcock & Mutiro, 2007) attempted to gather additional information from the implementing partners to fill this gap. For small livestock interventions, factoring in DFID and household investment costs, and likely pass-on rates, milk and egg production, offtake and disease-related losses and herd/flock reproduction over a 25-year horizon, the projected benefit–cost ratio was estimated at an impressive 8.4. For all the PRP activities for which such benefit–cost ratios could be calculated, this was one of the highest. Furthermore, the study supported the conclusion that such interventions also have a high potential 'relief-effectiveness' on account of their ready adaptability to the situation of poor and vulnerable households.

MARKET EFFECTS

The CRS Small Livestock Transfers scheme has several potentially important and positive relationships with markets at local levels. First, the scheme attempts wherever possible to source the livestock required for its transfers in the same or closely adjacent districts. This helps to support local livestock prices, and expands the sale opportunities of small livestock in those places. Second, successful multiplication up from the initial transfer results in sale of stock for a variety of purposes, thus again expanding the size of the market for that stock in the local economy. Third, possession of livestock assets can to some degree insulate families from the ravages of hyperinflation, since livestock values are likely to keep pace with the rate of inflation, except in rare cases (such as widespread enforced sales because of drought). Fourth, the holding of fairs is often argued to stimulate local exchange going beyond the value of the vouchers exchanged by beneficiaries at each fair. This is because numerous buyers and sellers take advantage of the holding of the fair to turn up at that venue.

ASSET BUILDING

The Small Livestock Transfers scheme is consciously and deliberately about building livelihood assets. The multiple roles of livestock in successful rural livelihoods in sub-Saharan Africa are well known, and have been empirically verified in numerous studies. Livestock can provide the key to the successful construction of pathways out of poverty, and a moderate to high level of livestock ownership confers resilience in the face of livelihood shocks.

STRENGTHS

The Small Livestock Transfers scheme displays some important strengths as a means of building the assets of the most vulnerable, providing them with resilience in the face of risks, and also giving them the potential for accumulation and better livelihoods in the future:

    i. The project identifies an important niche amongst different ways of supporting vulnerable rural families through social transfers.

    ii. The project targets geographical zones in Zimbabwe where depletion of livestock holdings due to drought and disease has been severe.

    iii. The project incorporates some innovative ideas, including the concept of 'pass-on' in order to expand the number of final beneficiaries that can be reached with a given budget, and also the use of livestock fairs to stimulate local markets in small livestock and other goods and services (for example, livestock medicines and veterinary services).

    iv. As far as can be ascertained, the project is well coordinated between funding agency (DFID PRP programme), implementing agency (CRS) and partnership organization (ORAP).

    v. The activity on which the project focuses appears to have the potential for high returns to investment.

WEAKNESSES

The Small Livestock Transfers project is also found to possess some weaknesses, as seen from interviews with key informants and beneficiaries at delivery locations:

    i. Livestock delivery is perhaps a comparatively high risk form of social transfer: this is because owning and successfully breeding livestock require water, adequate grazing (for goats and sheep), vaccination against common and preventable diseases (like Newcastle disease in chickens), and skills in animal or bird husbandry.

    ii. Where these preconditions are not met, relatively high rates of loss in the initial transfers may occur, with disease losses being the most likely reason for scheme failure in individual cases.

    iii. As occurs in many social protection projects of this kind, the monitoring of delivery seems to have been considerably stronger than the monitoring of outcomes, so it is not possible to ascertain scheme success (in terms of the pass-on component, and the multiplication up of stock through breeding) with any degree of accuracy.

iv. As also occurs in many social protection projects in places character-ized by widespread poverty and vulnerability, the Small Livestock Transfers project may have caused social friction owing to the percep-tion of non-beneficiaries that they were as deserving of support as the beneficiaries.

POLICY LESSONS

The CRS Small Livestock Transfers project is one among a substantial portfolio of projects that seeks to address the worsening circumstances of vulnerable people in the unstable economic and political environment of Zimbabwe. It has the advantage of delivering tangible assets, the values of which are likely to keep pace with the rate of inflation, and indeed success-ful breeding and multiplying up of small livestock can potentially enable families to accumulate even in the face of such disadvantageous economic circumstances.

Very little is known more generally about the true success rates of live-stock transfer projects in Africa. Over the years, there have been many such projects across the continent, sometimes specializing in exotic species (for example, exotic goat projects) and sometimes delivering local animals or birds that should already be well adapted to their environments. However, evidence that these have resulted in sustained rises in livestock ownership by beneficiaries is seriously lacking. Unfortunately, and despite a high pro-jected rate of return on investment, the CRS Small Livestock Transfers project in Zimbabwe is no different in this regard, and therefore we do not know, say three years later, the success rate amongst direct transferees in keeping their livestock alive, nor the number and type of pass-ons achieved by the project, nor the addition to overall livestock numbers that have resulted from the project. The chief lesson here, then, is that, for a project of this type that depends on asset accumulation in order to be counted a success, outcomes need to be monitored well beyond the season or year of original transfer delivery and preferably for several subsequent years.

References

Abdulai, A., C.B. Barrett and J. Hoddinott (2005), 'Does Food Aid *Really* Have Disincentive Effects? New Evidence from Sub-Saharan Africa', *World Development*, Vol.33, No.10, pp. 1689–1704.

Barnett, T., A. Whiteside and C. Desmond (2001), 'The Social and Economic Impact of HIV/AIDS in Poor Countries: A Review of Studies and Lessons', *Progress in Development Studies*, Vol.1, No.2, pp. 151–170.

Barrett, C.B. and B.M. Swallow (2005), 'Dynamic Poverty Traps and Rural Livelihoods', Ch.2 in F. Ellis and H.A. Freeman (eds), *Rural Livelihoods and Poverty Reduction Policies*, London: Routledge, pp. 16–28.

Bergeron, G. and J.M. Del Rosso (2001), *Food for Education Indicator Guide*, Washington, DC: Academy for Educational Development.

Britto, T. (2008), 'The Emergence and Popularity of Conditional Cash Transfers in Latin America', Ch.9 in A. Barrientos and D. Hulme (eds), *Social Protection for the Poor and Poorest: Concepts, Policies and Politics*, London: Palgrave Macmillan.

CARE Zambia (2007), *Social Cash Transfer Semi-Annual Report, October 2006 to March 2007*, Lusaka, Zambia: CARE.

Carter, M.R. and C.B. Barrett (2006), 'The Economics of Poverty Traps and Persistent Poverty: An Asset-Based Approach', *Journal of Development Studies*, Vol.42, No.2, pp. 178–199.

Carter, M.R. and C.B. Barrett (2007), 'Asset Thresholds and Social Protection: A "Think-Piece"', *IDS Bulletin*, Vol.38, No.3, pp. 34–38.

Carter, M.R., P. Little, T. Mogues and W. Negatu (2008), 'Poverty Traps and Natural Disasters in Ethiopia and Honduras', Ch.5 in A. Barrientos and D. Hulme (eds), *Social Protection for the Poor and Poorest: Concepts, Policies and Politics*, London: Palgrave Macmillan.

Chaka, N., L. Ranko, M. Sebatane and M. Matsoai (2007), 'Impact and Effectiveness of School Feeding Programme on Hunger and Vulnerability in Lesotho', Report prepared for the Regional Evidence Building Agenda (REBA) of the Regional Hunger and Vulnerability Programme (RHVP), May.

Chambers, R. (1989), 'Editorial Introduction: Vulnerability, Coping and Policy', *IDS Bulletin*, Vol.20, No.2, pp. 1–7.

Chambers, R., R. Longhurst and A. Pacey (eds) (1981), *Seasonal Dimensions to Rural Poverty*, London: Frances Pinter.

Chapoto, A. and T.S. Jayne (2005), 'Impact of HIV/AIDS-Related Mortality on Rural Farm Households in Zambia: Implications for Poverty Reduction Strategies', Paper presented at the IUSSP Seminar on 'Interactions between Poverty and HIV/AIDS', Cape Town, South Africa, December, document available at: http://www.aec.msu.edu/agecon/fs 2/zambia/.

Chirwa, E.W. (2007), 'Targeting and Exclusion Experiences in Public Works Programmes in Malawi', Report prepared for the Regional Evidence Building Agenda (REBA) of the Regional Hunger and Vulnerability Programme (RHVP), April.

Cliffe, L. (2006), 'Politics and the Feasibility of Initiatives on Hunger and Vulnerability', Regional Hunger and Vulnerability Programme (RHVP), document available at: www.wahenga.net/uploads/documents/reports/Politics_HV_Aug 2006.pdf.

Coady, D., M. Grosh and J. Hoddinott (2002), 'Targeting Outcomes, Redux', *Safety Nets Primer,* Washington, DC: World Bank.

Conway, T. and A. Norton (2002), 'Nets, Ropes, Ladders and Trampolines: The Place of Social Protection within Current Debates on Poverty Reduction', *Development Policy Review*, Vol.20, No.5, pp. 533–540.

Corbett, J. (1988), 'Famine and Household Coping Strategies', *World Development*, Vol.16, No.9, pp. 1099–1112.

Croome, D. and A. Nyanguru (2007), 'The Impact of the Old Age Pension on Hunger and Vulnerability in a Mountain Area of Lesotho', Report prepared for the Regional Evidence Building Agenda (REBA) of the Regional Hunger and Vulnerability Programme (RHVP).

Croome, D., M. Letsie and M. Nteso (2007), 'Asset Protection, Asset Building and Hunger Vulnerability in Lesotho', Report prepared for the Regional Evidence Building Agenda (REBA) of the Regional Hunger and Vulnerability Programme (RHVP).

Davies, M., B. Guenther, J. Leavy, T. Mitchell and T. Tanner (2008), *Climate Change Adaptation, Disaster Risk Reduction and Social Protection: Complementary Roles in Agriculture and Rural Growth?*, Brighton: Centre for Social Protection and Climate Change and Disasters Group, Institute of Development Studies, April.

Davies, S. (2007), *Making the Most of It: A Regional Multiplier Approach to Estimating the Impact of Cash Transfers on the Market*, Lilongwe: Concern Worldwide, May.

Del Rosso, J. (1999), *School Feeding Programs: Improving Effectiveness and Increasing the Benefit to Education. A Guide for Program Managers*, Imperial College, London: Partnership for Child Development.

Dercon, S. (2002), 'Income Risk, Coping Strategies, and Safety Nets', *The World Bank Research Observer*, Vol.17, No.2, pp. 141–166.

Dercon, S. (ed.) (2005), *Insurance against Poverty*, UNU-WIDER Studies in Development Economics, Oxford: Oxford University Press.

Devereux, S. (2002), 'Can Social Safety Nets Reduce Chronic Poverty?', *Development Policy Review*, Vol.20, No.5, November, pp. 657–675.

Devereux, S. (2006), 'The Impact of Droughts and Floods on Food Security and Policy Options to Alleviate Negative Effects', Paper presented at the International Association of Agricultural Economists (IAAE) Conference, Queensland, Australia, 12–18 August.

Devereux, S. (2007), 'Lessons from Ethiopia on a Scaled-Up National Safety Net Programme', *Wahenga Brief*, No.14, August, document available at: www.wahenga.net.

Devereux, S. and S. Coll-Black (2007), 'Review of Evidence and Evidence Gaps on the Effectiveness and Impacts of DFID-supported Pilot Social Transfer Schemes', Department for International Development Evaluation Working Paper/ Evaluation Report A1/A3, October.

Devereux, S. and R. Sabates-Wheeler (2004), *Transformative Social Protection*, IDS Working Paper No.232, Brighton: Institute of Development Studies.

Devereux, S. and R. Sabates-Wheeler (2007), 'Editorial Introduction: Debating Social Protection', *IDS Bulletin*, Vol.38, No.3, pp. 1–7.

Devereux, S., P. Mvula and C. Solomon (2006a), *After the FACT: An Evaluation of Concern Worldwide's Food and Cash Transfers Project in Three Districts of Malawi, 2006*, Concern Worldwide Malawi, June, document available at: http://www.concern.net/documents/324/fact_external_evaluation_report.pdf.

Devereux, S., B. Baulch, I. Macauslan, A. Phiri and R. Sabates-Wheeler (2006b), *Vulnerability and Social Protection in Malawi*, IDS Discussion Paper No.387, Brighton: Institute of Development Studies, October.

Devereux, S., C. Mthinda, F. Power, P. Sakala and A. Suka (2007), *Smart Cards for Smart Women: An Evaluation of Concern Worldwide's Dowa Emergency Cash Transfer Project (DECT) in Malawi, 2006/07*, Brighton: Institute of Development Studies, July.

de Waal, A. and A. Whiteside (2003), '"New Variant Famine": AIDS and Food Crisis in Southern Africa', *The Lancet*, No.362, pp. 1234–1237.

DFID Kenya (2007a), 'The Hunger Safety Net Programme', unpublished briefing note.

DFID Kenya (2007b), 'SOS Brief – Social Protection', unpublished briefing note.

DFID Kenya (2007c), 'Reducing Extreme Poverty, Vulnerability and Hunger in Kenya: Developing a National Social Protection Framework – Frequently Asked Questions', unpublished briefing note.

Dlamini, S. (2007), 'Neighbourhood Care Points in Swaziland: A Case Study', Report prepared for the Regional Evidence Building Agenda (REBA) of the Regional Hunger and Vulnerability Programme (RHVP), March.

Dorward, A., E. Chirwa, V. Kelly, T. Jayne, R. Slater and D. Boughton (2008), *Evaluation of the 2006/7 Agricultural Input Supply Programme, Malawi: Final Report*, Ministry of Agriculture and Food Security, Lilongwe, March, document available at: www.future-agricultures.org/pdf%20files/MalawiAISPFinalReport31March.pdf.

Dzingirai, V. (2007), 'Lessons from CRS's Small Livestock Programme', Report prepared for the Regional Evidence Building Agenda (REBA) of the Regional Hunger and Vulnerability Programme (RHVP).

Ellis, F. (2006a), 'Review Paper on Community Coping, Vulnerability and Social Protection', Regional Hunger and Vulnerability Programme (RHVP), February, document available at: www.wahenga.net/uploads/documents/reports/Review_paper_on_SP_060329.pdf.

Ellis, F. (2006b), 'Vulnerability and Coping', in D. Clarke (ed.), *The Elgar Companion to Development Studies*, Cheltenham, UK and Northampton, MA, USA : Edward Elgar, pp. 671–675.

Ellis, F. (2007a), 'REBA Case Study Brief Number 6: Old Age and Public Assistance Grants, Swaziland', Regional Hunger and Vulnerability Programme (RHVP), November, document available at: www.wahenga.net/index.php/evidence/case_study_briefs/.

Ellis, F. (2007b), 'REBA Case Study Brief Number 20: Rural Micro Finance, Zimbabwe', Regional Hunger and Vulnerability Programme (RHVP), November, document available at: www.wahenga.net/index.php/evidence/case_study_briefs/.

Ellis, F. (2008), '"We Are All Poor Here": Economic Difference, Social Divisiveness, and Targeting Cash Transfers in Sub-Saharan Africa', Paper prepared for the conference 'Social Protection for the Poorest in Africa: Learning from Experience', Kampala, Uganda, 8–10 September.

Ethiopia (2004), *Productive Safety Net Programme: Programme Implementation Manual*, Addis Ababa: Ministry of Agriculture and Rural Development, December.

FAO Mozambique (2007a), note entitled 'Input Trade Fairs FAO Mozambique', FAO, Maputo.

FAO Mozambique (2007b), *Emergency Relief and Rehabilitation Country Overview, March – April 2007*, Maputo: FAO.

FAO Mozambique (2007c), *Support to Small-Holding Farming Production through Agricultural Inputs Trade Fairs in Mozambique*, Report No. UTF/MOZ/071/MOZ, Maputo: FAO.

Farrington, J. and R. Slater (2006), 'Introduction: Cash Transfers: Panacea for Poverty Reduction or Money Down the Drain?', *Development Policy Review*, Vol.24, No.5, pp. 499–511.

FEWSNET (2006), 'Ethiopia: Food Security Update June 2006', pp. 2–4, briefing paper available at website www.fews.net.

Freeland, N. (2007), 'Superfluous, Pernicious, Atrocious and Abominable? The Case against Conditional Cash Transfers', *IDS Bulletin*, Vol.38, No.3, pp. 75–78.

Gentilini, U. (2007a), *Cash and Food Transfers: A Primer*, Rome: World Food Programme.

Gentilini, U. (2007b), 'Food Transfers and Food Insecurity', *IDS Bulletin*, Vol.38, No.3, pp. 82–86.

Ghana (2007), 'Livelihood Empowerment Against Poverty (LEAP) Social Grants Pilot Implementation Design', Final Draft Report, Ministry of Manpower, Youth and Employment, Accra, November.

Guhan, S. (1994), 'Social Security Options for Developing Countries', *International Labour Review*, Vol.133, No.1, pp.35–53.

Handa, S. and B. Davis (2006), 'The Experience of Conditional Cash Transfers in Latin America and the Caribbean', *Development Policy Review*, Vol.24, No.5, pp. 513–536.

Hlanze, Z. (2007), 'Chiefs' Fields (Indlunkhulu)', Report prepared for the Regional Evidence Building Agenda (REBA) of the Regional Hunger and Vulnerability Programme (RHVP), April.

Hoddinott, J. (2007), 'Social Protection: To Target or Not to Target', *IDS Bulletin*, Vol.38, No.3, pp. 90–94.

IDL Group (2007), *Building Consensus for Social Protection: Insights from Ethiopia's Productive Safety Nets Programme (PSNP)*, London: DFID.

Jayne, T.S., J. Govereh, Z. Xu, J. Ariga and E. Mghenyi (2006), 'Factors Affecting Small Farmers' Use of Improved Maize Technologies: Evidence from Kenya and Zambia', Paper presented at the Symposium on Seed-Fertilizer Technology, Cereal Productivity and Pro-Poor Growth in Africa: Time for New Thinking?, International Association of Agricultural Economics Tri-Annual Meetings, Gold Coast, Australia, 12–18 August.

Jones, S., P. Mataure, B. Mlalazi and S. Wiggins (2006), *Protracted Relief Programme Output to Purpose Review*, DFID Zimbabwe, October.

Kadzandira, J.M. (2007), 'REBA Case-Study on the Input Subsidy Program, Malawi', Report prepared for the Regional Evidence Building Agenda (REBA) of the Regional Hunger and Vulnerability Programme (RHVP), June.

Kenya National Bureau of Statistics (2007), *Basic Report on Well-Being in Kenya*, Nairobi: Ministry of Planning and National Development, April.

Lesotho (2007), *School Feeding Guidelines*, Maseru: Ministry of Education and Training, January.

McCord, A. (2008), 'The Social Protection Function of Short-Term Public Works Programmes in the Context of Chronic Poverty', Ch.8 in A. Barrientos and D. Hulme (eds), *Social Protection for the Poor and Poorest: Concepts, Policies and Politics*, London: Palgrave Macmillan.

Malawi (2007), 'A Framework of Principles and Guidelines for Social Protection in Malawi', Department of Poverty and Disaster Management Affairs, Ministry of Economic Planning and Development, April (unpublished).

Malawi, Government of (2005), *Integrated Household Survey 2004–05, Volume 1: Household Socio-economic Characteristics*, Zomba: National Statistics Office, October.

Malawi, Government of and World Bank (2006), *Malawi Poverty and Vulnerability Assessment: Investing in Our Future*, Washington, DC: World Bank, June.

Manjengwa, J. and B. Mukamuri (2007), 'Lessons from Action Aid International's Urban Food Programme', Report prepared for the Regional Evidence Building Agenda (REBA) of the Regional Hunger and Vulnerability Programme (RHVP), June.

Matin, I. and D. Hulme (2003), 'Programs for the Poorest: Learning from the IGVGD Program in Bangladesh', *World Development*, Vol.31, No.3, pp. 647–665.

Midgley, J. (1997), *Social Welfare in Global Context*, London: Sage.

Mkandawire, T. (2005), *Targeting and Universalism in Poverty Reduction*, Social Policy and Development Programme Paper No. 23, UNRISD, December, document available at: www.unrisd.org/80256B3C005 BCCF9/(httpPublications)/955FB8A594EEA0B0C12570FF00493EAA ?OpenDocument.

Mole, P. and N. Giva (2007), 'REBA Education Materials Fairs Case-Study, Mozambique', Report prepared for the Regional Evidence Building Agenda (REBA) of the Regional Hunger and Vulnerability Programme (RHVP), May.

Mole, P. and R. Vasco (2007), 'REBA Input Trade Fairs Case-Study, Mozambique', Report prepared for the Regional Evidence Building Agenda (REBA) of the Regional Hunger and Vulnerability Programme (RHVP), May.

Molyneux, M. (2007), 'Two Cheers for CCTs', *IDS Bulletin*, Vol.38, No.3, pp. 69–74.

Morduch, J. (1999), 'Between the Market and State: Can Informal Insurance Patch the Safety Net?', *World Bank Research Observer*, Vol.14, No.2, pp. 187–208.

Morduch, J. and M. Sharma (2002), 'Strengthening Public Safety Nets from the Bottom Up', *Development Policy Review*, Vol.20, No.5, pp. 569–588.

Mulumbi, M. (2007), 'Case Study on the Chipata and Kazungula Social Cash Transfer Schemes', Report prepared for the Regional Evidence Building Agenda (REBA) of the Regional Hunger and Vulnerability Programme (RHVP), July.

Munro, L. (2008), 'Risks, Needs and Rights: Compatible or Contradictory Bases for Social Protection?', Ch.2 in A. Barrientos and D. Hulme (eds), *Social Protection for the Poor and Poorest: Concepts, Policies and Politics*, London: Palgrave Macmillan.

Mvula, P.M. (2007), 'The Dowa Emergency Cash Transfer (DECT) Project: A Study of the Social Impacts', Report prepared for the Regional Evidence Building Agenda (REBA) of the Regional Hunger and Vulnerability Programme (RHVP), Zomba, May.

Norton, A., T. Conway and M. Foster (2002), 'Social Protection: Defining the Field of Action and Policy', *Development Policy Review*, Vol.20, No.5, pp. 541–567.

Rawlings, L. and G. Rubio (2005), 'Evaluating the Impact of Conditional Cash Transfer Programs', *World Bank Economic Observer*, Vol.20, No.1, pp. 29–55.

Renton, A. (2007), 'How America Is Betraying the Hungry Children of Africa', *The Observer*, 27 May, document available at: http://lifeand-health.guardian.co.uk/food/story/0,,2086467,00.html.

Sabates-Wheeler, R. and S. Devereux (2007), 'Social Protection for Transformation', *IDS Bulletin*, Vol.38, No.3, pp. 23–28.

Sabates-Wheeler, R. and S. Devereux (2008), 'Transformative Social Protection: The Currency of Social Justice', Ch.4 in A. Barrientos and D. Hulme (eds), *Social Protection for the Poor and Poorest: Concepts, Policies and Politics*, London: Palgrave Macmillan, pp. 64–84.

Sahn, D.E. (ed.) (1989), *Seasonal Variability in Third World Agriculture: The Consequences for Food Security*, Baltimore: Johns Hopkins University Press.

Samson, M. and K. Mac Quene (2006), *Approaches to Social Protection: An Evaluation of Donor-Supported and NGO-Implemented Social Protection Initiatives in Zimbabwe*, Cape Town: Economic Policy Research Institute.

Schubert, B. and J. Goldberg (2004), 'The Pilot Social Cash Transfer Scheme, Kalomo District – Zambia', Lusaka, December, document available at: www.socialcashtransfers-zambia.org.

Schubert, B. and M. Huijbregts (2006), 'The Malawi Social Cash Transfer Pilot Scheme: Preliminary Lessons Learned', Paper presented at a conference on 'Social Protection Initiatives for Children, Women and

Families: An Analysis of Recent Experiences', New York, 30–31 October, document available at: www.socialcashtransfers-malawi.org.

Scoones, I. (1998), *Sustainable Rural Livelihoods: A Framework for Analysis*, IDS Working Paper, No.72.

Sen, A.K. (1981), *Poverty and Famines: An Essay on Entitlements and Deprivation*, Oxford: Clarendon Press.

Sen, A. (1995), 'The Political Economy of Targeting', Ch.2 in D. van de Walle and K. Nead (eds), *Public Spending and the Poor*, Baltimore: Johns Hopkins University Press.

Sharp, K. (2001), 'An Overview of Targeting Approaches for Food-Assisted Programming', Paper prepared for CARE's PHLS Unit, Atlanta, Georgia: CARE.

Silaula, S.M. (2007), 'Food and Inputs for OVC Child-Headed Households as a Social Protection Intervention: A Case Study', Report prepared for the Regional Evidence Building Agenda (REBA) of the Regional Hunger and Vulnerability Programme (RHVP), April.

Slater, R. (2008), 'HIV/AIDS, Social Protection and Chronic Poverty', Ch.7 in A. Barrientos and D. Hulme (eds), *Social Protection for the Poor and Poorest: Concepts, Policies and Politics*, London: Palgrave Macmillan.

Slater, R. and B. Schubert (2006), 'Social Cash Transfers in Low-Income African Countries: Conditional or Unconditional?', *Development Policy Review*, Vol.24, No.5, pp. 571–578.

Sultan, S. and T.T. Schrofer (2008), 'Building Support to Have Targeted Social Protection Interventions for the Poorest: The Case of Ghana', Paper prepared for the conference 'Social Protection for the Poorest in Africa: Learning from Experience', Kampala, Uganda, 8–10 September.

Swaziland, Kingdom of (2006), *National Plan of Action for Orphans and Vulnerable Children 2006–2010*, Mbabane: Government of Swaziland.

Swaziland Vulnerability Assessment Committee (2006), *Swaziland National Vulnerability Assessment*, Mbabane: SwaziVAC, September.

Taimo, N.V. and R. Waterhouse (2007a), 'REBA Case-Study of the Food Subsidy Programme of the National Institute for Social Action (INAS)', Report prepared for the Regional Evidence Building Agenda (REBA) of the Regional Hunger and Vulnerability Programme (RHVP), June.

Taimo, N.V. and R. Waterhouse (2007b), 'REBA Case-Study of the WFP Food Assistance Programme for Care and Treatment of HIV/AIDS, Inhambane and Manhica', Report prepared for the Regional Evidence Building Agenda (REBA) of the Regional Hunger and Vulnerability Programme (RHVP), June.

Tembo, S. (2007), 'REBA Case Study on Food Security Packs Implemented by the Programme against Malnutrition', Report prepared for the Regional Evidence Building Agenda (REBA) of the Regional Hunger and Vulnerability Programme (RHVP), September.

UNAIDS (2006a), *2006 Report on the Global AIDS Epidemic: Annex 2 HIV and AIDS Estimates and Data, 2003 and 2005,* Geneva: UNAIDS.

UNAIDS (2006b), *Lesotho: Country Situation Analysis*, document available at: http://www.unaids.org/en/Regions_Countries/Countries/lesotho.asp.

UNAIDS (2007), *Swaziland: Country Situation Analysis*, document available at: http://www.unaids.org/en/Regions_Countries/Countries/swaziland.asp.

UNICEF Swaziland (2006), *Report on the Assessment of Neighbourhood Care Points*, Mbabane, Swaziland: UNICEF, October.

Waterhouse, R. (2007), 'Coordination and Coverage Module Paper: Mozambique', Report prepared for the Regional Evidence Building Agenda (REBA) of the Regional Hunger and Vulnerability Programme (RHVP), May.

White, P. and A. McCord (2006), 'Cost Comparison of Cash, Food and Agricultural Input Transfer Schemes in Malawi and Zambia', unpublished paper, DFID Policy Division (Equity and Rights Team), London, January, document available at: www.wahenga.net/uploads/documents/library/Transfer_Schemes_Malawi_Zambia_2006.pdf.

Woldehanna, T., J. Hoddinott, F. Ellis and S. Dercon (2008), *Ethiopia Dynamics of Growth and Poverty Reduction 1995/96–2004/05*, Addis Ababa: Development Planning and Research Department, Ministry of Finance and Economic Development, April.

Woolcock, R. and K. Mutiro (2007), *Cost-Benefit Analysis of PRP*, Report No.33, Harare: Protracted Relief Programme Technical Learning and Coordination Unit, June.

World Bank (2005), *Zambia Poverty and Vulnerability Assessment*, Washington, DC: World Bank, June, document available at: www.sarpn.org.za/documents/d0001457/index.php.

World Bank (2006), *Swaziland Public Expenditure Review: Strengthening Public Expenditure and Management for Service Delivery and Poverty Reduction*, Report No.35318-SW, Washington, DC: World Bank, August.

World Bank (2007), *World Development Report 2008: Agriculture for Development*, Washington, DC: World Bank.

World Food Programme (2003), *Development Project – Lesotho 10266.0*, Projects for Executive Board Approval, Rome: WFP, April.

World Food Programme (2006), *World Hunger Series 2006: Hunger and Learning*, Rome: WFP.

Zambia (2006), *The Pilot Social Cash Transfer Scheme – Kalomo District, Zambia: Summary Report*, 3rd edn, Lusaka: MCDSS/GTZ, January.

Zambia (2007), *The Pilot Social Cash Transfer Scheme Zambia, Summary Report*, 5th edn, Lusaka: MCDSS/GTZ, May.

Author Index

Abdulai, A. 18

Barnett, T. 7
Barrett, C.B. 7
Bergeron, G. 35
Britto, T. 17

Carter, M.R. 7
Chaka, N. 212
Chambers, R. 6, 28
Chapoto, A. 7
Chirwa, E.W. 171
Cliffe, L. 52
Coady, D. 52
Coll-Black, S. 136
Conway, T. 7
Corbett, J. 6
Croome, D. 120, 158

Davies, M. 19
Davies, S. 104, 184
Davis, B. 17
de Waal, A. 7
Del Rosso, J.M. 35
Dercon, S. 6, 7, 23
Devereux, S. 6, 7, 8, 23, 29, 32, 47, 104,
    108, 113, 132, 136
Dlamini, S. 219
Dorward, A. 33, 34, 94, 234, 237, 239,
    240
Dzingirai, V. 269, 271

Ellis, F. 7, 23, 28, 68, 91, 95, 111, 120,
    132

Farrington, J. 17, 57
Freeland, N. 17

Gentilini, U. 17, 58
Giva, N. 228, 230, 231
Goldberg, J. 27
Guhan, S. 7

Handa, S. 17
Hlanze, Z. 265
Hoddinott, J. 47
Huijbregts, M. 18, 28
Hulme, D. 18

Jayne, T.S. 7, 249
Jones, S. 272

Kadzandira, J.M. 239

Mac Quene, K. 200, 202
Manjengwa, J. 197, 201
Matin, I. 18
McCord, A. 5, 7, 93, 178, 249
Midgley, J. 4
Mkandawire, T. 96
Mole, P. 228, 230, 231, 256
Molyneux, M. 17
Morduch, J. 7, 8
Mukamuri, B. 197, 201
Mulumbi, M. 188
Munro, L. 8
Mutiro, K. 273
Mvula, P.M. 183

Norton, A. 7
Nyanguru, A. 158

Rawlings, L. 17
Renton, A. 105
Rubio, G. 17

Sabates-Wheeler, R. 7, 8
Sahn, D.E. 28
Samson, M. 200, 202
Schrofer, T.T. 83
Schubert, B. 17, 27, 28
Scoones, I. 111
Sen, A.K. 6, 47
Sharma, M. 7
Sharp, K. 40

Slater, R. 7, 17, 57
Sultan, S. 83
Swallow, B.M. 7

Taimo, N.V. 161, 204
Tembo, S. 244

UNAIDS 36, 155, 198, 221, 227

Vasco, R. 256

Waterhouse, R. 74, 161, 204
White, P. 93, 249
Whiteside, A. 7
Woldehanna, T. 132
Woolcock, R. 273
World Bank 34, 132, 221

Subject Index

The key treatment of a particular topic or theme is indicated in the index by page numbers in bold print.

age threshold 25–6, 43, 125, 138, 155–6, 159
alpha ratio 86
  see also cost-effectiveness; efficiency ratio
asset building 11, 63–4, 111–12, **114–23**, 152–3
  financial assets 118
  human assets 117
  issues arising 120–21
  lesson learning 122–3
  natural assets 114
  physical assets 114–17
  social assets 118–20
asset depletion 6, **36–7**
  coping and 6
  distress disposal 111
asset protection 15–16, **111–23**, 152–3
  social transfer effects 112–14
  issues arising 120–21
  lesson learning 122–3

Bolsa Familia 17, 82
Brazil 17, 82

case studies 20–23, 143–53
  Chiefs' Fields for OVC, Swaziland 22, 37, 93, **261–8**
  Dowa Emergency Cash Transfer, Malawi 20, 29, **179–86**
  Education Material Fairs, Mozambique 21, 34, 55, 148, **226–33**
  Food Assistance Programme, Mozambique 21, 35–6, 58, 117, 148, **204–10**
  Food Security Pack, Zambia 21–2, 48, 51, 63, 93–4, 114, 128, 129, **244–52**

  Food Subsidy Programme, Mozambique 20, 49, 50, 91, 103, 121, **161–8**
  Input Subsidy Programme, Malawi 21, 33, 63, 65, 94, 105, 136, 138, **234–43**
  Input Trade Fairs, Mozambique 22, 34, 38–9, 55, 94, 117, 148, **253–60**
  Neighbourhood Care Points for OVC, Swaziland 21, 44, 117, **219–25**
  Old Age Pension, Lesotho 20, 25, 48, 103–4, 120, 138, **154–60**
  Public Works Programmes, Malawi 20, 29–30, 94–5, **169–78**
  School Feeding, Lesotho 21, 34–5, 58, 65, 93, 104–5, 109, **211–28**
  Small Livestock Transfers, Zimbabwe 22, 106, **269–75**
  Social Cash Transfers, Zambia 20, 49, 65, **187–94**
  Urban Food Programme, Zimbabwe 20–21, 55, 108, **195–203**
cash transfers 10, 16–17, 91–2, 125, 135–6
  see also conditional cash transfers
  contrasted to food transfers 17
  cost-effectiveness 91–2
  delivery 55–8
  market effects 103–4
Chiefs' Fields for OVC, Swaziland 22, 37, 93, **261–8**
  asset building 266
  coordination 264–5
  cost-effectiveness 265
  cost-efficiency 90, 265
  coverage 263–4
  market effects 265–6

overview 261–2
policy lessons 267–8
strengths 266
targeting 262–3
vulnerability 262
weaknesses 267
chronic hunger 16, 22, 30, 59
community cohesion 127, 130–35
Community Welfare Assistance
    Committees 48, 120, 187–94,
    245–6
coordination 15, **70–84**, 150–52
    central 70, 72–4
    coverage and 77–80
    intermediate level 75–7
    lesson learning 80–84
    Livelihoods Empowerment Against
      Poverty, Ghana, 81–3
    Mozambique 73–4
    scheme level 75–7
    overview 70–71
conditional cash transfers 17–18, 81–3,
    89
coping 6, 112–13, 122, 153
cost-effectiveness 15, **85–97**
    analysis 85–8
    cash transfers 91–2
    cost efficiency 86–8, 90
    case studies and 88–91
    food transfers 92–3
    input transfers 93–4
    policy lessons 96–7
    public works 94–5
    targeting and 95–6
coverage 15, **77–80**, 145–6
    geographical 77–9
    group 79
    lesson learning 80–84
    predictability 79

delivery 14–15, **54–69**
    asset building 63–4
    cash transfers 55–8
    food transfers 58
    Hunger Safety Net Programme
      59–62
    innovation 127, 137
    input transfers 63
    lesson learning 66–9
    methods 55–64

motivation and incentives 64–6
Old Age Grant, Swaziland 67–8
Department for International
    Development *x*, *xi*
dependency 18, 44, 51, 83, 168
destitution 26–8, 149–50, 190
disaster response 9
    see also emergency response;
      humanitarian response
distress disposal
    see asset depletion; asset protection
donors 3, **12**, 13
Dowa Emergency Cash Transfer,
    Malawi 20, 29, **179–86**
    asset building 184
    coordination 181
    cost-effectiveness 181
    cost-efficiency 90, 181
    coverage 180–81
    market effects 181–4
    overview 179
    policy lessons 186
    social impacts 183, 185
    strengths 184
    targeting 180
    weaknesses 185–6

Education Material Fairs,
    Mozambique 21, 34, 55, 148,
    226–33
    asset building 231
    coordination 229
    cost-effectiveness 229–30
    cost efficiency 90, 229–30
    coverage 228–9
    market effects 230–31
    overview 226–7
    policy lessons 232–3
    strengths 231–2
    targeting 227–8
    vulnerability 227
    weaknesses 232
efficiency ratio **86–7**, 89
emergency response 4, 9, 30, 38
empowerment 7, 17, 124, 125
Engel's Law 121
entitlements 6, 25, 98
Ethiopia 22, 29, 30–32, 131
exclusion errors
    see targeting

fertilizer subsidies 6, 7, 33, **234–43**
food aid 3–5, 12, 16, 58, 59, 89, 99–103,
        107
    see also food transfers
Food Assistance Programme,
        Mozambique 21, 35–6, 58, 117,
        148, **204–10**
    asset building 208
    coordination 207–8
    cost-effectiveness 208
    cost-efficiency 90, 208
    coverage 206–7
    market effects 208
    overview 204–5
    policy lessons 210
    strengths 209
    targeting 206
    vulnerability 205
    weaknesses 209–10
food consumption gap 25, 27, 28–9
food-for-work 5, 6, 7, 100, 176
    see also Public Works Programmes,
        Malawi
Food Security Pack, Zambia 21–2, 48,
        51, 63, 93–4, 114, 128, 129, **244–52**
    asset building 250
    coordination 248–9
    cost-effectiveness 249
    cost-efficiency 90, 249
    coverage 246–8
    market effects 249–50
    overview 244–5
    policy lessons 252
    strengths 251
    targeting 246
    vulnerability 245
    weaknesses 251
food subsidies 4–5
Food Subsidy Programme,
        Mozambique 20, 49, 50, 91, 103,
        121, **161–8**
    asset building 166
    coordination 164–5
    cost-effectiveness 165–6
    cost-efficiency 90, 165–6
    coverage 164
    market effects 166
    overview 161–2
    policy lessons 168
    strengths 166–7

    targeting 162–4
    vulnerability 162
    weaknesses 167
food transfers 3, 10, 17
    cost effectiveness 92–3
    delivery 58
    market effects 104–5

Ghana
    see Livelihoods Empowerment
        Against Poverty
Ghana Living Standards Survey 81
good practice principles **124–5**, 135
graduation 18, 31–2, 40, 81–3

HIV/AIDS 7, 25–6, **35–6**
    Swaziland 26
Hunger Safety Net Programme, Kenya
    iv, 22, 57, **59–62**

inclusion errors
    see targeting
India 5
indlunkhulu 76, 79, 244–52
innovation 127, 137
input subsidies
    see input transfers
Input Subsidy Programme, Malawi 21,
        33, 63, 65, 94, 105, 136, 138,
        234–43
    asset building 241
    coordination 237
    cost-effectiveness 237–40
    cost-efficiency 90, 237–40
    coverage 237
    experiences 238–9
    market effects 240–41
    overview 234–5
    policy lessons 243
    strengths 241–2
    targeting 236–7
    vulnerability 235–6
    weaknesses 238–9, 242
Input Trade Fairs, Mozambique 22, 34,
        38–9, 55, 94, 117, 148, **253–60**
    asset building 257–8
    coordination 255–6
    cost-effectiveness 256
    cost-efficiency 90, 256
    coverage 255, 256

market effects 256–7
overview 253–4
policy lessons 259–60
strengths 258
targeting 254–5
vulnerability 254
weaknesses 258–9
input transfers 10–11
see also Food Security Pack,
   Zambia; Input Subsidy
   Programme, Malawi; Input
   Trade Fairs, Mozambique
cost effectiveness 93–4
delivery 63
market effects 105

Kalomo scheme 27–8, 187–8
Kenya
see Hunger Safety Net Programme,
   Kenya

Latin America 17
Lesotho 25, 26, 34–5, 43, 48, 57, 58, 65,
   91, 93, 103–5, 117, 120, 138
Old Age Pension 20, 25, 48, 103–4,
   120, 138, **154–60**
School Feeding 21, 34–5, 58, 65, 93,
   104–5, 109, **211–28**
lesson learning **124–39**
see also policy lessons under each
   case study title
asset impacts 122–3
coordination and coverage 80–84
cost effectiveness 96–7
delivery 66–9
good practice principles 124–5
market effects 108–110
NGOs 137
politics 137–8
targeting 52–3
vulnerability 37–9
Livelihoods Empowerment Against
   Poverty, Ghana, *xi*, 22, **81–3**
livelihoods framework 111–12
livestock transfers 11, 22, 37, 269–75

Malawi 29, 33, 36, 41, 47, 63, 65, 74,
   77, 94–5, 104–5, 113–14
Dowa Emergency Cash Transfer 20,
   29, **179–86**

Input Subsidy Programme 21, 33,
   63, 65, 94, 105, 136, 138,
   234–43
Public Works Programmes 20,
   29–30, 94–5, **169–78**
Malawi Social Action Fund (MASAF)
   77, 95
see also Input Subsidy Programme,
   Malawi
market effects 15, **98–110**
asset transfers 106
case studies and 100–101
cash transfers 103–4
food transfers 104–5
input transfers 105
lesson learning 108–110
market impacts on social transfers
   98, 107–8
social transfer impacts on markets
   98, 99–106
Mexico 17
microfinance 118, **119–20**
Mozambique 49, 50, 72, 73–4, 91
coordination and coverage 73–4
Education Material Fairs 21, 34, 55,
   148, **226–33**
Food Assistance Programme 21,
   35–6, 58, 117, 148, **204–10**
Food Subsidy Programme 20, 49, 50,
   91, 103, 121, **161–8**
Input Trade Fairs 22, 34, 38–9, 55,
   94, 117, 148, **253–60**

National Rural Employment
   Guarantee Scheme, India 5
Neighbourhood Care Points for OVC,
   Swaziland 21, 44, 117, **219–25**
asset building 224
coordination 222–3
cost-effectiveness 223
cost-efficiency 90, 223
coverage 222
market effects 223
overview 219–20
policy lessons 225
strengths 224
targeting 221–2
vulnerability 220–21
weaknesses 224–5
NGOs 11, **13**, 41, 60, 64–5, 83–4, 137

Old Age Grant, Swaziland 26, **67–8**, 91
Old Age Pension, Lesotho 20, 25, 48,
   103–4, 120, 138, **154–60**
   asset building 158
   coordination 157
   cost-effectiveness 157
   cost-efficiency 90, 157
   coverage 156–7
   market effects 157–8
   overview 154
   policy lessons 159–60
   strengths 158–9
   targeting 155–6
   vulnerability 155
   weaknesses 159
Oportunidades 17

pensions 25–6, 128, 138–9
   see also Old Age Grant, Swaziland;
      Old Age Pension, Lesotho
   age threshold 25–6, 43, 125, 138,
      155–6, 159
   strengths 128
   vulnerability and 25–6
politics 137–8, 139
poverty 131–2
   intergenerational transmission of 25,
      34–5, 148
   poverty traps 7
   proxy means tests 44, 45
   ultra poverty 23
predictable funding for predictable
      needs 3, 9, 16, 28, 30, 39, 125, 138,
      144, 160
private sector **13**, 62, 69, 137
Productive Safety Net Programme,
      Ethiopia *xi*, 16, 22, **30–32**
Protracted Relief Programme,
      Zimbabwe 28, 79, 126, 195–203,
      269–75
proxy criteria
   see targeting
public works programmes 5, 11, 29–33,
      94–5, 112, 117, 122
   see also Productive Safety Net
      Programme, Ethiopia
Public Works Programmes, Malawi 20,
      29–30, 94–5, **169–78**
   asset building 176
   coordination 174

cost-effectiveness 175
cost-efficiency 90, 175
coverage 174
market effects 176
overview 169–72
policy lessons 178
strengths 176–7
targeting 173–4
vulnerability 172
weaknesses 177

Regional Evidence Building Agenda *x*
Regional Hunger and Vulnerability
      Programme *x-xii*
   country coordinators *xi*

safety nets **5–7**
   see also public works programmes;
      Public Works Programmes,
      Malawi
   cash-for-work 6, 7
   food-for-work 6, 7
   limitations of 7
School Feeding, Lesotho 21, 34–5, 58,
      65, 93, 104–5, 109, **211–28**
   asset building 216
   coordination 215
   cost-effectiveness 215–16
   cost-efficiency 90, 215–16
   coverage 214–15
   market effects 216
   overview 211–13
   policy lessons 218
   strengths 216–17
   targeting 214
   vulnerability 213
   weaknesses 217
seasonality 16, **28–33**, 38, 109, 147
   food deficits and 28–9
   Productive Safety Net Programme
      30–32
shocks 7, 9, 23, 36–7, 149
Small Livestock Transfers, Zimbabwe
      22, 106, **269–75**
   asset building 273–4
   coordination 272
   cost-effectiveness 272–3
   cost-efficiency 90, 272–3
   coverage 271–2
   market effects 273

overview 269–70
policy lessons 275
strengths 274
targeting 270–71
vulnerability 270
weaknesses 274–5
Social Cash Transfers, Zambia 20, 49,
   65, **187–94**
asset building 192
coordination 190
cost-effectiveness 191
cost-efficiency 90, 191
coverage 190
market effects 191–2
overview 187–8
policy lessons 191, 193–4
strengths 192
targeting 189–90
vulnerability 188–9
weaknesses 193
social interactions 127, **130–35**
community reciprocity 134
elite capture 46, 48, 133–4
'we are all poor here' 130–32, 134
social pensions
see pensions
social protection 4–7
actors 11–13
definition **8**
functions 7–8
good practice principles **124–5**, 135
graduation from 18, 31–2, 40, 81–3
growth and 19
institutions 11–13
lesson learning **135–8**
needs approach 8
rights approach 8
social interactions 127, **130–35**
strategic issues 16–19
strengths 126–8
themes 14–16
transformative 7
weaknesses 128–30
social transfers **9–11**
asset transfers 11, 63–4, 111–12,
   114–23, 152–3
cash transfers 10, 16–17, 91–2, 125,
   135–6
food transfers 3, 10, 17, 58, 92–3,
   104–5

forms 9–11
input transfers 10–11, 63, 93–4, 104–5
vulnerability and 23–4
strengths 126–8
see also strengths under each case
   study title
sustainable livelihoods framework
see livelihoods framework
Swaziland 25–6, 35–6, 44, 57, 67–8, 77,
   79, 112
Chiefs' Fields for OVC 22, 37, 93,
   261–8
indlunkhulu 76, 79, 261–8
King of Swaziland 26
Old Age Grant 26, **67–8**, 91
Neighbourhood Care Points for
   OVC 21, 44, 117, **219–25**
Post Office 67

targeting 14, **40–53**, 149–50
categorical 43
community selection 44, 46
cost-effectiveness 95–6
exclusion errors 14, 41, 43, 46,
   48–50, 52, 53, 88, 173
geographic 41
inclusion errors 14, 43, 46, **49–50**,
   52, 88, 173
lesson learning 52–3
mechanisms 41–6
means tests 43–4
politicisation 51–2
principles 46–52
proxy means tests 44, 45
self-targeting 46
universal coverage **47–8**, 95
themes 14–16
asset protection and building 11,
   63–4, **111–23**, 152–3
coordination and coverage 15,
   70–84, 145–6, 150–52
cost-effectiveness 15, **85–97**
delivery 14–15, **54–69**
market effects 15, **98–110**
targeting 14, **40–53**, 149–50
vulnerability 6, 14, **23–39**, 146–9

universal coverage **47–8**, 95
Urban Food Programme, Zimbabwe
   20–21, 55, 108, **195–203**

asset building 201
coordination 199
cost-effectiveness 200
cost-efficiency 90, 200
coverage 199
market effects 200–201
overview 195–7
policy lessons 203
strengths 202
targeting 198–9
vulnerability 197–8
weaknesses 202–3

vulnerability 6, 14, **23–39**, 146–9
asset depletion 36–7
concepts of **27**
definition 23–4
destitution and 26–8
HIV/AIDS and 35–6
inputs and 33–4
lesson learning 37–9
older people and 25–6
seasonality and 28–9, 33

wahenga x–xi
weaknesses 128–30
see also weaknesses under each case
study title
complexity 129

cost-effectiveness 129–30
input timing 130
lack of continuity 128–9
limited scope 129
monitoring 130
motivation 129
World Food Programme 12, 16, 58, 93,
105, 204–10, 211–18

Zambia 27–8, 33, 35–6, 47–8, 49, 51,
63, 65, 72–3, 93–4, 120,
131
Community Welfare Assistance
Committees 48, 120, 187–94,
245–6
Food Security Pack 21–2, 48, 51, 63,
93–4, 114, 128, 129, **244–52**
Kalomo scheme 27–8, 187–8
Social Cash Transfers 20, 49, 65,
187–94
Zimbabwe 28, 35–6, 37, 43, 46, 47, 64,
114, 117, 118
microfinance 118, **119–20**
Protracted Relief Programme 28, 79,
126, 195–203, 269–75
Small Livestock Transfers 22, 106,
269–75
Urban Food Programme 20–21, 55,
108, **195–203**